D1613578

THE SOCIOLOGY OF AGING

GARLAND BIBLIOGRAPHIES IN SOCIOLOGY
General Editor Dan A. Chekki
(Vol. 5)

GARLAND REFERENCE LIBRARY
OF SOCIAL SCIENCE
(Vol. 206)

GARLAND BIBLIOGRAPHIES IN SOCIOLOGY

General Editor: Dan A. Chekki

1. *Conflict and Conflict Resolution: A Historical Bibliography*
   by Jack Nusan Porter

2. *Sociology of Sciences: An Annotated Bibliography of Invisible Colleges, 1972–1981*
   by Daryl E. Chubin

3. *Race and Ethnic Relations: An Annotated Bibliography*
   by Graham C. Kinloch

4. *Friendship: A Selected, Annotated Bibliography*
   by J.L. Barkas

5. *The Sociology of Aging: An Annotated Bibliography and Sourcebook*
   by Diana K. Harris

THE SOCIOLOGY OF AGING
An Annotated Bibliography and Sourcebook

Diana K. Harris

GARLAND PUBLISHING, INC. • NEW YORK & LONDON
1985

Library of Congress Cataloging in Publication Data

Harris, Diana K.
The sociology of aging.

(Garland bibliographies in sociology ; v. 5)
(Garland reference library of social science ; v. 206)
Includes index.
1. Gerontology—Bibliography. 2. Aged—Bibliography.
3. Aging—Bibliography. I. Title. II. Series.
III. Series: Garland reference library of social
science ; v. 206.
Z7164.04H374 1985 [HQ1061] 016.3052′6 83-48220
ISBN 0-8240-9046-2 (alk. paper)

Printed on acid-free, 250-year-life paper
Manufactured in the United States of America

CONTENTS

FOREWORD

North Americans are living longer today than ever before. The number and proportion of older people in the population have been rising sharply as life expectancy increases and as birth, death, and immigration rates decline. These forces have tended to create a geriatric society. The twenty-first century, it is projected, will see a doubling in the proportion, and a tripling in the absolute numbers of people over the age of sixty-five. The implications of the changing age structure for the lives of both old and younger people are now being recognized by social scientists and policy makers. Policies related to health care, housing, work, retirement, social security, and leisure have major consequences for the old and the young. What are the patterns of aging and what are the problems of aging?

The sociology of aging or social gerontology, though interdisciplinary in its content, incorporates data from social sciences, medicine, nursing, epidemiology, health planning and administration and focuses upon sociological aspects of aging. In an attempt to understand the processes and problems of aging most sociologists who specialize in this area seem to have examined "activity" and "disengagement" theories. Researchers have also tested role theory, subculture theory, and age-stratification theory. During the past two decades there has been a major development in social gerontology. Despite the tremendous upsurge of interest in aging, our knowledge of aging is still limited in many ways.

Sociology of aging can make a significant contribution to a better understanding of the characteristics and needs of the elderly. It can also suggest appropriate plans and services to help them age successfully.

The aged often face prejudice and discrimination from the rest of society. Sterotypical beliefs about the elderly are being perpetuated. Institutional policies and practices transform the natural process of aging into a social problem. Ageism, like racism and sexism, is pervasive in our society. The aged who have lost jobs, income, power and prestige, relatives, and friends are a minority group. A disproportionate percentage of the elderly live below the poverty line and are lonely, in ill health, malnourished, poorly housed and isolated. A large majority of them are women who suffer from an additional disadvantage. It is predicted that by the year 2000, there will be 154 women for every 100 men in the age group 65 plus. It is reasonable to expect then that poverty, fear of crime, victimization, and institutionalization would be increasingly linked to older females as compared to elderly males. Also, women are expected to care for old people in their homes, in institutions, and in the community. In this sense, aging may also be considered a woman's issue.

It is recognized that older persons experience more stresses than any other age cohort. The excessive prescription and overuse of drugs adversely affects the older person. Likewise, mandatory and unprepared retirement, loss of income and health, inadequate housing and transportation facilities, prejudice and discrimination, all may lead to consequences that can be misdiagnosed as effects of aging when examined outside of their societal context. While the elderly in urban communities have been receiving better health care and housing facilities in recent years, the neglect of the elderly in rural communities has persisted. By and large, older people are excluded from the policy and planning process.

In the next several decades dramatic changes in the population of the elderly will take place. As a special need and interest group, they are likely to gain more political power, thereby influencing the decision-making process. These changes will have a major impact on their roles and needs, on society's perception of the elderly and old age, and the services provided to senior citizens.

Is institutionalization of the elderly the only efficient means of providing for an aging population? Is it an ideal situation? What are the alternative service delivery mechanisms? Should we make an effort to adjust the old to the changing environment or change the environment to meet the needs of the elderly?

Should we or can we revivify intergenerational family ties and family care of the aged by the young? These questions demand further reflection and research. There is a need for studies of the aging process focusing upon an interaction between individual characteristics and social milieu. Sociological research should not only deal with the problems of the older people in terms of how they face their changed physical, social, and emotional capacities but also examine the limitations imposed upon older persons by the structure of society. Furthermore, it is necessary to suggest policies aimed at removing these limitations and perhaps assisting the elderly in strengthening their capacities for adaptive creative behavior.

There is a wide variation of life styles among the elderly. There are multiple patterns of successful aging and enormously diverse patterns of disengagement. The major issue facing government today is how to provide and pay for quality service to the elderly. The question of mandatory retirement and the various implications of new and innovative options such as early or partial retirement/pensions, phased, late or non-retirement are being discussed, experimented with, and assessed in West Germany, France, Norway, Sweden, and Denmark. In the United States the elderly along with other disadvantaged groups are those most affected by the reduction of social benefits. In Britain the belief that assistance for the old and the underprivileged is a major responsibility of government has come under serious attack. Even in Sweden, they are having second thoughts about the practicality of limitless public support of social programs. In most Third World countries social security programs for the elderly are either non-existent or cover a limited segment of senior citizens in a marginal way.

Today's young elders, that is, the 55- to 75-year-olds, have a higher level of education, are in better health, and have a longer life expectancy than previous generations of the same age group. They tend to avoid retirement communities, senior citizen homes, and the traditional retirement lifestyle of full-time leisure. These young elders intend to remain active and wish to engage themselves in meaningful and creative work. "Re-engagement" appears to be a new form of involvement in life—in many ways different from that in earlier years and best suited to the interests, energies, and capacities of one's later years. The elderly can volunteer to render community service when increasing numbers of younger women are entering the labor force.

The future generations of old, it is predicted, will be better educated, healthier, in higher occupation levels, possess improved accommodations and longer life, be politically organized and actively involved in community affairs. In the postindustrial society, chronological age may become less important, with young, middleaged, and old contributing according to their unique abilities and experience. The elderly in the twenty-first century may be exposed to a variety of opportunities, and continuing education, work, and leisure flexibilities should result in a greater adaptability to changing environments. With rapid advances in technology, and the bio-medical and social sciences, the status of the old may improve as they become young in body and mind. If the presently declining birth rate continues to decline, older individuals may have to assume many new and different roles. Business and industry will have to cater to the diverse lifestyles of later years. Governments may be compelled to reform the pension system. Our attitudes toward work and toward the concept of retirement itself will most likely change in the future.

This sourcebook assembles a broad spectrum of materials on aging. Although contributions are drawn from many sources, the author's major focus is on sociological studies of aging. Diana Harris of the University of Tennessee presents an overview of significant theories and research methods. Each chapter includes substantive data on specific aspects of aging. This reference volume would be very useful to students of social sciences, social work and service and health care personnel, research scholars, and policy-makers in this field.

Dan A. Chekki
University of Winnipeg

PREFACE

Today sociologists are becoming increasingly aware of the later years of life as a strategic area of research. This bibliography has been designed to assist such present and future research ventures. It is also intended to serve students, teachers, and practitioners in their study and work with the elderly.

Procedures and Methods

This annotated bibliography covers the years 1960 through 1980. Rather than being multidisciplinary as most bibliographies on aging tend to be, this work attempts to focus primarily on the sociology of aging. To compile the material for this volume, I first surveyed the literature on aging from a wide variety of journals, monographs, and books. Then using only the original sources, I selected for annotation those works which had a sociological emphasis throughout or contained substantial parts relating to the sociological aspects of aging. Also for a work to be included it had to be accessible in that it could be found in most university libraries. Finally, the work had to have some bibliographic value.

Organization

The bibliographic material is divided into five parts. Part One provides annotations from general works and from theory and research methods. Part Two deals with culture and society, and the annotations focus on the social and cultural forces that influence the social behavior and personal experience of older persons. This part contains chapters on culture, socialization, life satisfaction, social groups, and deviance. The annotations in Part Three deal with various forms of social inequality. The first chapter in this part concerns the inequalities of social class and age and the second the inequalities of race and ethnicity as they relate to the elderly. Part Four covers some important social institutions and includes chapters on the family, religion and education, politics and economy, and work, retirement, and leisure. Finally, Part Five focuses on social problems and specific concerns associated with aging and the aged. It contains chapters with annotations concerning demography, health and transportation, living environments, institutionalization, and death and dying.

Features

A number of features have been used to increase the effectiveness of the bibliography as a research tool. As mentioned earlier, this bibliography contains no annotations from secondary sources. All works were read in their original form to determine whether they should be included. Probably one of the unique features of this work is that when an annotation relates to two or more areas such as social class and the family, it is listed in its entirety under each heading to save the researcher the chore of looking up cross references. Next, the annotations are intended not only to be easy to find but also easy to read and to be as free from jargon as possible. Finally, in the annotations reporting research, especially journal articles, the major findings are given.

Resource Materials

Beginning in Part Six, this work provides current resources and information in the field of aging. Selected periodicals and some pertinent information about them are contained in this section. Part Seven provides information on bibliographies, abstracts, handbooks, and other references related to aging as well as some useful statistical sources. Finally, Part Eight lists the names and addresses of offices on aging, gerontological associations, and university centers and institutes for the study of aging.

In thinking back over the three years that I have worked on

this project, I am reminded of what Dr. Johnson said about dogs who walked on their hind legs—not that it was done well, but that it was done at all.

D.K.H.

PART 1

INTRODUCTION

Chapter 1

GENERAL

Albrecht, Ruth E. "The Sociological Parameters in the Ecology of the Aging Process and of the Aging Human." *The Gerontologist*, 1968, 8(2), pp. 94-99.

Attempts to define the scope and limits of the sociological aspects of aging. The author then selects some of these areas and discusses them in greater detail.

Atchley, Robert C. "Aging." In Rodney Stark (Ed.), *Social Problems.* New York: CRM/Random House, 1975, pp. 391-415.

Addresses income, housing, transportation, and retirement problems of the elderly. Discusses some sources of these problems and programs for dealing with them.

Atchley, Robert C. *Social Forces in Later Life: An Introduction to Social Gerontology,* 3d. ed. Belmont, Calif.: Wadsworth, 1980.

Offers a general introduction to social gerontology with an emphasis on the social and sociopsychological aspects of aging.

Atchley, Robert C., and Seltzer, Mildred M. (Eds.). *The Sociology of Aging: Selected Readings.* Belmont, Calif.: Wadsworth, 1976.

Provides a set of readings from the sociology of aging literature to accompany the first edition of *The Social Forces in Later Life* (Atchley, 1972, see above).

Barron, Milton L. *The Aging American: An Introduction to Social Gerontology.* New York: Thomas Y. Crowell, 1961.

Contains theories on social gerontology as well as gerontological research. The main focus is on retirement and health problems of the elderly.

Barrow, Georgia M., and Smith, Patricia A. *Aging, Ageism and Society.* St. Paul: West Publishing, 1979.

The theme of this book is ageism, the prejudice and discrimination that is suffered by the elderly. Offers many suggestions on what can be done to end ageism.

Barry, John R., and Wingrove, C. Ray (Eds.). *Let's Learn About Aging: A Book of Readings.* Cambridge, Mass.: Schenkman, 1977.

Consists of articles on social gerontology from both scientific journals and popular magazines. Also included are several papers written specifically for this volume.

Baum, Martha, and Baum, Rainer C. *Growing Old: A Societal Perspective.* Englewood Cliffs, N.J.: Prentice Hall, 1980.

Discusses six aspects of contemporary old age: income, political participation, retirement, family, dying, and death. Applies three theoretical perspectives to each of these aspects.

Bell, Bill D. (Ed.). *Contemporary Social Gerontology: Significant Developments the Field of Aging.* Springfield, Ill.: Charles C. Thomas, 1976.

Contains a collection of articles, mainly from the *Gerontologist* and the *Journal of Gerontology.* The focus is on theoretical and methodological developments in social gerontology after 1968.

Bengtson, Vern L. *The Social Psychology of Aging.* Indianapolis, Ind.: The Bobbs-Merrill Company, 1973.

Examines change and continuity in both the personal systems and social systems of individuals as they age.

Bengtson, Vern L., and Haber, David A. "Sociological Approaches to Aging." In Diana S. Woodruff and James E. Birren (Eds.), *Aging: Scientific Perspectives and Social Issues.* New York: D. Van Nostrand Co., 1975, pp. 70-91.

Focuses on the sociological definitions of aging and time and how aging and time can be analyzed from a sociological perspective. Also discusses the ways in which the elderly can be viewed as a social problem.

Bengtson, Vern L., and Manuel, Ron C. "The Sociology of Aging." In Richard H. Davis (Ed.). *Aging: Prospects and Issues*, 3d ed. Los Angeles: Ethel Percy Andrus Gerontology Center, University of Southern California, 1976, pp. 41-57.

Discusses social losses and their consequences for the individual and his or her social network, competence in coping with losses, and responsibility in assisting the older person. These issues are examined from the perspective of social theory and research.

Binstock, Robert H., and Shanas, Ethel (Eds.). *Handbook of Aging and the Social Sciences.* New York: Van Nostrand Reinhold, 1976.

Provides comprehensive knowledge, major reference sources, and suggestions for further research on the social aspects of aging. The social aspects of aging are approached and developed within the framework of the subject matter of various social science disciplines.

Blau, Zena Smith. *Old Age in a Changing Society.* New York: New Viewpoints, 1973.

A major thesis of the book is that many problems of old age are the result of role exits that occur in later life. Outlines some of the elements in role exit theory and explores its relationship to identity.

Boyd, Rosamonde R., and Oakes, Charles G. (Eds.). *Foundations of Practical Gerontology*, 2d ed. Columbia, South Carolina: University of South Carolina Press, 1973.

Consists of a collection of papers written by laypersons and professionals from various disciplines including sociology, psychology, and economics.

Brantl, Virginia M., and Brown, Sister Marie Raymond (Eds.). *Readings in Gerontology*. St. Louis: C. V. Mosby, 1973.

This selection of a dozen papers provides an understanding of the relationship between practice, theory, and research.

Burgess, Ernest W. "Aging in Western Culture." In Ernest W. Burgess (Ed.), *Aging in Western Societies*. Chicago: The University of Chicago Press, 1960, pp. 3-28.

This chapter serves as an introduction to the volume and provides the background for the chapters that follow. Discusses social trends and their effects upon aging as well as societal concerns for the elderly.

Busse, Ewald W., and Pfeiffer, Eric (Eds.). *Behavior and Adaptation in Late Life*, 2d ed. Boston: Little, Brown and Company, 1977.

Presents a multidisciplinary approach to how people adapt to growing old. It was written mainly by members of the Duke Center for the Study of Aging and Human Development.

Cottrell, Fred. *Aging and the Aged*. Dubuque, Iowa: Wm. C. Brown, 1974.

Concentrates on the problems of the elderly in our society and some of the social action that is being taken to alleviate them.

Cowgill, Donald O. "Aging in American Society." In Donald O. Cowgill and Lowell D. Holmes (Eds.), *Aging and Modernization*. New York: Appleton-Century-Crofts, 1972, pp. 243-261.

Describes the present position of the elderly in our society. Discusses topics such as the demographic aspects of aging, rites of passage, status of the aged, rights and privileges of the aged, and the aged and family structure.

Cox, Harold (Ed.). *Aging, Second Edition.* Guilford, Conn.: Dushkin, 1980.

Consists of 44 widely varied articles from magazines, newspapers, and journals which relate to aging.

Crandall, Richard C. *Gerontology: A Behavioral Science Approach*. Reading, Mass.: Addison Wesley, 1980.

A gerontology text that includes chapters on the "History of Gerontology" and "Aging in Preliterate Societies".

Decker, David L. *Social Gerontology: An Introduction to the Dynamics of Aging*. Boston: Little, Brown, 1980.

Provides an overview of social gerontology while viewing the aging process from a variety of perspectives.

Harris, Diana K., and Cole, William E. *The Sociology of Aging*. Boston: Houghton Mifflin Co., 1980.

As the title indicates, the emphasis in this volume is upon the sociological aspects of aging. This book represents the first attempt to integrate the subject of aging into a systematic, sociological framework.

Hendricks, Jon, and Hendricks, C. Davis. *Aging in Mass Society: Myth and Realities*, Cambridge, Mass.: Winthrop, 1977.

Presents an interdisciplinary overview of the dimensions of aging in modern mass societies. Focuses on the biological, psychological, and sociological aspects of the aging process.

Hendricks, Jon, and Hendricks, C. Davis. *Dimensions of Aging: Readings*. Cambridge, Mass.: Winthrop Publishers, 1979.

Designed to complement the authors' text, *Aging in Mass Society*, this reader contains articles from varied sources and disciplines (see above).

Hess, Beth B. (Ed.). *Growing Old in America*. New Brunswick, N.J.: Transaction Books, 1976.

The major section of this book, "Varieties of the Aging Experience," deals with the many settings in which the elderly attempt to generate support systems. Other sections examine the elderly within a cross-cultural and time perspective, focus on the transition to old age and its role adjustments, and illustrate some of the uses of social gerontology.

Hess, Beth B., and Markson, Elizabeth W. *Aging and Old Age: An Introduction to Social Gerontology*. New York: Macmillan, 1980.

Focuses on the changes that have taken place in the past for the elderly and the prospects for change in the future. Emphasizes the larger social systems in which aging takes place as well as some of the problems of aging.

Hoffman, Adeline M. (Ed.). *The Daily Needs and Interests of Older People.* Springfield, Ill.: Charles C. Thomas, 1970.

Although this multi-authored book was written primarily for home economists, it contains a wide selection of topics on aging of interest to social scientists.

Jarvik, Lissy F. (Ed.). *Aging into the 21st Century: Middle-Agers Today.* New York: Gardener Press, 1978.

Looks at the future of aging and the aged from the perspectives of various disciplines.

Johnson, Elizabeth S., and Williamson, John B. *Growing Old: The Social Problems of Aging.* New York: Holt, Rinehart and Winston, 1980.

Analyzes categories of injustice--victimization, exploitation, discrimination, and oppression--that confront the aging and the aged.

Kalish, Richard A. *Late Adulthood: Perspectives on Human Development.* Monterey, Calif.: Brooks/Cole, 1975.

Written from a psychological and psychosocial perspective, this book offers a concise overview of the information, ideas, and issues related to aging and the aged.

Kalish, Richard A. (Ed.). *The Later Years: Social Application of Gerontology.* Belmont, Calif.: Wadsworth, 1978.

Geared primarily for those persons who plan to work with the elderly, this book uses material from many varied sources. Each of the chapters, as well as the selections within them, is preceded by a discussion which coordinates and gives continuity to the book.

Kart, Cary S., and Manard, Barbara B. *Aging in America: Readings in Social Gerontology.* Port Washington, N.Y.: Alfred Publishing Co., 1976.

Providing an introduction to social gerontology, the articles in this reader were selected on the basis of their being issue and problem oriented.

Kennedy, Caroll E. "Old Age." In Caroll Kennedy, *Human Development: The Adult Years and Aging.* New York: Macmillan, 1978, pp. 290-339.

Deals with the activities, attitudes, and characteristics of older people.

Kimmel, Douglas C. *Adulthood and Aging: An Interdisciplinary Developmental View,* 2d ed. New York: John Wiley, 1980.

Adulthood is approached from an interdisciplinary, interactionist perspective. Chapter 6, "Work, Retirement and Leisure" and Chapter 9, "Growing Old in a Changing World" deal with the sociological aspects of aging.

Koller, Marvin R. *Social Gerontology.* New York: Random House, 1968.

Presents an overview of some of the key ideas in the field of social gerontology.

Loether, Herman J. *Problems of Aging: Sociological and Social Psychological Perspectives,* 2d ed. Encino, Calif.: Dickenson Publishing Co., 1975.

Discusses some of the critical problems associated with the aging process, including health, housing, retirement, and widowhood.

McFarland, David D. "The Aged in the 21st Century: A Demographer's View." In Lissy Jarvik F. (Ed.), *Aging into the 21st Century: Middle-Agers Today.* New York: Gardner Press, 1978, pp. 5-22.

Makes some projections about the elderly population in the future.

McKinney, John C., and de Vyver, Frank T. (Eds.). *Aging and Social Policy.* New York: Appleton-Century-Crofts, 1966.

A collection of papers on the socioeconomic aspects of aging which approaches the subject from the perspective of policy implications.

Maddox, George L. (Ed.). *The Future of Aging and the Aged.* Durham, N.C.: Duke University Press, 1971.

Contains a group of papers on various topics in the field of aging from a Duke University seminar for southern journalists.

Maddox, George L. "Sociology of Later Life." In Alex Inkeles, James Coleman, and Ralph H. Turner (Eds.), *Annual Review of Sociology,* vol. 5. Palo Alto, Calif.: Annual Reviews, Inc., 1979, pp. 113-135.

The first part of the article presents a sociological characterization of later life reviewing the major issues of social scientific research on aging. The second part emphasizes how sociological interests and social gerontology are increasingly intersected. Common issues include the impact of demographic and social change on the individual and society, and age differentiation over the life course. Points out the growing interest of sociologists in aging as a strategic site for sociological research.

Manney, James D. *Aging in American Society: An Examination of Concepts and Issues.* Ann Arbor: Institute of Gerontology, University of Michigan-Wayne State University, 1975.

Provides a succinct overview of the major concepts in aging along with programs and policies for improving the lives of the elderly.

Monk, Abraham (Ed.). *The Age of Aging: A Reader in Social Gerontology.* Buffalo, N.Y.: Prometheus Books, 1979.

Offers the undergraduate and beginning graduate student a sampling of issues, problems, policies, and services concerning the elderly.

Neugarten, Bernice L. "The Aged in American Society." In Howard S. Becker (Ed.), *Social Problems: A Modern Approach.* New York: John Wiley & Sons, 1966, pp. 167-196.

Discusses the aged as a social problem, their position in society, their economic status, and their family life.

Neugarten, Bernice L. (Ed.). *Middle Age and Aging: A Reader in Social Psychology.* Chicago: The University of Chicago Press, 1968.

Focuses upon the social and psychological processes of individuals as they move from middle age to old age.

Neugarten, Bernice. "The Old and the Young in Modern Societies." *American Behavioral Scientist,* 1970, 14(1), pp. 13-24.

Predicts that the position of the old will improve in the distant future as they become successively younger in mind and body. The author sees the importance of chronological age as a distinguishing feature between individuals diminishing.

Neugarten, Bernice. (Interviewed by Elizabeth Hall) "Acting One's Age: New Rules for Old." *Psychology Today,* 1980, 13(11), pp. 66-80.

Discusses the social and economic consequences of the graying of America. The perception of what kind of behavior is appropriate at various ages today is changing and, according to Neugarten, we are becoming a truly age-irrelevant society.

Palmore, Erdman B. (Ed.). *Normal Aging,* vol. 1. Durham, N.C.: Duke University Press, 1970.

This collection of published papers reports the findings from the Longitudinal Study of Aging at the Duke Center for the Study of Aging.

Palmore, Erdman B. (Ed.). *Normal Aging,* vol. 2. Durham, N.C.: Duke University Press, 1974.

In this sequel to *Normal Aging,* the previous findings that were reported in the first volume are extended and updated. Some papers written especially for this volume are included as well as reports from the adaptation study of middle-aged persons (see above).

Palmore, Erdman B., and Maddox, George L. "Sociological Aspects of Aging." In Ewald W. Busse and Eric Pfeiffer (Eds.), *Behavior and Adaptation in Late Life,* 2d. ed. Boston: Little, Brown and Company, 1977, pp. 31-58.

Views aging as a social process and discusses such topics as cross-cultural differences in the status of the aged, differences among the aged in our society, and the aged as a minority group.

Quadagno, Jill S. *Aging, the Individual and Society: Readings in Social Gerontology.* New York: St. Martin's Press, 1980.

Focuses primarily on the sociological changes that accompany aging and that have occurred as a result of modernization.

Riesman, Frank (Ed.). *Older Persons: Unused Resources for Unmet Needs.* Beverly Hills, Calif.: Sage Publications, 1977.

Originally appearing in a special issue of *Social Policy* (November/December 1976), the articles in this book cover a variety of topics on aging and the aged.

Riley, Matilda W., et al. *Aging and Society: An Inventory of Research Findings, vol. 1.* New York: Russell Sage Foundation, 1968.

Organizes and summarizes the findings of social scientific research on middle-aged and older people. It interprets these findings in the light of sociological theory and professional practice.

Riley, Matilda W. *Aging from Birth to Death: Interdisciplinary Perspectives.* Boulder, Colo.: Westview Press, 1979, pp. 153-166.

Contains a two-part collection of papers from various disciplines on the aging process. The first part of the book deals with the life course of the individual, and the second with the impact of social and environmental changes as they shape the life-course patterns of individuals.

Rose, Arnold M., and Peterson, Warren A. (Eds.). *Older People and Their Social World.* Philadelphia: F.A. Davis, 1965.

The interaction of research, theory, and interpretation in a wide range of topics in social gerontology characterizes the collection of articles in this volume. The theme of subculture of the aging is a common thread throughout the book.

Schwartz, Arthur N., and Peterson, James A. *Introduction to Gerontology.* New York: Holt, Rinehart and Winston, 1979.

Emphasizing the practical application of gerontology, rather than a theoretical or academic approach, this book is intended to provide an overview of gerontology for those persons who work with the elderly.

Shanas, Ethel (Ed.). *Aging in Contemporary Society.* Beverly Hills, Calif.: Sage Publications, 1970.

Written by persons from various disciplines, these papers address a number of topics in the aging field. The material in this book originally appeared as a special issue of *American Behavioral Scientist,* 1970, 14(1).

Shanas, Ethel. "The Sociology of Aging and the Aged." *The Sociological Quarterly,* 1971, 12(2), pp. 159-176.

Reviews the state of the field of the sociology of aging. Discusses landmark works and significant contributions of recent years.

Shanas, Ethel. "Gerontology and the Social and Behavioral Sciences: Where Do We Go from Here?" *The Gerontologist,* 1975, 15(6), pp. 499-502.

Reviews some of the major research findings in the social and behavioral sciences and discusses some promising areas of research for the future.

Simpson, Ida H., and McKinney, John C. (Eds.). *Social Aspects of Aging.* Durham, N.C.: Duke University Press, 1966.

Focuses on four problems of old age: retirement, the family, the community, and life space. Examines the ways in which variations in the life circumstances of the elderly affect adaptation to these problems.

Sweetser, Dorrian A. "Sociologic Perspectives on Aging." In Marian G. Spencer and Caroline J. Dorr (Eds.), *Understanding Aging: A Multidisciplinary Approach.* New York: Appleton-Century-Crofts, 1975.

Identifies change over generations in regard to demography, the family, and the distributive process.

Talmon, Yonina. "Aging: Social Aspects." In *International Encyclopedia of the Social Sciences.* New York: Macmillan, 1968, pp. 19-26.

Aging and the modern kinship system and the occupational system are discussed as well as the elderly's participation in formal organizations, informal relations, and leisure. Concludes with two major issues in the study of aging: the disengagement and activity theories and the controversy between community integration and age-group segregation.

Tibbitts, Clark. "Social Gerontology: A New Approach to Understanding Aging." *Geriatrics,* 1960, 15(10), pp. 705-717.

Discusses the biological, psychological and societal approaches to the study of aging. Points out problems arising in these areas and the need for further research.

Tibbitts, Clark (Ed.). *Handbook of Social Gerontology.* Chicago: The University of Chicago Press, 1960.

Seeks to identify and structure the field of aging as well as providing a comprehensive view of it.

Tibbitts, Clark. "Origin, Scope, and Fields of Social Gerontology." In Clark Tibbitts (Ed.), *Handbook of Social Gerontology.* Chicago: The University of Chicago Press, 1960, pp. 3-26.

This introductory chapter traces the origins of social gerontology and provides a framework for the chapters that follow.

Tibbitts, Clark and Donahue, Wilma. *Social and Psychological Aspects of Aging.* New York: Columbia University Press, 1962.

Papers in this volume provide a report of a worldwide scientific investigation of the social and psychological aspects of aging. Includes research that is currently in process in many parts of the world.

Tibbitts, Clark. "Some Social Aspects of Gerontology." *The Gerontologist,* 1968, 8(2), pp. 131-133.

Reviews some of the concerns of social gerontology for the retirement role as well as the family and intergenerational relationships of older persons.

Vander Zanden, James W. "Adulthood: The Later Years." *In Human Development.* New York: Alfred A. Knopf, 1978, pp. 577-609.

Contains a summary of some of the theories advanced by sociologists to describe the changes in the elderly in terms of changes in their social environment. Includes a section on the social aspects of aging.

Vedder, Clyde B. *Gerontology: A Book of Readings.* Springfield, Ill.: Charles C. Thomas, 1963.

Provides selections from a wide variety of disciplines with a chapter devoted to the sociology of aging.

Ward, Russell A. *The Aging Experience: An Introduction to Social Gerontology.* New York: Harper and Row, 1979.

Providing an introduction to the knowledge and issues in social gerontology, this book focuses on the aging experience as it is shaped by the social context within which it occurs.

Watson, Wilbur H., and Maxwell, Robert J. (Eds.). *Human Aging and Dying: A Study of Sociocultural Gerontology.* New York: St. Martin's Press, 1977.

Focusing on society and culture as the initial level of analysis, this book examines the influence of differing social contexts upon the processes of aging and dying.

Williams, Richard H.; Tibbitts, Clark; and Donahue, Wilma (Eds.), *Processes of Aging: Social and Psychological Perspectives,* 2 vols. New York: Atherton Press, 1963.

These volumes contain papers that are an inventory of the principal fields of gerontological research and deal with the psychological and social aspects of aging in relation to mental health.

Williamson, John B., et al. *Aging and Society: An Introduction to Social Gerontology.* New York: Holt, Rinehart and Winston, 1980.

Analyzes aging as a process with an emphasis on its social and psychological aspects.

Woodruff, Diana S., and Birren, James E. (Eds.). *Aging: Scientific Perspectives and Social Issues.* New York: D. Van Nostrand Co., 1975.

Using a multidisciplinary approach, this text contains chapters on the sociological, biological, and psychological aspects of aging.

Youmans, E. Grant. "Some Views on Human Aging." In Rosamonde R. Boyd, and Charles G. Oakes (Eds.), *Foundations of Practical Gerontology,* 2d ed. Columbia, South Carolina: University of South Carolina Press, 1973, pp. 17-26.

Discusses the sociology of the life course.

Zarit, Steven H. (Ed.). *Readings in Aging and Death: Contemporary Perspectives.* New York: Harper and Row, 1977.

Written from a wide variety of perspectives, the articles in this reader have been selected from both the popular and scholarly literature. They include articles on social problems of the elderly, culture and aging, and death and dying.

Chapter 2

THEORY AND RESEARCH METHODS

A. Theory

Baum, Rainer C., and Baum, Martha. "The Aged and Diachronic Solidarity in Modern Society." *International Journal of Aging and Human Development,* 1975, 6(4), pp. 329-346.

After reviewing four sociological theories of aging, this paper explores the issue of how the aged can be used as a valuable societal resource in the production of intergenerational solidarity.

Bell, Bill D. "The Limitations of Crisis Theory as an Explanatory Mechanism in Social Gerontology." *International Journal of Aging and Human Development,* 1975, 6(2), pp. 153-168.

Using a longitudinal sample of older persons, this study investigates five assumptions of crisis theory as they relate to the prediction of life satisfaction following retirement from work. The correlation between work commitment and the desire for subsequent employment is negative and significant. It was the only assumption out of the five which received support.

Bell, Bill D. "Role Set Orientations and Life Satisfaction: A New Look at an Old Theory." In Jaber F. Gubrium (Ed.), *Time, Roles, and Self in Old Age.* New York: Human Sciences Press, 1976, pp. 148-164.

Examines the assumptions and predictions of the continuity theory with regard to life satisfaction. Finds that the more time invested in the family after retirement, the more negative the life satisfaction. However, interaction in the community and involvement in voluntary associations is found to be positively associated with life satisfaction. Bell concludes that his findings do not substantiate the continuity hypothesis and sees an activity orientation as a more appropriate explanation.

Bengtson, Vern L., and Dowd, James J. "Sociological Functionalism, Exchange Theory and Life Cycle Analysis: A Call for More Explicit Theoretical Bridges." *International Journal of Aging and Human Development,* 1980-1981, 12(1), pp. 55-73.

Focuses on an application of structural-functionalism and the exchange theory to the later years of the life cycle. Suggests that these theories possess potential contributions to an understanding of behavior associated with aging.

Cowgill, Donald O., and Holmes, Lowell D. (Eds.). *Aging and Modernization.* New York: Appleton-Century-Crofts, 1972.

Contains 18 papers that deal with aging in various societies and settings, ranging from primitive to highly modern. These papers provide the basis for the testing of a number of hypotheses. The general conclusion is that the status of the aged is inversely associated with modernization.

Cowgill, Donald O. "A Theory of Aging in Cross-Cultural Perspective." In Donald O. Cowgill and Lowell D. Holmes (Eds.), *Aging and Modernization.* New York: Appleton-Century-Crofts, 1972, pp. 1-3.

Proposes a number of hypotheses about aging. Some of these hypotheses pertain to universal conditions while others specify the variations found in different societies. The major hypothesis is that the role and status of the elderly vary inversely with the degree of modernization of a society.

Cowgill, Donald O., and Holmes, Lowell D. "Summary and Conclusions: The Theory in Review." In Donald O. Cowgill and Lowell D. Holmes (Eds.), *Aging and Modernization.* New York: Appleton-Century-Crofts, 1972, pp. 305-323.

In this final chapter, the authors discuss the hypotheses advanced in the first part of the book. They conclude that their theory of modernization has been extended and strengthened by the societies studied in the preceding chapters.

Cumming, Elaine, and Henry, William E. *Growing Old: The Process of Disengagement.* New York: Basic Books, 1962.

The authors present the disengagement theory. This social- psychological theory of aging, derived from a portion of the data gathered in the Kansas City Studies of Adult Life, maintains that aging is a gradual, mutually beneficial process in which the individual and society withdraw from one another.

Cumming, Elaine. "New Thoughts on the Theory of Disengagement." In Robert Kastenbaum (Ed.), *New Thoughts on Old Age.* New York: Springer, 1964, pp. 3-18.

Adds new elements to the disengagement theory of aging and elaborates on its basic propositions.

Cumming, Elaine. "Engagement with an Old Theory." *International Journal of Aging and Human Development,* 1975, 6(3), pp. 187-191.

Discusses some controversies, misunderstandings, and misapplications of the disengagement theory.

Dowd, James J. "Aging as Exchange: A Preface to Theory." *Journal of Gerontology,* 1975, 30(5), pp. 584-594.

The exchange theory of aging, as developed by Dowd, views the problems of aging as problems of declining power resources. This decline in power restricts the elderly from entering into balanced exchange relationships with other individuals or groups.

George, Linda K. *Role Transitions in Later Life.* Monterey, Calif.: Brooks/Cole, 1980.

The first part of the book is devoted to the development of a model of adjustment to social stress in later life. The second half assesses the utility of the social stress model for increasing our understanding of the nature of role transitions and role changes that usually occur in late adulthood.

Gordon, Judith B. "A Disengaged Look at Disengagement Theory." *International Journal of Aging and Human Development,* 1975, 6(3), pp. 215-227.

Argues that the disengagement theory could be useful if used as a theory of the middle range and not as a general theory about aging.

Gubrium, Jaber F. "Toward a Socio-Environmental Theory of Aging." *The Gerontologist,* 1972, 12(3), pt. 1, pp. 281-284.

Proposes a new theory of aging built around the interrelationship of the social and individual environments of the elderly. The social environment refers to the normative effects of homogeneity, residential proximity, and local protectiveness, while the individual environment refers to health, solvency, and social support that influence behavior flexibility.

Gubrium, Jaber F. *The Myth of the Golden Years: A Socio-Environmental Theory of Aging.* Springfield, Ill.: Charles C. Thomas, 1973.

Develops a socio-environmental approach to aging which is used to analyze other theories, existing data on the elderly, and popular images of old age.

Hochschild, Arlie R. "Disengagement Theory: A Critique and Proposal." *American Sociological Review,* 1975, 40(5), pp. 553-569.

Discusses three problems that appear in the disengagement theory and proposes an alternative theory to solve these problems.

Hochschild, Arlie R. "Disengagement Theory: A Logical, Empirical, and Phenomenological Critique." In Jaber F. Gubrium (Ed.), *Time, Roles, and Self in Old Age.* New York: Human Sciences Press, 1976, pp. 53-87.

The logic of the disengagement theory is criticized from the perspective of a social phenomenologist. Suggests we try to locate social types of older persons based on what they say is meaningful in the daily acts that compose their social life. Also that we explain why these types are distributed as they are in the social structure.

Kalish, Richard A. "Of Social Values and the Dying: A Defense of Disengagement." *The Family Coordinator,* 1972, 21(1), pp. 81-94.

Argues that although the adaptive functions of disengagement have been widely debated, they tend to be more acceptable for the dying older person. Disengagement at this point is highly adaptive in that it permits persons to reduce the effect of what they are leaving behind so that dying is less painful.

Kutner, Bernard. "The Social Nature of Aging." *The Gerontologist,* 1962, 2(1), pp. 5-8.

Suggests that social aging may be conceived of as a process of re-differentiation (transition and change) and re-integration (stabilization and homeostasis) of social roles and functions occurring as one ages chronologically.

Loeb, Rita. "Disengagement, Activity or Maturity." *Sociology and Social Research,* 1973, 57(3), pp. 367-382.

Proposes and tests a model of sociocultural aging. This model is based on the cumulative process of decision-making and the narrowing of choice alternatives as persons grow older.

Lowenthal, Marjorie F. "Toward a Sociopsychological Theory of Change in Adulthood and Old Age." In James E. Birren, and K. Warner Schaie (Eds.), *Handbook of the Psychology of Aging.* New York: Van Nostrand Reinhold, 1977, pp. 116-127.

Contends that while contributions have been made by theorists who have extended the personality and stage theories of childhood development beyond adolescence, as yet there is no integrated sociopsychological theory of aging.

Maddox, George L. "Disengagement Theory: A Critical Evaluation." *The Gerontologist,* 1964, 4(2), pp. 80-82.

In reviewing the evidence regarding the disengagement theory, the author concludes that it does support the contention that social and psychological disengagement adequately characterize the modal response for elderly persons.

Marshall, Victor W., and Tindale, Joseph A. "Notes for a Radical Gerontology." *International Journal of Aging and Human Development,* 1978-1979, 9(2), pp. 163-175.

Provides a critique of the predominant theoretical perspectives in social gerontology for their normative assumptions. A radical scholarship in gerontology is proposed as an alternative.

Marshall, Victor W. "No Exit: A Symbolic Interactionist Perspective on Aging." *International Journal of Aging and Human Development,* 1978-1979, 9(4), pp. 345-358.

As an alternative to the normative perspective in studying socialization for old age, suggests the use of the symbolic interactionist perspective. According to Marshall, the concepts of "status passage" and "career", contained within the symbolic interactionist perspective, have considerable utility in gerontology.

Martin, J. David. "Power, Dependence, and the Complaints of the Elderly: A Social Exchange Perspective." *Aging and Human Development,* 1971, 2(2), pp. 108-112.

The social exchange theory is used to explain the complaining of many elderly persons as behavior that is reinforced by social interaction. The behavior pattern is paradoxical in that the more unpleasant the aged person is, the more that person is rewarded by the very persons who are being annoyed by his or her complaining.

Mercer, Jane R., and Butler, Edgar W. "Disengagement of the Aged Population and Response Differentials in Survey Research." *Social Forces,* 1967, 46(1), pp. 89-96.

The aged who refused to be interviewed were more "disengaged" than those who were cooperative. The authors suggest that a correlation factor for age bias should be used when precise estimates are needed.

Neugarten, Bernice L., and Havighurst, Robert J. "Disengagement Reconsidered in a Cross-National Context." In Robert J. Havighurst, et al. (Eds.), *Adjustment to Retirement: A Cross-National Study.* New York: Humanities Press, 1969, pp. 138-146.

Using cross-national data from retired men in different occupations, the authors find that psychological well-being is positively related to the level of social interaction. This finding does not support a portion of the disengagement theory and raises some important research questions.

Payne, Raymond. "Some Theoretical Approaches to the Sociology of Aging." *Social Forces,* 1960, 38(4), pp. 359-362.

Deals with the process by which the aging male assumes and maintains appropriate statuses and roles in his social world. It attempts to approach the phenomenon of aging through theories of socialization.

Prasad, S. Benjamin. "The Retirement Postulate of the Disengagement Theory." *The Gerontologist,* 1964, 4(1), pp. 20-23.

No empirical support is found for the postulate of the disengagement theory--that most men are ready to disengage or retire--when it is translated in terms of industrial workers.

Reingold, Jacob, and Dobrof, Rose. "Organization Theory and Homes for the Aged." *The Gerontologist,* 1965, 5(2), pp. 88-95 and p. 112.

Maintains that a productive approach to studying institutions for the aged is through organizational theory. Shows how the specialization that exists among staff members in homes for the aged can be utlilzed for organizational analysis.

Rifai, Marlene A.Y., and Ames, Sheila A. "Social Victimization of Older People: A Process of Social Exchange." In Marlene A.Y. Rifai (Ed.), *Justice and Older Americans.* Lexington, Mass.: Lexington Books, 1977, pp. 47-62.

Applies the social exchange model to help explain why inequalities exist and persist among older persons. The model is also used to offer strategies for preventing victimization of the elderly.

Riley, Matilda W., et al. "Socialization for Middle and Later Years." In David A. Goslin (Ed.), *Handbook of Socialization Theory and Research.* Chicago: Rand McNally, 1969, pp. 951-982.

As an aid to interpreting some of the relevant empirical data, a model of the socialization process is developed. This model regards socialization as a process which occurs not only within the individual being socialized but also between the individual and the social systems to which he or she belongs. The discussion emphasizes the important place society holds in the socialization process.

Rose, Arnold M. "A Current Theoretical Issue in Social Gerontology." *The Gerontologist,* 1964, 4(1), pp. 46-50.

Criticizes the Cumming and Henry theory of disengagement and points to some new trends which are counteracting the forces that make for the disengagement of older persons.

Rosenblatt, Daniel, and Taviss, Irene. "The Home for the Aged - Theory and Practice." *The Gerontologist,* 1966, 6(3), pp. 165-168.

Discusses the major points of the theories of Goffman, and Cumming and Henry dealing with aging and total institutions and examines them in the light of a study in a home for the aged.

Spence, Donald L. "The Meaning of Engagement." *International Journal of Aging and Human Development,* 1975, 6(3), pp. 193-198.

Although the author agrees with the general postulates of the disengagement theory, he does not agree with its interpretation and proposes an interactional analysis approach instead.

Trela, James E. "Status Inconsistency and Political Action in Old Age." In Jaber F. Gubrium (Ed.), *Time, Roles, and Self in Old Age.* New York: Human Sciences Press, 1976, pp. 126-147.

Develops a framework to view the process of aging in terms of status consistency theory. This framework is then used to explore the effects of the aging experience on political attitudes and beliefs, and to analyze the potential of the aged for unified political action.

Youmans, E. Grant. "Some Perspectives on Disengagement Theory." *The Gerontologist,* 1969, 9(4), pt. 1, pp. 254-257.

Discusses some of the limitations concerning the adequacy of the disengagement theory as a guide for research in gerontology. Suggests that a more fruitful approach would be to use a developmental concept such as the life course.

B. Research

Anderson, John E. "Research on Aging." In Ernest W. Burgess (Ed.), *Aging in Western Societies.* Chicago: The University of Chicago Press, 1960, pp. 354-376.

Describes social and psychological research projects in various European countries.

Anderson, Nancy N. "The Significance of Age Categories for Older Persons." *The Gerontologist,* 1967, 7(3), pp. 164-67 and p. 224.

Before further research is done on the significance of age categories, the author suggests that it would be fruitful to study the existence and characteristics of age groups within such contexts as day centers or living units.

Atchley, Robert C. "Respondents vs. Refusers in an Interview Study of Retired Women: An Analysis of Selected Characteristics." *Journal of Gerontology,* 1969, 24(1), pp. 42-47.

Examines differences between respondents and refusers in an interview study of retired women. Refusers tend to be in poor health, to have a perceived lack of sufficient income, are loners, and have a good opinion of themselves.

Atchley, Robert C., and George, Linda K. "Symptomatic Measurement of Age." *The Gerontologist,* 1973, 13(3), pt. 1, pp. 332-336.

Presents a four-item Guttman scale of withdrawal from the job. This scale illustrates the feasibility of measuring other social dimensions of aging by this technique.

Atchley, Robert C. "Issues in Retirement Research." *The Gerontologist,* 1979, 19(1), pp. 44-54.

Identifies some key issues, pertinent variables, and research questions concerning retirement. These issues and variables include: consideration of how retirement is defined and the types of retirement factors affecting the decision and timing of retirement, and the effects of retirement on couples, work organizations, communities, and society.

Back, Kurt W., and Bourque, Linda B. "Life Graphs: Aging and Cohort Effect." *Journal of Gerontology,* 1970, 25(3), pp. 249-255.

Reports on a "Draw-a-Graph" technique for collecting gerontological data. A random national sample of the population was asked to draw a graph representing their life. Results indicate that the curve of life satisfaction is mainly dependent on age and that generational effects have little influence.

Bennett, Ruth. "Social Context--A Neglected Variable in Research on Aging." *Aging and Human Development,* 1970, 1(2), pp. 97-116.

An analysis of social gerontological literature from 1959 to 1969 reveals that while the elderly were studied in a variety of social systems, these systems do not play an important role either as dependent or independent variables. Stresses the need for more gerontological research based on samples of social systems rather than individuals.

Bloom, Martin. "Measurement of the Socioeconomic Status of the Aged: New Thoughts on an Old Subject." *The Gerontologist,* 1972, 12(4), pp. 375-378.

Attempts to clarify the meaning of socioeconomic status for the elderly and offers a procedure for measuring it.

Borgatta, Edgar F., and McCluskey, Neil G. (Eds.). *Aging and Society: Current Research and Policy Perspectives.* Beverly Hills, Calif.: Sage Publications, 1980.

Designed to stimulate interest and research on some central issues in gerontology, this book includes essays on the economic, political, health, and psychological perspectives of aging.

Breen, Leonard Z. "The Aging Individual." In Clark Tibbitts (Ed.), *Handbook of Social Gerontology.* Chicago: The University of Chicago Press, 1960, pp. 145-162.

Gives an overview of some of the research in several of the disciplines concerned with aging.

Brehm, Henry P. "Sociology and Aging: Orientation and Research." *The Gerontologist,* 1968, 8(2), pt. 2, pp. 24-31.

Discusses some of the areas of social research on the aging process and the results of that research.

Britton, Joseph H. "Dimensions of Adjustment of Older Adults." *Journal of Gerontology,* 1963, 18(1), pp. 60-65.

Investigates the problem of measuring adjustment by determining the dimensions which underlie several measures of adjustment. Three dimensions emerge: an activity factor, a sociability factor, and a composure-serenity-integrity factor.

Carp, Frances M. "Compound Criteria in Gerontological Research." *Journal of Gerontology,* 1969, 24(3), pp. 341-347.

Presents two sets of data analyses, one involving adjustment and the other disengagement. The findings indicate that some inconsistencies from study to study concerning disengagement and adjustment may result from the use of different partial and compound criteria with different elements.

Carp, Frances M. "Position Effects on Interview Responses." *Journal of Gerontology,* 1974, 29(5), pp. 581-587.

Two types of position effects upon the response tendencies of older persons are: (1) serial order of response options for an item; and (2) position of items in the interview schedule. Findings indicate that it may not be necessary to present general questions before specific ones to avoid response contamination. Also to obtain valid group values, a counterbalanced presentation is necessary.

Cutler, Stephen J. "An Approach to the Measurement of Prestige Loss among the Aged." *Aging and Human Development,* 1972, 3(3), pp. 285-292.

Suggests a method for measuring the status of the elderly in industrial societies. By employing this method, tentative findings indicate the existence and recognition of prestige loss among the aged.

Dobson, Cynthia, et al. "Anomia, Self-Esteem, and Life Satisfaction: Interrelationships among Three Scales of Well-Being." *Journal of Gerontology,* 1979, 34(4), pp. 569-572.

The analysis revealed some overlap among the scales. While Srole's anomia scale and Rosenberg's scale of self-esteem measures distinct dimensions, some of the LSI-Z items combined with the anomia and self-esteem items.

Filsinger, Erik, and Sauer, William J. "An Empirical Typology of Adjustment to Aging." *Journal of Gerontology,* 1978, 33(3), pp. 437-445.

Constructs a typology of adjustors to age. Derives three male types of adjustors and two female types through cluster analysis.

George, Linda K. "The Happiness Syndrome: Methodological and Substantive Issues in the Study of Social Psychological Well-Being in Adulthood." *The Gerontologist,* 1979, 19(2), pp. 210-216.

Advocates the use of available survey data as a starting point for examining life satisfaction and related concepts from the perspective of aging. Describes six major national surveys.

George, Linda K., and Bearon, Lucille B. *Quality of Life in Older Persons: Meaning and Measurement.* New York: Human Sciences Press, 1980.

Presents a conceptual context for the accessment of quality of life and introduces a set of criteria to use in selecting a measuring instrument. Describes 22 measuring instruments in terms of psychometric properties and conceptual and methodological issues.

Glenn, Norval D., and Zody, Richard E. "Cohort Analysis with National Survey Data." *The Gerontologist,* 1970, 10(3), pt. 1, pp. 233-240.

Points out how cohort analysis of existing survey sample data can be a valuable resource for social gerontologists. Reviews the procedures that must be followed in this type of analysis and provides an example of a cohort study.

Graney, Marshall J., and Graney, Edith E. "Scaling Adjustment in Older Persons." *International Journal of Aging and Human Development,* 1973, 4(4), pp. 351-359.

Discusses the advantages and disadvantages of several scaling procedures. A scaling procedure is developed and used to collect data to test the hypothetical relationship between happiness and personal adjustment. The data indicate the two are unrelated.

Graney, Marshall. "The Aged and Their Environment: The Study of Intervening Variables." In Jaber F. Gubrium (Ed.), *Late Life: Communities and Environmental Policy.* Springfield, Ill.: Charles C. Thomas, 1974, pp. 5-16.

Suggests a strategy for theory development and data analysis applicable to the sociology of aging.

Havighurst, Robert J. "Successful Aging." *The Gerontologist,* 1961, 1(1), pp. 8-13.

Describes the various measures of successful aging, their validity, and use.

Henretta, John C.; Campbell, Richard T.; and Gardocki, Gloria. "Survey Research in Aging: An Evaluation of the Harris Survey." *The Gerontologist,* 1977, 17(2), pp. 160-167.

Proposes the use of national surveys instead of local samples to obtain a representative sample of the elderly in this country. The authors suggest that this can best be done through a supplement to a survey similar to the NORC General Social Survey every 2 or 3 years.

Jeffers, Frances C.; Eisdorfer, Carl; and Busse, Ewald. "Measurement of Age Identification: A Methodologic Note." *Journal of Gerontology,* 1962, 17(4), pp. 437-439.

Using a card-sort technique, the subjects who had previously answered the Activities and Attitudes Inventory (Burgess, et al., 1948) placed the terms "young," "middle-aged," "elderly," "old," and "aged" in an ordered sequence. Differences were found between the order defined by Burgess and the card-sort order of the subjects. The authors conclude that it might be more appropriate for a card-sort to be arranged in terms of major life events and in this way the subjects' attitudes toward the different stages of life also could be studied.

Kafer, Rudolph A., et al. "Aging Opinion Survey: A Report on Instrument Development." *International Journal of Aging and Human Development,* 1980, 11(4), pp. 319-333.

Describes the development of the Aging Opinion Survey, a multidimensional attitude instrument regarding aging and the elderly.

Kahana, Eva, and Kahanna, Boaz. "Theoretical and Research Perspectives on Grandparenthood." *Aging and Human Development,* 1971, 2(4), pp. 261-268.

Based on a review of the literature and several exploratory studies, the authors summarize some of the issues and problems relating to research on grandparenthood. They propose a scheme for sorting out some of the findings about grandparents and grandchildren.

Kahana, Eva. "Matching Environments to Needs of the Aged: A Conceptual Scheme." In Jaber F. Gubrium (Ed.), *Late Life: Communities and Environmental Policy.* Springfield, Ill.: Charles C. Thomas, 1974, pp. 201-214.

Offers a conceptual model for matching environments to the needs of the aged and shows how this model has been used in a study of three nursing homes.

Kahana, Eva; Liang, Jersey; and Felton, Barbara J. "Alternative Modes of Person-Environment Fit: Prediction of Morale in Three Homes for the Aged." *Journal of Gerontology,* 1980, 35(4), pp. 584-595.

Presents person-environment fit (P-E Fit) conceptualizations for the elderly and provides different methods for operationalizing them. Findings from a study to test these theoretical models indicate that P-E fit scores along the dimensions of impulse control, congregation, and segregation make a significant contribution to the understanding of the morale of the elderly in homes for the aged.

Kent, Donald P.; Kastenbaum, Robert; and Sherwood, Sylvia (Eds.), *Research Planning and Action for the Elderly: The Power and Potential of Social Science.* New York: Behavioral Publications, 1972.

Attempts to integrate theory, research, and practice in social gerontology.

Lee, Gary R., and Finney, John M. "Sampling in Social Gerontology: A Method of Locating Specialized Populations." *Journal of Gerontology,* 1977, 32(6), pp. 689-693.

Describes a two-stage sampling method for obtaining large probability samples of specialized populations such as the elderly.

Lipman, Aaron. "Latent Function Analysis in Gerontological Research." *The Gerontologist,* 1969, 9(1), pp. 33-36.

Shows how latent functions can play a crucial role in gerontological research and offers a theoretical strategy.

Lohmann, Nancy. "Correlations of Life Satisfaction, Morale, and Adjustment Measures." *Journal of Gerontology,* 1977, 32(1), pp. 73-75.

Using Pearson Product Moment correlation coefficients, results show a high level of correlation among several measures of life satisfaction, morale, and adjustment.

Lohmann, Nancy. "A Factor Analysis of Life Satisfaction, Adjustment and Morale Measures with Elderly Adults." *International Journal of Aging and Human Development,* 1980, 11(1), pp. 35-43.

Examines seven frequently used measures of life satisfaction by the technique of construct validation. The results reveal that there is a construct, called "life satisfaction," which is shared by six of the seven measures and that no instrument best encompasses that construct.

Maddox, George L. "Sociological Perspectives in Gerontological Research." In Donald P. Kent, Robert Kastenbaum, and Sylvia Sherwood (Eds.), *Research Planning and Action for the Elderly: The Power and Potential of Social Science.* New York: Behavioral Publications, 1972, pp. 315-333.

Points out the theoretical and methodological limitations found in Cumming and Henry's disengagement theory and, more specifically, their deliberate nonuse of a sociological perspective in analyses of data. These limitations illustrate some persistent research problems in social gerontology.

Maddox, George L., and Wiley, James. "Scope, Concepts and Methods in the Study of Aging." In Robert H. Binstock, and Ethel Shanas (Eds.), *Handbook of Aging and the Social Sciences.* New York: Van Nostrand Reinhold, 1976, pp. 3-34.

This introductory chapter traces the recent history of the social scientific study of aging, and highlights major themes and issues that will be discussed in the following chapters.

Makarushka, Julia L., and McDonald, Robert D. "Informed Consent, Research, and Geriatric Patients: The Responsibility of Institutional Review Committees." *The Gerontologist,* 1979, 19(1), pp. 61-66.

Examines the responsibilities of the Institutional Review Committee to the older patient as a potential research subject. Discusses the functions of the informed consent process and the effects of inappropriate informed consent procedures.

Neugarten, Bernice L.; Havighurst, Robert J.; and Tobin, Sheldon S. "Measurement of Life Satisfaction." *Journal of Gerontology,* 1961, 16(2), pp. 134-143.

Presents a set of scales for rating life satisfaction.

Palmore, Erdman. "Potential Demographic Contributions to Gerontology." *The Gerontologist,* 1973, 13(2), pp. 236-242.

Asserts that demography could make an important contribution to gerontology. Suggests some types of demographic analysis that could lead to significant advances in gerontology.

Palmore, Erdman. "When Can Age, Period, and Cohort Be Separated?" *Social Forces,* 1978, 57(1), pp. 282-295.

Presents a model for dealing with the problem of separating age effects from period and cohort effects. Compares the model to other methods and discusses its usefulness.

Payne, Barbara P. "The Older Volunteer: Social Role Continuity and Development." *The Gerontologist,* 1977, 17(4), pp. 355-361.

Offers a theoretical model of new social role reconstructuring. The model is illustrated by data from a longitudinal study of the older volunteer.

Pihlblad, C. Terence; Rosencranz, Howard A.; and McNevin, Tony E. "An Examination of the Effects of Perceptual Frames of Reference in

Interviewing Older Respondents." *The Gerontologist,* 1967, 7(2), pt. 1, pp. 125-127.

Although measurable differences were found to exist among interviewers in attitudes toward the elderly, these did not significantly affect the interviewers subjective evaluations of the older respondents.

Pippin, Roland N. "Assessing the Needs of the Elderly with Existing Data." *The Gerontologist,* 1980, 20(1), pp. 65-70.

Gives a technique for the use of secondary data to determine priorities in regard to the needs of the elderly. Discusses the advantages and disadvantages of utilizing secondary data.

Powers, Edward A., and Bultena, Gordon L. "Characteristics of Deceased Dropouts in Longitudinal Research." *Journal of Gerontology,* 1972, 27(4), pp. 530-535.

Compares persons in a longitudinal study lost through death and those reinterviewed. Characteristics of subjects lost through death included being older, lower family incomes, and a greater number of health difficulties. Also they did not generally differ from reinterviewed respondents in life satisfaction, self-assessment of health, or attitudes about their lives.

Ridley, Jeanne C.; Backrach, Christine A.; and Dawson, Deborah A. "Recall and Reliability of Interview Data from Older Women." *The Journal of Gerontology,* 1979, 34(1), pp. 99-105.

Finds that older respondents have little problem in recalling information about personal events. The proportion that gave responses was over 90%. Also the study indicates that there is little evidence of differentials in recall ability and reliability by respondents' age, education, or health status.

Rose, Arnold M. "The Subculture of the Aging: A Topic for Sociological Research." *The Gerontologist,* 1962, 2(3), pp. 123-127.

Observes that there are certain conditions in our society such as the formation of group identity among the elderly which are creating and influencing the development of an aging subculture. Rose stresses the need for systematic studies in this area which has been neglected by sociological researchers.

Rose, Arnold M. "The Subculture of Aging: A Framework for Research in Social Gerontology." In Arnold M. Rose and Warren A. Peterson (Eds.), *Older People and Their Social World.* Philadelphia: F.A. Davis, 1965, pp. 3-16.

An elaboration of an earlier draft in 1962 (see above). Discusses some of the ways in which older people in this country are developing a subculture and how they are becoming conscious of themselves as a distinctive group.

Rose, Charles L. "The Measurement of Social Age." *Aging and Human Development,* 1972, 3(2), pp. 153-168.

Provides a technique for the measurement of social age. Demonstrates the usefulness of this concept and presents a specific example.

Rosencranz, Howard A., and McNevin, Tony E. "A Factor Analysis of Attitudes toward the Aged." *The Gerontologist,* 1969, 9(1), pp. 55-59.

Constructs and analyzes an instrument to measure stereotypic attitudes toward the elderly and to determine the content of such attitudes.

Rosencranz, Howard A., and Pihlblad, C. Terence. "Measuring the Health of the Elderly." *Journal of Gerontology,* 1970, 25(2), pp. 129-133.

Attempts to construct a health index based on self-reported statements. Validation of the index was made by relating it to the degree of physical mobility or physical impairment and to the individual's self perception of his or her health.

Rosow, Irving, and Breslau, Naomi. "A Guttman Health Scale for the Aged." *Journal of Gerontology,* 1966, 21(4), pp. 556-559.

Presents a Guttman scale of the functional health of older people. The scale is based on respondents' judgments and relies on objective referents of people's activities and specific functional capacities.

Seltzer, Mildred M. "Suggestions for the Examination of Time-Disordered Relationships." In Jaber F. Gubrium (Ed.), *Time, Roles, and Self in Old Age.* New York: Human Sciences Press, 1976, pp. 111-125.

Based on a model developed by Merton, the author discusses the causes and consequences of time-disordered relationships that occur in middle age and old age.

Shanas, Ethel. "National Studies of Older People in the United States.: In Richard H. Williams, Clark Tibbitts, and Wilma Donahue (Eds.), *Processes of Aging: Social and Psychological Perspectives,* vol. 2. New York: Atherton Press, 1963, pp. 9-24.

Discusses the value and techniques of national surveys of older people. Notes that the data from such surveys provide a framework for the study of special age groups and can measure changes in the characteristics of the elderly population.

Sherman, Susan R. "Methodology in a Study of Residents of Retirement Housing." *Journal of Gerontology,* 1973, 28(3), pp. 351-358.

Describes the methodology used in a longitudinal study of residents of six retirement housing sites. Gives the criteria for selection of the sites, interview construction, as well as matching procedures and methods used to minimize attrition.

Streib, Gordon F. "Longitudinal Studies in Social Gerontology." In Richard H. Williams, Clark Tibbitts, and Wilma Donahue (Eds.), *Processes of Aging: Social and Psychological Perspectives,* vol. 2. New York: Atherton Press, 1963, pp. 25-39.

Examines longitudinal studies in social gerontology and some of the problems involved in this type of research.

Streib, Gordon F. "Participants and Drop-Outs in a Longitudinal Study." *Journal of Gerontology,* 1966, 21(2), pp. 200-209.

Analyzes demographic information for the participants and the drop-outs in the Cornell Study of Occupational Retirement. Results show that foreign-born persons are more likely to drop out of the study than native-born, and males are more likely to drop out than females. Persons of lower socioeconomic levels are more likely to leave the study than those in higher socioeconomic levels.

Sussman, Marvin B. "Use of the Longitudinal Design in Studies of Long-Term Illness: Some Advantages and Limitations." *The Gerontologist,* 1964, pt. 2, 4(2), pp. 25-29.

Discusses several reasons for selecting a longitudinal design and some of the methological problems encountered in this type of study.

Tissue, Thomas L. "A Guttman Scale of Disengagement Potential." *Journal of Gerontology,* 1968, 23(4), pp. 513-516.

Proposes an instrument to operationalize psychological disengagement.

Van Es, J.C., and Bowling, Michael. "A Model for Analyzing the Aging of Local Populations: Illinois Counties between 1950 and 1970." *International Journal of Aging and Human Development,* 1978-1979, 9(4), pp. 377-387.

Develops and applies a model relating migration and its effect on age structure to those community characteristics which are most likely to influence decisions on migration.

PART 2

CULTURE AND SOCIETY

Chapter 3

CULTURE

A. Values and Attitudes

Ansello, Edward F. "Age and Ageism in Children's First Literature." *Educational Gerontology,* 1977 2(3), pp. 255-274.

A survey of children's first literature reveals that little or no effect, negatively or positively, typifies the older characters. The elderly are portrayed as noncreative and boring.

Antonucci, Toni; Gillett, Nancy; and Hoyer, Frances W. "Values and Self-Esteem in Three Generations of Men and Women." *Journal of Gerontology,* 1979, 34(3), pp. 415-422.

Studies similarities and differences in values within families across three generations. Findings reveal that the oldest generation rates instrumental values higher than the youngest generation. Also the oldest generation rates values appropriate for retirement higher, while maintaining values associated with work and success.

Auerbach, Doris N., and Levenson, Richard L. "Second Impressions: Attitude Change in College Students toward the Elderly." *The Gerontologist,* 1977, 17(4), pp. 362-366.

Finds that there are parallels between research models in ethnic contact studies and intergenerational contact. The attitudes of young college students toward their elderly classmates became significantly more negative after a semester in the classroom together. Discusses reasons for the negative attitudes of the young toward the old.

Bekker, L. DeMoyne, and Taylor, Charles. "Attitudes toward the Aged in a Multi-Generational Sample." *Journal of Gerontology,* 1966, 21(1), pp. 115-118.

Reveals that students who have living great-grandparents perceive their grandparents as having fewer characteristics of old age than those students who have no living great-grandparents.

Bell, Bill D., and Stanfield, Gary G. "Chronological Age in Relation to Attitudinal Judgments: An Experimental Analysis." *Journal of Gerontology,* 1973, 28(4), pp. 491-496.

A group of college students and a group of older persons heard and rated a recorded discussion by a stimulus person described as being either 25 or 65 years of age. The findings show a slight but nonsignificant tendency for the younger subjects to rate an older stimulus person more positively than the older subjects. All subjects reflect a tendency, though not statistically significant, to rate the younger stimulus person more positively than the older person.

Bell, Bill D., and Stanfield, Gary G. "The Aging Stereotype in Experimental Perspective." *The Gerontologist,* 1973, 13(3), pt. 1, pp. 341-344.

Examines the influence of age designations upon ratings of a recorded discussion by a stimulus person described as being either 25 or 65 years of age. The data show no significant differences in the rating of the stimulus person in either the experimental or the control group.

Brubaker, Timothy H., and Powers, Edward A. "The Stereotype of 'Old': A Review and Alternative Approach." *Journal of Gerontology,* 1976, 31(4), pp. 441-447.

Studies on the stereotype of old age contain both positive and negative elements. Instead of assuming that an elderly person accepts a negative stereotype of old age from which a negative self-definition is derived, the authors propose a model in which the self-concept mediates between the definition of the self as old and the acceptance of a positive or negative stereotype of old age.

Christenson, James A. "Generational Value Differences." *The Gerontologist,* 1977, 17(4), pp. 367-373.

Finds that adults of different age groups show no major variations in their adherence to social values. However, there is a variation in terms of personal values. Younger adults attach greater importance to work, leisure, and achievement than do older adults.

Clark, Margaret, and Anderson, Barbara G. *Culture and Aging: An Anthropological Study of Older Americans.* Springfield, Ill.: Charles C. Thomas, 1967.

This study is based on a sample of 435 elderly persons in San Francisco. Some of the subjects are considered mentally healthy while others have undergone treatment for mental disorders. The major focus is on the personal and social factors relevant to a good or poor adaptation in old age.

Clark, Margaret. "Cultural Values and Dependency in Later Life." In Richard Kalish (Ed.), *Dependencies of Old People.* Ann Arbor and Detroit: Institute of Gerontology, University of Michigan and Wayne State University, 1969, pp. 59-83.

Discusses six types of dependencies in old age and their relationship to different cultural values and the meaning that dependency has in American society.

Clark, Margaret. "Cultural Values and Dependency in Later Life." In Donald O. Cowgill and Lowell D. Holmes (Eds.), *Aging and Modernization.* New York: Appleton-Century-Crofts, 1972, pp. 263-274.

Describes the concept of dependency in old age and its relationship to varying cultural values and environments and distinguishes various types of dependencies.

Clemente, Frank. "Age and the Perception of National Priorities." *The Gerontologist,* 1975, 15(1), pp. 61-63.

Reveals that in terms of spending more money to solve national problems, older persons are more conservative than younger persons even on issues that are of direct benefit to them.

Collette-Pratt, Clara. "Attitudinal Predictors of Devaluation of Old Age in a Multigenerational Sample." *Journal of Gerontology,* 1976, 31(2), pp. 193-197.

Focuses on the devaluation of old age as compared to age in general by college students, middle-aged persons, and the elderly. The most consistent predictor of devaluation is negative attitudes toward poor health. Negative attitudes toward death are a significant predictor of devaluation among the young and middle-aged.

Crockett, Walter H.; Press, Allen N.; and Osterkamp, Marilyn. "The Effect of Deviations from Stereotyped Expectations upon Attitudes toward Older Persons." *Journal of Gerontology,* 1979, 34(3), pp. 368-374.

An interview about the way a woman aged 36 and a woman aged 76 spent the preceding day and described their lives was read by two groups of subjects. The subjects consistently rated the older woman more favorably than the younger woman even when her actions were socially undesirable and corresponded to negative stereotypes of older persons.

Cryns, Arthur G., and Monk, Abraham. "Attitudes of the Aged toward the Young: A Multivariate Study in Intergenerational Perception." *The Journal of Gerontology,* 1972, 27(1), pp. 107-112.

Examines the attitudes of older males toward three categories of young people: the generalized young, American soldiers in Vietnam, and college students. Men who had a high level of life satisfaction and a good relationship with their own children had significantly more favorable attitudes toward the young than those men of low life satisfaction and poor filial relationships. Also the respondents were more positively inclined toward the young men in Vietnam than toward the generalized young or college students.

Cryns, Arthur G., and Monk, Abraham. "Attitudes toward Youth as a Function of Adult Age: A Multivariate Study in Intergenerational Dynamics." *International Journal of Aging and Human Development,* 1973, 4(1), pp. 23-33.

Investigates the social attitudes of young adult males, middle-aged males, and elderly males toward young people in general, American soldiers in Vietnam, and college students. Findings reveal that tolerance of youth and a significantly more positive attitude toward them tends to increase linearly with age.

Cutler, Stephen J., et al. "Aging and Conservatism: Cohort Changes in Attitudes about Legalized Abortion." *Journal of Gerontology,* 1980, 35(1), pp. 115-123.

Attitudes about the availability of legal abortion are used to evaluate the aging-conservatism hypothesis. Survey data obtained from four cohorts were traced over a twelve-year period, 1965-1977. Results indicated that attitudes about the availability of legal abortions became more liberal during 1965 to 1973 and public opinion became relatively stable after that. This general pattern characterized all cohorts. There is no evidence of attitudinal rigidity, growing conservatism, or change at a slower rate among the older cohorts.

Dowd, James J. "The Problems of Generations: A Generational Analysis." *International Journal of Aging and Human Development,* 1979-1980, 10(3), pp. 213-230.

Investigates the degree to which longitudinal, cross-sectional, and time lag differences contribute to any observed change in values and attitudes over time. Findings suggest that individuals do not necessarily become less tolerant as they age. Also during periods of increased tolerance, all age groups including the elderly, respond in the same direction.

Fengler, Alfred P., and Wood, Vivian. "The Generation Gap: An Analysis of Attitudes on Contemporary Issues." *The Gerontologist,* 1972, 12(2), pt. 1, pp. 124-128.

Studies attitude differences among three generations, a college student, his two parents, and one grandparent. Age provides the most consistent explanation for the generational differences that are found in their values and attitudes.

Fillenbaum, Gerda G. "On the Relation Between Attitude to Work and Attitude to Retirement." *Journal of Gerontology,* 1971, 26(2), pp. 244-248.

Finds a very limited relationship between job attitude and retirement attitude among non-academic employees at a university and medical center. Suggests that only where work holds the central position in a person's life should job attitude affect retirement attitude.

Gelfand, Donald E., and Fandetti, Donald V. "Suburban and Urban White Ethnics: Attitudes toward Care of the Aged." *The Gerontologist,* 1980, 20(5), pp. 588-594.

Compares a sample of Italian-American suburban residents and a sample of Italian and Polish inner-city residents regarding attitudes toward their continued use of traditional structures for the care of aged family members. The suburban group is more likely than the inner-city group to turn to purchasing care for the bedridden elderly in the private sector. Both groups show continued respect for services under church auspices.

Gergen, Kenneth J., and Back, Kurt W. "Cognitive Constriction in Aging and Attitudes toward International Issues." In Ida H. Simpson and John C. McKinney (Eds.), *Social Aspects of Dying.* Durham, N.C.: Duke University Press, 1966, pp. 322-334.

Examines the relationship between age and preferences for certain types of solutions to problems in international relations. Results indicate that the elderly tend to prefer solutions to problems which would terminate the problems as rapidly as possible. The evidence suggests that such preferences are a function of the aged person's restricted time perspective.

Goudy, Willis J.; Powers, Edward A.; and Keith, Patricia. "Work and Retirement: A Test of Attitudinal Relationships." *Journal of Gerontology,* 1975, 30(2), pp. 193-198.

Analyzes the relationship between work satisfaction and retirement attitudes. The results offer only marginal support for an inverse relationship between work satisfaction and retirement attitude.

Guemple, D. Lee. "Human Resource Management: The Dilemma of the Aging Eskimo." *Sociological Symposium,* No. 2, Spring 1969, pp. 59-74.

Discusses the social position of the elderly among the Eskimos and makes some comparisons between Eskimos and Americans in their treatment of the problems of the aged.

Hansen, Gary D., et al. "Older People in the Midwest: Conditions and Attitudes." *Older People and Their Social World.* Philadelphia: F.A. Davis, 1965, pp. 311-322.

Focuses on older persons in five Midwestern states and gives an assessment of their self-image and environment. Topics which are discussed include health, income, housing, family and friends, and social participation.

Harris, Louis and Associates. *The Myth and Reality of Aging in America.* Washington, D.C.: National Council on the Aging, 1975.

This nationwide survey provides information on public beliefs about old age and the elderly. Some topics covered include: public attitudes toward old age, the public's image of "most" people over 65, and perceived social and economic contributions of the elderly.

Hendricks, Jon, and Hendricks, C. Davis. "The Age Old Question of Old Age: Was It Really So Much Better Back When?" *International Journal of Aging and Human Development*, 1977-1978, 8(2), pp. 139-154.

Based on historical, literary, and archaelogical reports from ancient Greece to the present, the evidence suggests that negative attitudes toward the elderly were as pervasive in the past as they are now.

Hess, Beth B. "Stereotypes of the Aged." *Journal of Communication*, 1974, 24(4), pp. 76-85.

Hess discusses the mass media representations of the elderly and how they result in the perpetuation of myths regarding the aged.

Hickey, Tom, and Kalish, Richard A. "Young People's Perceptions of Adults. *Journal of Gerontology*, 1968, 23(2), pp. 215-219.

A 20-item questionnaire was administered to persons between the ages of eight and twenty to examine their attitudes and perceptions toward the elderly. The data reveal that children and young persons perceive age-related differences between adult age groups. The fact that these differences become greater as the child becomes older was borne out for the descriptive items on the questionnaire but not for the evaluative items. Also the older the adult, the less pleasant image of him or her is held by the child.

Hickey, Tom, et al. "Attitudes toward Aging as a Function of In-Service Training and Practitioner Age." *Journal of Gerontology*, 1976, 31(6), pp. 681-686.

Focuses on attitude change toward aging that are associated with a three-hour training program. Results show no negative attitudes toward aging and the aged in all age groups. Finds younger women to have less cynicism toward aging and less social distance from the aged.

Holden, Karen C. "Comparability of the Measured Labor Force of Older Women in Japan and the United States." *Journal of Gerontology*, 1978, 33(3), pp. 422-426.

Older women in Japan are more likely to be employed than women in the U.S., but labor force data for the two countries are not entirely comparable. One reason is the difference in the definition of unpaid family workers which contributes to the higher measured labor force participation in Japan, especially for the women and elderly. Another reason is that the Japanese census is taken during one of the peak agricultural seasons. While older women are more likely to be only part-time and seasonal workers at this period, they report themselves as working because of instructions to do so.

Invester, Connie, and King, Karl. "Attitudes of Adolescents toward the Aged." *The Gerontologist*, 1977, 17(1), pp. 85-89.

Although the majority of adolescents showed a positive attitude toward the aged, adolescents of the lower classes were less favorable toward the aged than those in the upper class.

Johnson, Gregory, and Kamara, J. Lawrence. "Growing Up and Growing Old: The Politics of Age Exclusion." *International Journal of Aging and Human Development,* 1977-1978, 8(2), pp. 99-110.

Discusses the exclusion of the young and the old from the productive life of society and how this exclusion has resulted in economic discrimination, age stereotyping, and territorial segregation.

Kafer, Rudolph A., et al. "Aging Opinion Survey: A Report on Instrument Development." *International Journal of Aging and Human Development,* 1980, 11(4), pp. 319-333.

Describes the development of a multidimensional attitude instrument regarding aging and the aged.

Kalish, Richard A. "Of Children and Grandfathers: A Speculative Essay on Dependency." In Richard A. Kalish (Ed.), *Dependencies in Old People.* Ann Arbor and Detroit: Institute of Gerontology, University of Michigan and Wayne State University, 1969, pp. 73-83.

Explores the ways in which the values internalized by the elderly make their increasing need for dependence a painful thing.

Kalish, Richard A., and Johnson, Ann I. "Value Similarities and Differences in Three Generations of Women." *Journal of Marriage and the Family,* 1972, 34(1), pp. 49-54.

Using a sample of young women, their mothers, and maternal grandmothers, a Likert-type questionnaire composed of six scales was employed to investigate similarities and differences in values and attitudes between generations. The results show that mother-daughter correlations are higher than mother-grandmother or daughter-grandmother correlations on some scales but lower on others. Grandmothers and mothers seem farthest apart and daughters and mothers the closest.

Kastenbaum, Robert, and Durkee, Nancy. "Young People View Old Age." In Robert Kastenbaum (Ed.), *New Thoughts on Old Age.* New York: Springer, 1964, pp. 237-249.

Explores the attitudes of young adults toward old age. Finds that there is some evidence indicating a predominantly negative appraisal of older people. Also the capacity for emphatic identification of young people with persons who are already old is diminished by their lack of contemplation of their own later years.

Kidwell, I. Jane, and Booth, Alan. "Social Distance and Intergenerational Relations." *The Gerontologist,* 1977, 17(5), pp. 412-420.

Finds social distance to exist between all age groups and is a linear function of age difference. People appear to feel more socially distant from older people regardless of their own age.

Kleemeier, Robert W. "Attitudes toward Special Settings for the Aged." In Richard H. Williams, Clark Tibbitts, and Wilma Donahue (Eds.), *Processes of Aging: Social and Psychological Perspectives,* vol. 2. New York: Atherton Press, 1963, pp. 101-121.

Discusses special settings for the elderly, the place of special settings, and the attitudes toward them.

Kogan, Nathan. "Beliefs, Attitudes, and Stereotypes about Old People: A New Look at Old Issues." *Research on Aging,* 1979, 1(1), pp. 11-36.

Discusses the body of research on beliefs, attitudes, and stereotypes about the elderly. Raises a number of conceptual and methodological issues.

Ludwig, Edward G., and Eichhorn, Robert L. "Age and Disillusionment: A Study of Value Changes Associated with Aging." *Journal of Gerontology,* 1967, 22(1), pp. 59-65.

Focuses on some changes and modifications in values which accompany aging. Aging tends to undermine one's faith in science and technology and leads to a rejection of an optimistic approach to life. Also there is a strict adherence to the work-activity orientation by the elderly at a time when society expects it to be relinquished.

Lutsky, Neil S. "Attitudes toward Old Age and Elderly Persons." In C. Eisdorfer (Ed.), *Annual Review of Gerontology and Geriatrics,* vol. 1. New York: Springer, 1980, pp. 287-331.

Presents a review of attitude studies in gerontology, concentrating on the literature published between January 1976 and June 1979.

Maddox, George L. "Growing Old: Getting Beyond the Stereotypes." In Rosamonde R. Boyd and Charles G. Oakes (Eds.), *Foundations of Practical Gerontology,* 2d ed. Columbia, South Carolina: University of South Carolina Press, 1973, pp.2-16.

Reviews and assesses the stereotypes that are supposed to characterize the elderly along with their implications for social policy.

Meddin, Jay. "Generations and Aging: A Longitudinal Study." *International Journal of Aging and Human Development,* 1975, 6(2), pp. 85-101.

Focuses on the relationship between age and subjective outlook. To account for or to minimize differences in attitudes, values, and beliefs between persons of different ages, three models are proposed: the "age status" model, the "generations" model, and the "illusion of differences" model. Tests hypotheses derived from these models and strong support is found for the "generations" hypothesis which predicts that young adults will show greater attitude changes than older persons.

Messer, Mark. "Race Differences in Selected Attitudinal Dimensions of the Elderly." *The Gerontologist,* 1968, 8(4), pp. 245-249.

Reveals that the elderly blacks have higher morale, less of a feeling of integration with the overall society, and are less likely to deny their actual age status than their white counterparts.

Neugarten, Bernice L. "Grow Old Along with Me! The Best Is Yet to Be." *Psychology Today,* 1971, 5(7), pp. 45-48, 79-81.

Some of the myths and stereotypes about aging are dispelled.

O'Gorman, Hubert J. "False Consciousness of Kind: Pluralistic Ignorance among the Aged." *Research on Aging,* 1980, 2(1), pp. 105-128.

Using data from the 1974 survey conducted by Harris and Associates for the National Council on the Aging, patterns of perceived similarity and dissimilarity among the elderly are examined. The findings show that the more serious the respondents thought a problem to be in their lives, the more likely they are to identify it as being very serious among other elderly persons. Pluralistic ignorance among the aged, the author concludes, is based on misconceptions of similarity and dissimilarity.

Orbach, Harold L. "Social Values and the Institutionalization of Retirement." In Richard H. Williams, Clark Tibbitts, and Wilma Donahue (Eds.), *Processes of Aging: Social and Psychological Perspectives,* vol. 2. New York: Atherton Press, 1963, pp. 389-402.

Considers the historical dynamics of retirement as a social phenomenon and analyzes the character of the basic value systems which have developed on the societal level to deal with retirement.

Palmore, Erdman B. "Attitudes toward Aging as Shown by Humor." *The Gerontologist,* 1971, 2(3), pt. 1, pp. 181-186.

The content analysis of jokes about aging reveals that over half reflect a negative view of aging. Those jokes dealing with aged men are more positive than those dealing with aged women.

Peterson, David A., and Eden, Donna Z. "Teen-agers and Aging: Adolescent Literature as an Attitude Source." *Educational Gerontology,* 1977, 2(3), pp. 311-325.

A content analysis of adolescent literature was done to determine the ways in which older persons are portrayed. The study found few negative stereotypes of the elderly and blatant ageism did not seem to be present. However, the lack of development and the routinizing of older persons' activities made them seem dull and uninteresting.

Query, Joy M.N., and Steines, Meriel. "Disillusionment, Health Status and Age: A Study of Value Differences of Midwestern Women." *International Journal of Aging and Human Development,* 1974, 5(3), pp. 245-256.

Data were collected from young, middle-aged, and elderly females living in a metropolitan area to test the theory that as age increases, so does disillusionment with American values. Findings suggest that religious optimism decreases with age, while the work-activity orientation does not. Optimism is expressed about the belief in the mastery of science and technology over nature.

Robin, Ellen P. "Old Age in Elementary School Readers." *Educational Gerontology,* 1977, 2(3), pp. 275-292.

A content analysis about old age was undertaken on elementary textbooks which were published from 1953 to 1968 and those published in 1975. Little change was found in the earlier and later books; both were similar in their portrayal of the elderly.

Rodin, Judith, and Langer, Ellen. "Aging Labels: The Decline of Control and the Fall of Self-Esteem." *Journal of Social Issues,* 1980, 36(2), pp. 12-29.

Explores the extent to which negative labeling is associated with aging and the consequences of this labeling on the elderly.

Rosencranz, Howard A., and McNevin, Tony E. "A Factor Analysis of Attitudes toward the Aged." *The Gerontologist,* 1969, 9(1), pp. 55-59.

Constructs and analyzes an instrument to measure stereotypic attitudes toward the elderly and to determine the content of such attitudes.

Rosow, Irving. "Old Age: One Moral Dilemma of an Affluent Society." *The Gerontologist,* 1962, 2(4), pp. 182-191.

Compares the position of the elderly in our society with that of nonindustrial societies. Rosow shows how our values and institutions undermine the position of older people and offers some solutions to the problem.

Ross, Robert F., Jr., and Freitag, Carl B. "Comparison of Adolescent and Adult Attitudes toward the Aged." *Educational Gerontology,* 1976, 1(3), pp. 291-295.

Compares the attitudes of adolescent subjects aged 13 and 14 and young adult subjects between the ages of 20 and 23 toward the elderly. The study finds that the adolescent population has a more favorable attitude toward the aged than do the young adults.

Schuerman, Laurell E.; Eden, Donna Z.; and Peterson, David A. "Older People in Women's Periodical Fiction." *Educational Gerontology,* 1977, 2(3), pp. 327-351.

Finds the image of aging as presented through fiction in nine women's periodicals to be both positive and inaccurate. While older persons perform important roles, they are shown as extensions of the readers themselves and not as realistic older persons. Old age is described more through external appearance than through status and role changes.

Seefeldt, Carol, et al. "Children's Attitudes toward the Elderly: Educational Implications." *Educational Gerontology,* 1977, 2(3), pp. 301-310.

Interviews children between the ages of three and eleven to assess their attitudes toward the elderly. The results indicate that children's attitudes toward the elderly are generally negative and stereotypic. Few children gave positive responses about growing old themselves. However, the children expressed strong affective feelings toward the elderly.

Seltzer, Mildred M., and Atchley, Robert C. "The Concept of Old: Changing Attitudes and Stereotypes." *The Gerontologist,* 1971, 2(3), pt. 1, pp. 226-230.

A content analysis of children's literature from 1870 to 1960 did not support a generally negative picture about older people. It may be that gerontologists are overly sensitized to the negative attitudes about old age.

Stinnett, Nick, and Montgomery, James E. "Youths' Perception of Marriages of Older Persons." *Journal of Marriage and the Family,* 1968, 30(3), pp. 392-401.

Examines the attitudes of college students toward older marriages. The findings show that women have a more favorable attitude toward older persons marrying than do men. Positive attitudes toward older marriages are also related to being Protestant, living in a rural area, and having a considerable amount of contact with aged persons.

Thorson, James A. "Attitudes toward the Aged as a Function of Race and Social Class." *The Gerontologist,* 1975, 15(4), pp. 343-344.

Finds a significant difference in the attitude of the respondents toward the elderly by education: those respondents having more education have more positive attitudes toward the elderly. Finds no difference in the attitude of the respondents toward the elderly by age, race, or social class.

Wake, Sandra B., and Sporakowski, Michael J. "An Intergenerational Comparison of Attitudes towards Supporting Aged Parents." *Journal of Marriage and the Family,* 1972, 34(1), pp. 42-48.

Studies generational differences between students and their parents regarding filial responsibilities. The findings reveal that students show more willingness to support aged parents than their parents. Religious affiliation evidences greater within-generation differences for parents than for students or between generations.

Weinberger, Arthur. "Stereotyping of the Elderly: Elementary School Children's Response." *Research on Aging,* 1979, 1(1), pp. 113-136.

Examines children's impressions of aging and the aged. Results reveal that the negative stereotypes that elementary school children have toward the elderly mirror those of adults. The children express both favorable and unfavorable reactions about interacting with older people.

Weinberger, Linda E., and Millham, Jim. "A Multi-Dimensional Multiple Method Analysis of Attitudes toward the Elderly." *Journal of Gerontology,* 1975, 30(3), pp. 343-348.

Investigates attitudes toward a "representative" 25-year-old and a "representative" 70-year-old. Results reveal that college students express significantly more negative attitudes toward the representative older person than the representative younger person, but judge a personalized 70-year-old more favorably than a personalized 25-year-old.

Youmans, E. Grant. "Generation and Perceptions of Old Age: An Urban-Rural Comparison." *The Gerontologist,* 1971, 2(4), pt. 1, pp. 284-288.

Compares generational differences in perceptions of old age of those living in a metropolitan center and those in a rural county. The older generation show more concern about worries and work problems and a stronger conviction about the positive aspects of age than do younger persons.

Youmans, E. Grant. "Age Stratification and Value Orientations." *International Journal of Aging and Human Development,* 1973, 4(1), pp. 53-65.

Compares value orientations of younger and older adults in a rural and metropolitan area. Results reveal significant differences between the two age groups in both geographical areas on such values as authoritarianism, dependency, achievement, religiosity, and anomia.

Youmans, E. Grant. "Age Group, Health, and Attitudes." *The Gerontologist,* 1974, 14(3), pp. 249-254.

Examines the attitudes of four age groups living in both urban and rural areas as to perceived health status. The findings reveal that in the urban area negative attitudes toward health show only a modest increase with the onset of old age, while in the rural area in each of the age groups there are more ailments and negative attitudes.

Youmans, E. Grant. "Attitudes: Young-Old and Old-Old." *The Gerontologist,* 1977, 17(2), pp. 175-178.

Compares the attitudes of young-old and old-old persons living in rural and urban communities. In the urban community more favorable attitudes as well as substantial differences in attitude scores are found betwen the old-old and the young-old. In the rural community there are only slight differences between the attitude scores of the young-old and old-old.

B. Norms

Atchley, Robert C. "The Life Course, Age Grading, and Age-Linked Demands for Decision Making." In Nancy Datan and Leon Ginsberg (Eds.), *Life Span Developmental Psychology: Normative Life Crises.* New York: Academic Press, 1975, pp. 261-278.

Views age as a variable that cuts across all areas of social life through three highly interrelated social mechanisms: the life course, the system of age-grading, and age-linked demands for decision making. Presents a paradigm for the study of age norms and discusses some sources of age norms and the criteria for applying them.

Breen, Leonard Z. "Retirement--Norms, Behavior, and Functional Aspects of Normative Behavior." In Richard H. Williams, Clark Tibbitts, and Wilma Donahue (Eds.), *Processes of Aging: Social and Psychological Perspectives,* vol. 2. New York: Atherton Press, 1963, pp. 381-388.

Discusses expectations about and approaches to retirement. Enumerates four areas in which there are functional aspects of retirement.

Britton, Joseph H.; Mather, William G.; and Lansing, Alice K. "Expectations for Older Persons in a Rural Community: Living Arrangements and Family Relationships." *Journal of Gerontology,* 1961, 16(2), pp. 156-162.

Most of the residents of the rural community investigated believe that older persons should live alone in their own homes unless they are not able to care for themselves, have financial difficulties, or are lonely. Under these conditions, they think it is appropriate for the elderly to live with their family or in a home for the aged. Some of the other expectations for the elderly are that they should maintain responsibility for themselves, enjoy their children and grandchildren, and do as they wish for their own enjoyment.

Bultena, Gordon, and Wood, Vivian. "Normative Attitudes toward the Aged Role among Migrant and Nonmigrant Retirees." *The Gerontologist,* 1969, 9(3), pt. 1, pp. 204-208.

Indicates that the elderly who move to retirement areas are more liberal in their assessment as to what constitutes proper behavior among the aged than those persons retiring in their home communities.

Davis, Robert W. "Social Influences on the Aspiration Tendency of Older People." *Journal of Gerontology,* 1967, 22(4), pt. 1, pp. 510-516.

Contrasts a group of older men (ages 66-85) with two younger groups (ages 20-30 and 40-58) to determine differences in the achievement motivation and response to a fictitious group norm. Both the older and younger men maintained a high level of aspiration and were equally responsive to failure. However, after experiencing success, the older men decreased their aspiration level while the younger men increased theirs. The study indicates that older men conform more closely to group norms, while young men tend to diverge when a standard is asserted.

Elder, Glen H., Jr. "Age Differentiation and The Life Course." In Alex Inkeles (Ed.), *Annual Review of Sociology,* vol. 1. Palo Alto, Calif.: Annual Reviews, Inc., 1975, pp. 165-190.

Focuses on social change in the life course. It draws mainly upon the age stratification perspective (cohort-historical) found in the work of Riley and from the age-status systems and age norms perspective (sociocultural) found in the work of Neugarten.

Havighurst, Robert J. "Life beyond Family and Work." In Ernest W. Burgess (Ed.), *Aging in Western Societies,* Chicago: The University of Chicago Press, 1960, pp. 299-353.

Compares the social roles of older persons in selected Western societies in regard to what each society expects of people as they grow older and how well they meet these expectations.

Kahana, Eva, and Coe, Rodney M. "Dimensions of Conformity: A Multidisciplinary View." *Journal of Gerontology,* 1969, 24(1), pp. 76-81.

Deals with individual and situational determinants of conforming behavior of 33 residents in a home for the aged. The findings show that the individual factors related to conformity are integration in the informal social organization of the home and adjustment. Among the situational factors eliciting conformity are the saliency of rules for the individual and for the home.

Kerckhoff, Alan C. "Nuclear and Extended Family Relationships: A Normative and Behavioral Analysis." In Ethel Shanas and Gordon F. Streib (Eds.), *Social Structure and the Family: Generational Relations.* Englewood Cliffs, N.J.: Prentice-Hall, 1965, pp. 93-112.

Based on data obtained from interviews with older couples having adult children, Kerckhoff analyzed the normative and behavioral aspects of extended family relationships. He found that there was considerable deviation between normative definitions and actual behavior in the families studied.

Kerckhoff, Alan C. "Norm-Value Clusters and the 'Strain toward Consistency' among Older Married Couples." In Ida H. Simpson and John C. McKinney (Eds.), *Social Aspects of Aging.* Durham, N.C.: Duke University Press, 1966, pp. 138-159.

Finds that among older married couples there is a strain toward consistency in the following measures: parent-child norms, normative definitions of husband-wife division of labor, the degree of acceptance of the value of changes, and the degree to which a conflict is seen between children's mobility and family values.

Klein, Ronald L. "Age, Sex, and Task Difficulty as Predictors of Social Conformity." *Journal of Gerontology,* 1972, 27(2), pp. 229-236.

Compares an old and young group of subjects in a laboratory visual perceptual judgment task to determine the relationship of conformity to age and sex, as well as the effect of age and task difficulty in relation to conformity. Findings reveal that older subjects conform more often than younger ones and that there is not a significant sex difference in conforming behavior. Also as the task becomes more difficult, the increase in conformity scores is greater for the older subjects.

Lozier, John, and Althouse, Ronald. "Social Enforcement of Behavior toward Elders in an Appalachian Mountain Settlement." *The Gerontologist,* 1974, 14(1), pp. 69-80.

Eight case histories of elderly persons in West Virginia illustrate how the circumstances of older persons can be viewed as a consequence of a social and historical process. This approach examines the degree to which the situations of the elderly are controlled by the strategic behavior of others. Successful aging is viewed as a result of the efforts of members of a collectivity on behalf of the older person and not simply as the result of an individual's own efforts.

Neugarten, Bernice L.; Moore, Joan W.; and Lowe, John C. "Age Norms, Age Constraints, and Adult Socialization." *The American Journal of Sociology,* 1965, 70(6), pp. 710-717.

Shows the consensus that exists concerning age-appropriate behavior in adults. It also reveals that different age groups perceive more and less age constraints operating in society.

Roff, Lucinda L., and Klemmack, David L. "Sexual Activity Among Older Persons: A Comparative Analysis of Appropriateness." *Research on Aging,* 1979, 1(3), pp. 389-399.

Compares the perceptions of the appropriateness of a variety of sexual behaviors for older persons and for the general population. Sexual activity among older persons is not seen as any more inappropriate than sexual activity in the general population.

Wood, Vivian. "Age-Appropriate Behavior for Older People." *The Gerontologist,* 1971, 2(4), pt. 2, pp. 74-78.

Although there is a lack of clear-cut norms for behavior in old age, norms for leisure-oriented kinds of behavior in retirement are emerging. Concludes with a list of questions for scientific research.

C. Subculture

Bultena, Gordon L. "Age Grading in the Social Interaction of an Elderly Male Population." *Journal of Gerontology,* 1968, 23(4), pp. 539-543.

Tests hypotheses from Rose's theory of an emergent subculture of the aged. The first hypothesis, older persons interact more with age mates than with younger persons, is supported. The second hypothesis, advancing age is associated with an increased degree of confinement of social interaction to age peers, is not supported.

Longino, Charles F., Jr.; McClelland, Kent A.; and Peterson, Warren A. "The Aged Subculture Hypothesis: Social Integration, Gerontophilia, and Self-Conception." *Journal of Gerontology,* 1980, 35(3), pp. 758-767.

To test Rose's aged subculture hypothesis, data from a national Harris survey of older persons are compared with data from residents of eight community settings. The findings partially support Rose's hypothesis. While the residents demonstrate higher levels of social integration and preference for interaction with the elderly, there is no evidence of an aging group consciousness.

Rose, Arnold M. "The Subculture of the Aging: A Topic for Sociological Research." *The Gerontologist,* 1962, 2(3), pp. 123-127.

Observes that there are certain conditions in our society such as the formation of group identity among the elderly which are creating and influencing the development of an aging subculture. Stresses the need for systematic studies in this area which has so far been neglected by sociological researchers.

Rose, Arnold M. "The Subculture of Aging: A Framework for Research in Social Gerontology." In Arnold M. Rose and Warren A. Peterson (Eds.), *Older People and Their Social World.* Philadelphia: F.A. Davis, 1965, pp. 3-16.

An elaboration of an earlier draft in 1962 (see above). Discusses some of the ways in which older people in this country are developing a subculture and how they are becoming conscious of themselves as a distinctive group.

Rutzen, S. Robert. "The Social Distribution of Primary Social Isolation among the Aged: A Subcultural Approach." *International Journal of Aging and Human Development,* 1980, 11(1), pp. 77-87.

Using a sample of older persons in an urban area, this research focuses on subcultural variations in primary social isolation or isolation from friends and relatives. Findings suggest that the two subcultures having extraordinary degrees of primary social isolation are white Catholic foreign born persons and black Protestant native-born persons; both fall into the lowest social positions in the sample.

Ward, Russell A. "Aging-Group Consciousness: Implications in an Older Sample." *Sociology and Social Research,* 1977, 61(4), pp. 496-519.

Focuses on two questions concerning the subculture of aging: when does such a subculture develop and what are the implications of such a subculture? Finds a positive relationship between aging-group consciousness and self-esteem for those who consider themselves as elderly. Feelings of aging-group consciousness are not widespread and are related to group interaction with age peers.

D. Cross-Culture

Albrecht, Ruth. "The Family and Aging Seen Cross-Culturally." In Rosamonde R. Boyd and Charles G. Oakes (Eds.), *Foundations of Practical Gerontology,* 2d ed., Columbia, South Carolina: University of South Carolina Press, 1973, pp. 27-34.

Deals with the meaning of age and the family relationships of the elderly in the United States and other countries.

Anderson, John E. "Research on Aging." In Ernest W. Burgess (Ed.), *Aging in Western Societies.* Chicago: The University of Chicago Press, 1960, pp. 354-376.

Describes social and psychological research projects in various European countries.

Boyd, Rosamonde R. "Preliterate Prologues to Modern Aging Roles." In Rosamonde R. Boyd and Charles G. Oakes (Eds.), *Foundations of Practical Gerontology,* 2d ed. Columbia, South Carolina: University of South Carolina Press, 1973, pp. 35-46.

Discusses ethnographic studies which show the high esteem of the elderly in many preliterate societies.

Burgess, Ernest W. (Ed.), *Aging in Western Societies.* Chicago: The University of Chicago Press, 1960.

Presents the problems of the elderly in six European countries and the policies and programs which have been developed by these countries to promote the elderly's welfare.

Burgess, Ernest W. "Resume and Implications." In Ernest W. Burgess (Ed.), *Aging in Western Societies.* Chicago: The University of Chicago Press, 1960, pp. 377-388.

Outlines the conclusions from a survey of aging in six European countries. Discusses the implications of the European experience for guiding the policies and programs for aging in the United States.

Cowgill, Donald. "The Social Life of the Aging in Thailand." *The Gerontologist,* 1968, 8(3), pp. 159-163.

Shows how the elderly in Thailand fit the theories that the status of the aged tends to be high in societies that are static, in societies in which there are few elderly, and in societies in which the elderly perform useful functions.

Cowgill, Donald, O., and Holmes, Lowell D. (Eds.). *Aging and Modernization.* New York: Appleton-Century-Crofts, 1972.

Contains 18 papers that deal with aging in various societies and settings, ranging from primitive to highly modern. These papers provide the basis for the testing of a number of hypotheses. The general conclusion is that the status of the aged is inversely associated with modernization.

Cowgill, Donald O. "A Theory of Aging in Cross-Cultural Perspective." In Donald O. Cowgill and Lowell D. Holmes (Eds.), *Aging and Modernization.* New York: Appleton-Century-Crofts, 1972, pp. 1-3.

Proposes a number of hypotheses about aging in this chapter. Some of these hypotheses pertain to universal conditions, while others specify the variations found in different societies. The major hypothesis is that the role and status of the elderly vary inversely with the degree of modernization of a society.

Cowgill, Donald O., and Holmes, Lowell D. "Summary and Conclusions: The Theory in Review." In Donald O. Cowgill and Lowell D. Holmes (Eds.), *Aging and Modernization.* New York: Appleton-Century-Crofts, 1972, pp. 305-323.

In this final chapter, the authors discuss the hypotheses advanced in the first part of the book. They conclude that their theory of modernization has been extended and strengthened by the societies studied in the preceding chapters.

Cowgill, Donald O. "Aging and Modernization: A Revision of the Theory." In Jaber F. Gubrium, *Late Life: Communities and Environmental Policy.* Springfield, Ill.: Charles C. Thomas, 1974, pp. 123-146.

The theory of aging and modernization is extended. New evidence suggests that in advanced stages of modernization the trend toward a decline in the relative status of the elderly may "bottom out" and at some point begin to improve.

Cutler, Stephen J. "An Approach to the Measurement of Prestige Loss among the Aged." *Aging and Human Development*, 1972, 3(3), pp. 285-292.

Suggests a method for measuring the status of the elderly in industrial societies. By employing this method, tentative findings indicate the existence and recognition of prestige loss among the aged.

Eaton, Joseph W. "The Art of Aging and Dying." *The Gerontologist*, 1964, 4(2), pp. 94-100, 103 and 112.

Contrasts the Hutterite culture with our own and discusses some reasons why the Hutterites make such a serene adjustment to aging and dying.

Harvey, Carol D., and Bahr, Howard M. "Widowhood, Morale, and Affiliation." *Journal of Marriage and the Family*, 1974, 36(1), pp. 97-106.

Based on data from sample surveys in five countries, morale and organizational ties of widowed and married persons were examined. The major finding is that neither the perspective of self-theory nor role-theory is adequate to explain differences between widowed and married persons in morale or affiliations. This study suggests that the widowed appear to have more negative attitudes than married persons. These attitudes may be due to other factors besides widowhood per se. For example, widows are poorer than married persons and they may be less affiliated for this reason.

Havighurst, Robert J.; Neugarten, Bernice L.; and Bengtson, Vern L. "A Cross-National Study of Adjustment to Retirement." *The Gerontologist*, 1966, 6(3), pp. 137-138.

Discusses the initial work of a comparative study of adjustment to retirement that is presently underway in seven countries.

Havighurst, Robert J., et al. (Eds.). *Adjustment to Retirement: A Cross-National Study.* New York: Humanities Press, 1969.

Deals with a pilot study of retired steelworkers and teachers from various countries. Offers a description of the types of adjustment to retirement and makes comparisons between occupations within each country.

Lipman, Aaron. "Prestige of the Aged in Portugal: Realistic Appraisal and Ritualistic Deference." *Aging and Human Development*, 1970, 1(2), pp. 127-136.

Differences in the prestige rankings of the aged in Portugal are discussed and placed in a cross-cultural gerontological perspective.

Lipman, Aaron. "Conference on the Potential for Japanese-American Cross-National Research on Aging." *The Gerontologist,* 1975, 15(3), pp. 248-253.

Contains a condensation of the proceedings of a conference to stimulate cross-national research in the field of aging. The following topics are designated as key areas for research: family and living arrangements, culture and personality, health and health services, work, retirement, and income; and institutions and social services.

Maxwell, Robert J., and Silverman, Philip. "Information and Esteem: Cultural Considerations in the Treatment of the Aged." *Aging and Human Development,* 1970, 1(4), pp. 361-392.

Using the Human Relations Area Files, the treatment of the aged in 26 societies was examined. Findings indicate that the degree of control that the elderly have over useful information does determine to some degree their treatment in the sociocultural system. Furthermore, high informational control among the aged is associated with their being held in high esteem.

Monk, Abraham; Cryns, Arthur G.; and Milbrath, Kirsten. "Personal and Social Value Concerns of Scandinavian Elderly: A Multivariate Study." *International Journal of Aging and Human Development,* 1976, 7(3), pp. 221-230.

A comparative study of the value concerns of Danish and Norwegian elderly finds that both samples expressed only limited concerns about their economic well-being. Also finds no correlation between life satisfaction and the acceptance of youth for both the Danes and Norwegians.

Neugarten, Bernice L., and Havighurst, Robert J. "Disengagement Reconsidered in a Cross-national Context." In Robert J. Havighurst, et al. (Eds.), *Adjust to Retirement: A Cross-National Study.* New York: Humanities Press, 1969, pp. 138-146.

Using cross-national data from retired men in different occupations, the authors find that psychological well-being is positively related to the level of social interaction. This finding does not support a portion of the disengagement theory and raises some important research questions.

Palmore, Erdman B. *The Honorable Elders: A Cross-Cultural Analysis of Aging in Japan.* Durham, N.C.: Duke University Press, 1975.

Examines the status of older persons in Japan. The results do not support the theory that a marked decline in status is an inevitable accompaniment of industrialization. Concludes that the status of the

Japanese elderly has had little decline and is significantly higher than the status of the elderly in other industrialized countries.

Palmore, Erdman B. "What Can the USA Learn from Japan about Aging?" *The Gerontologist,* 1975, 15(1), pt. 1, pp. 64-67.

Lists 16 ways in which the situation of older Americans can be improved. These include the ending of discrimination against the aged in employment, integration of the elderly into the family, and organized political action by the aged.

Palmore, Erdman B. "The Status and Integration of the Aged in Japanese Society." *Journal of Gerontology,* 1975, 30(2), pp. 199-208.

Despite a high degree of industrialization, the status and integration of the elderly in Japan has remained at relatively high levels. Discusses reasons for this.

Palmore, Erdman B. (Ed.), *International Handbook on Aging: Contemporary Developments and Research.* Westport, Conn.: Greenwood Press, 1980.

Contains information on the state of gerontology in 28 countries which have substantial organizations, programs and research on aging.

Palmore, Erdman B., and Manton, Kenneth. "Modernization and Status of the Aged: International Correlations." *Journal of Gerontology,* 1974, 29(2), pp. 205-210.

Examines aspects of modernization which are related to the status of the elderly in 31 countries. Reveals that the occupational and educational status of the aged decline in the advanced stages of modernization. However, after an initial period of rapid modernization, these aspects of status may begin to rise and the discrepancies between the aged and other age groups decrease.

Parsons, Talcott. "The Cultural Background of Today's Aged." In Wilma Donahue and Clark Tibbitts (Eds.), *Politics of Age.* Ann Arbor: Division of Gerontology, University of Michigan Press, 1962, pp. 3-15.

Gives some background considerations concerning the problem of the political aspects of aging along with a comparison of some of the characteristics of our society with those that have existed in other societies.

Press, Irwin, and McKool, Mike, Jr. "Social Structure and the Status of the Aged: Toward Some Valid Cross-Cultural Generalizations." *Aging and Human Development,* 1972, 3(4), pp. 297-305.

From their study of Meso-American communities the authors derive four "prestige generating" components which may vary independently, but one or more must be present for the aged to be accorded prestige. These components are advisory, contributory, control, and residual.

Shanas, Ethel. "Some Observations on Cross-National Surveys of Aging." *The Gerontologist,* 1963, 3(1), pp. 7-9.

Describes a cross-national survey of older people now in progress in Denmark, Great Britain, and the United States and discusses some of the contributions it may be expected to make.

Shanas, Ethel. "Family Help Patterns and Social Class in Three Countries." *Journal of Marriage and the Family,* 1967, 29(2), pp. 257-286.

Reports that family help patterns in Denmark, Britain, and the United States vary by the social class of the older person. In Britain and the United States, old people of white-collar backgrounds are the most likely to help their children, while old people of working-class backgrounds need help from their children.

Shanas, Ethel, et al. *Old People in Three Industrial Societies.* New York: Atherton Press, 1968.

Contains the findings of a cross-national survey of the living conditions and behavior of older people in Denmark, Britain, and the United States.

Simmons, Leo W. "Aging in Preindustrial Societies." In Clark Tibbitts (Ed.), *Handbook of Social Gerontology.* Chicago: University of Chicago Press, 1960, pp. 62-89.

Describes the approaches to aging in preindustrial societies. Concludes that successful aging depends upon the capacities and opportunities of individuals to fit well into the social framework and in ways that insure influence and security.

Treas, Judith. "Socialist Organization and Economic Development in China: Latent Consequences for the Aged." *The Gerontologist,* 1979, 19(1), pp. 34-43.

Many of the socialist developments have contributed to the continuation of high status among the aged Chinese. Although the elderly exert considerable influence in the community and in the family, high status in the industrial sector is associated more with skills and education than with age.

Wolfbein, Seymour L., and Burgess, Ernest W. "Employment and Retirement." In Ernest W. Burgess (Ed.), *Aging in Western Societies.* Chicago: The University of Chicago Press, 1960, pp. 54-75.

Discusses the factors that influence the decision to retire or to continue working in a cross-national context.

Chapter 4

SOCIALIZATION, ROLES, AND STATUSES

Anderson, Nancy N. "Institutionalization, Interaction, and Self-Conception in Aging." In Arnold M. Rose and Warren A. Peterson (Eds.), *Older People and Their Social World.* Philadelphia: F.A. Davis, 1965, pp. 245-257.

Suggests that interaction explains self-conception more adequately than does institutionalization.

Atchley, Robert C. "Selected Social and Psychological Differences between Men and Women in Later Life." *Journal of Gerontology,* 1976, 31(2), pp. 204-211.

Investigates sex differences in certain social and psychological characteristics. Reveals that older women value job success as a life goal as much as men, and are less likely than men to make a quick adjustment to retirement. Also older women report a higher incidence of psychological problems, while men are more prone to see changes in social participation.

Atchley, Robert C. "Disengagement among Professors." *Journal of Gerontology,* 1971, 26(4), 476-480.

The findings from a questionnaire study, administered to professors and professors emeritus, reveal that a high potential for disengagement is prevalent among all age and work status categories in the sample. However, psychological disengagement from work commitment or participant leisure preferences occur only among a small number of professors even in the older age groups.

Back. Kurt W., and Guptill, Carleton S. "Retirement and Self-Ratings." In Ida H. Simpson and John C. McKinney (Eds.), *Social Aspects of Aging.* Durham, N.C.: Duke University Press, 1966, pp. 120-129.

Examines some of the dimensions of the self-concept of retired and pre-retired men. Finds that if the retiree is healthy, had a middle- or upper-stratum occupation, and is highly involved, he feels less of a loss in the activity dimensions.

Back, Kurt W. "Transition to Aging and the Self-Image." *Aging and Human Development,* 1971, 2(4), pp. 296-304.

Focuses on the changes in self-concept brought about by old age. Neither retirement nor separation from children affects the context of the self-image as much as the aging process itself. With age, women tend to shift their self-image from their relationship to others to their own abilities and feelings. On the other hand, men are involved more personally in the work role and problems with this role through aging may make life more difficult for them.

Bell, Tony. "The Relationship between Social Involvement and Feeling Old among Residents in Homes for the Aged." *Journal of Gerontology,* 1967, 22(1), pp. 17-22.

Data obtained from 55 residents in three homes for the aged indicate that those individuals who are highly involved socially see themselves as not old, while those less involved tend to see themselves as old.

Bengtson, Vern L. "Generation and Family Effects in Value Socialization." *American Sociological Review,* 1975, 40(3), pp. 358-371.

Tests several propositions concerning generational contrasts and within-family similarities in value orientations. The findings indicate neither marked generational differences nor strong familial similarity in value orientations.

Bengtson, Vern L., and Black, K. Dean. "Intergenerational Relations and Continuities in Socialization." In Paul B. Baltes and K. Warner Schaie (Eds.), *Life-Span Developmental Psychology: Personality and Socialization.* New York: Academic Press, 1973, pp. 207-239.

Focuses on intergenerational relations and their affect on individual socialization and cultural continuity.

Bengtson, Vern L.; Kasschau, Patricia L.; and Ragan, Pauline K. "The Impact of Social Structure on Aging Individuals." In James E. Birren and K. Warner Schaie (Eds.), *Handbook of the Psychology of Aging.* New York: Van Nostrand Reinhold, 1977, pp. 327-353.

Reviews some ways in which location in the social structure influences patterns of behavior among aging persons. Stresses three major themes arising from current research in the sociology of aging. The first theme concerns the value of recognizing that aging is socially defined. The next, the importance of social differentiation as it relates to aging. Finally, the third theme focuses on the role which social and historical change play in shaping the patterns of human aging.

Bennett, Ruth, and Nahemow, Lucille. "Socialization and Social Adjustment in Five Residential Settings for the Aged." In Donald P. Kent, Robert Kastenbaum, and Sylvia Sherwood (Eds.), *Research Planning and Action for the Elderly: The Power and Potential of Social Science.* New York: Behavioral Publications, 1972, pp. 514-524.

Investigates socialization, social adjustment,and mental status to determine if they vary according to institutional totality. Finds socialization to be better in residential settings which are low in totality. Socialization is only slightly related to mental status.

Bultena, Gordon L., and Powers, Edward A. "Denial of Aging: Age Identification and Reference Group Orientations." *Journal of Gerontology,* 1978, 33(5), pp. 748-754.

Data from a 10-year longitudinal study (1960 to 1970) reveal that few subjects viewed themselves as old in 1960 and most thought of themselves as middle-aged. One-third of the subjects (despite being over 70) continue to think of themselves as middle-aged in 1970. Favorable self-evaluations which result from reference group comparisons are positively associated with younger self-images.

Cain, Leonard D. "Life Course and Social Structure." In Robert E.L. Faris (Ed.), *Handbook of Modern Sociology.* Chicago: Rand McNally, 1964, pp. 272-309.

Identifies and systematizes an age status frame of reference. Reviews research relating to age status in the major institutions and of interaction patterns between generations and of age peers.

Cain, Leonard D. "The Growing Importance of Legal Age in Determining the Status of the Elderly." *The Gerontologist,* 1974, 14(2), pp. 167-174.

Suggests that a formidable task facing gerontologists in the near future is establishing criteria, other than chronological age, for legal status differentiation.

Cavan, Ruth S. "Self and Role in Adjustment during Old Age." In Arnold M. Rose (Ed.), *Human Behavior and Social Processes.* Boston: Houghton Mifflin, 1962, pp. 526-536.

Illustrates how the concepts of self-conception, role-taking, and role-playing can be used to analyze adjustment to old age and suggests how better adjustment can be manipulated.

Coe, Rodney M. "Self-Conception and Institutionalization." In Arnold M. Rose and Warren A. Peterson (Eds.), *Older People and Their Social World.* Philadelphia: F.A. Davis, 1965, pp. 225-243.

Reveals that institutionalization has a tremendous impact on the self-conception of chronically ill, aged patients. A fairly large number of patients appear to be depersonalized to an extreme degree.

Coe, Rodney M., and Barnhill, Elizabeth. "Social Participation and Health of the Aged." In Arnold M. Rose and Warren A. Peterson (Eds.), *Older People and Their Social World.* Philadelphia: F.A. Davis, 1965, pp. 211-223.

Finds a moderately positive association between the degree of social participation and perceived level of health.

Davis, Robert W. "The Relationship of Social Preferability to Self-Concept in an Aged Population " *Journal of Gerontology,* 1962, 17(4), pp. 431-436.

Studies residents in a home for the aged to investigate the relationship of self-concept and social functioning in old age. The findings indicate that those elderly who are preferred by their peers have more positive self-concepts than those that are non-preferred. The preferred elderly have mostly physical and social complaints while the non-preferred have complaints of a psychological nature.

Fontana, Andrea. *The Last Frontier: The Social Meaning of Growing Old.* Beverly Hills, Calif.: Sage Publications, 1977.

Focuses on the meaning of growing old and how old people find meaning in their lives.

Friedman, Edward P. "Age, Length of Institutionalization, and Social Status in a Home for the Aged." *Journal of Gerontology,* 1967, 22(4), pt. 1, pp. 474-477.

Shows that age and length of institutionalization are related to friendship formation for residents in a home for the aged. A significant correlation is found between extreme old age and long length of institutionalization and high social status within the institution.

Friedmann, Eugene A. "The Impact of Aging on the Social Structure." In Clark Tibbitts (Ed.), *Handbook of Social Gerontology.* Chicago: The University of Chicago Press, 1960, pp. 120-144.

Considers the impact of aging upon the economy, the labor force, and the family as well as the integration of the aged in our society.

Geist, Harold. *The Psychological Aspects of the Aging Process: With Sociological Implications.* St. Louis: Warren H. Green, 1968, Chapter V1, pp. 132-155.

Discusses the impact of the aging process on the social structure and briefly compares aging in other countries.

George, Linda K. "The Impact of Personality and Social Status Factors upon Levels of Activity and Psychological Well-Being." *Journal of Gerontology,* 1978, 33(6), pp. 840-847.

Examines the effect of personality and social status variables upon levels of activity and psychological well-being. Reveals that personality factors are better predictors of psychological well-being than social status factors, and that activity levels are better predicted by social status variables.

Gubrium, Jaber F. (Ed.). *Time, Roles, and Self in Old Age.* New York: Human Sciences Press, 1976.

Contains a collection of papers which considers roles and the variations in them over time in relation to later life. Discusses retirement roles and intergenerational roles as well as role consistency.

Guptill, Carleton S. "A Measure of Age Identification." *The Gerontologist,* 1969, 9(2), pt. 1, pp. 96-102.

Attempts to develop a measure of age identification through the use of the sematic differential technique. Measures the meanings of three concepts, "middle-aged man," "myself," and "old man" to an individual. The individual's view of himself is then rated in relation to the meanings he holds of "middle-aged man" and "old man."

Hendricks, C. Davis, and Hendricks, Jon. "Concepts of Time and Temporal Construction among the Aged, with Implications for Research." In Jaber F.Gubrium (Ed.), *Time, Roles, and Self in Old Age.* New York: Human Sciences Press, 1976, pp. 13-49.

Focuses on the traditional concepts of time and suggests that more innovative conceptual frameworks are needed to understand the aging process.

Itzin, Frank. "Social Relations." In Adeline M. Hoffman (Ed.), *The Daily Needs and Interests of Older People.* Springfield, Ill.: Charles C. Thomas, 1970, pp. 137-164.

Describes the social roles of the elderly and discusses the theories of disengagement and the subculture of the aging.

Jeffers, Frances C.; and Eisdorfer, Carl; and Busse, Ewald. "Measurement of Age Identification: A Methodologic Note." *Journal of Gerontology,* 1962, 17(4), pp. 437-439.

Using a card-sort technique, the subjects who had previously answered the Activities and Attitudes Inventory (Burgess, et al., 1948) placed the terms "young," "middle-aged," "elderly," "old," and "aged" in an ordered sequence. Finds differences between the order defined by Burgess and the card-sort order of the subjects. The authors conclude that it might be more appropriate for a card-sort to be arranged in terms of major life events and in this way the subjects' attitudes toward the different stages of life could also be studied.

King, Charles E., and Howell, William. "Role Characteristics of Flexible and Inflexible Retired Persons." *Sociology and Social Research,* 1965, 49(2), pp. 153-165.

Examines the experiences of retired persons in the process of role change. Finds that occupational, marital, and organizational participation roles have an important influence on retirement.

Kline, Chrysee. "The Socialization Process of Women." *The Gerontologist,* 1975, 15(6), pp. 486-492.

Suggests that the impact of the socialization process on women in our society creates impermanence in the form of role loss and repeated adjustment to change which helps ease the adjustment of women to old age.

Lacy, William B., and Hendricks, Jon. "Developmental Models of Adult Life: Myth or Reality." *International Journal of Aging and Human Development,* 1980, 11(2), pp. 89-110.

Examines questions regarding sequential changes throughout the life cycle as a way of assessing the generalizability of developmental stages. Finds little empirical support for developmental stage models. The results challenge the existence of regularities of the life cycle.

Lipman, Aaron. "Role Conceptions and Morale of Couples in Retirement." *Journal of Gerontology,* 1961, 16(3), pp. 267-271.

At retirement role differentiation by sex is reduced. The preretirement roles of the couple that were mainly of an instrumental nature shift to supportive roles which require expressive qualities such as sharing, cooperation, love, and companionship.

Lipman, Aaron. "Role Conceptions of Couples in Retirement." In Clark Tibbitts and Wilma Donahue (Eds.), *Social and Psychological Aspects of Aging.* New York: Columbia University Press, 1962, pp. 475-485.

Analyzes preretirement role orientations and new role conceptions emerging as a result of retirement. Concludes that retirement brings a definite change in the traditional activities of the male which alters the preretirement division of males and females. It appears that role differentiation by sex is reduced with increased age and retirement. Because non-sex differentiated roles demand expressive rather than instrumental qualities, they tend to be well-adapted for the personality system of both husband and wife in retirement.

Lopata, Helena Z. "Role Changes in Widowhood: A World Perspective." In Donald O.Cowgill and Lowell D. Holmes (Eds.), *Aging and Modernization.* New York: Appleton-Century-Crofts, 1972, pp. 275-303.

Examines role shifts in the lives of widows in different societies and the types of lifestyles or alternatives which are available to them.

Lopata, Helena Z. "Self-Identity in Marriage and Widowhood." *The Sociological Quarterly,* 1973, 14(3), pp. 407-418.

Deals primarily with the relationship between education and identity reformulation among widows. Results reveal that widowhood is less disorganizing to the identities of lower-class women than to those of upper-class women. Lower-class women are less affected in their conscious identities by the world-view constructs and presence of their husbands.

Marshall, Victor W. "Socialization For Impending Death In A Retirement Village." *American Journal of Sociology,* 1975, 80(5), pp. 1124-1144.

Analyzes how the legitimation of death is successfully accomplished at a retirement village (Glen Brae). Contends that congregate living facilities can provide optimal settings for this type of socialization.

Multran, Elizabeth, and Burke, Peter J. "Personalism as a Component of Old Age Identity." *Research on Aging,* 1979, 1(1), pp. 37-63.

Tests a procedure for studying role identities as they relate to age. Findings show that old age identity is one of personalism which contains both positive and negative elements and is influenced by poor health, chronological age, income, and retirement.

Multran, Elizabeth and Burke, Peter J. "Feeling 'Useless': A Common Component of Young and Old Adult Identities." *Research on Aging,* 1979, 1(2), pp. 187-212.

Explores one dimension of age-related identities, uselessness-usefulness. Analyzes the variations in this dimension at various age levels. Results show that feelings of uselessness as a dimension of age/identity are caused by loneliness and poor health for older people and by lack of employment for younger persons.

Neugarten, Bernice L., and Moore, Joan W. "The Changing Age-Status System." In Bernice L. Neugarten (Ed.), *Middle Age and Aging: A Reader in Social Psychology.* Chicago: The University of Chicago Press, 1968, pp. 5-21.

Discusses how social change in regard to age patterns has taken place within the institutions of the family, the economy, and the political and legal system.

Neugarten, Bernice L., and Datan, Nancy. "Sociological Perspectives on the Life Cycle." In Paul B. Baltes and K. Warner Schaie (Eds.), *Life-Span Developmental Psychology: Personality and Socialization.* New York: Academic Press, 1973, pp. 53-69.

Reviews the concept of social system, social role, and socialization and discusses dimensions of time, age norms, and age stratification.

Palmore, Erdman B., and Whittington, Frank. "Trends in the Relative Status of the Aged." *Social Forces,* 1971, 50(1), pp. 89-91.

The comparison of similarity indexes from 1940 through 1969 supports the theory that the relative status of the elderly tends to decline in an industrial society. The evidence shows that gaps are steadily increasing in the areas of income, employment,and education between the older and younger population.

Palmore, Erdman B. "The Future Status of the Aged." *The Gerontologist,* 1976, 16(4), pp. 297-302.

Concludes that the status of the elderly, relative to that of younger groups, has clearly improved in the areas of health and income. It is predicted that the occupational status of the elderly should rise several points by 1990 and the educational status about eight to ten points by 1994.

Palmore, Erdman B. "Advantages of Aging." *The Gerontologist,* 1979, 19(2), pp. 220-223.

Cites 14 advantages of aging. The advantages fall into two types: those which primarily benefit society and those which primarily benefit the older person.

Payne, Barbara P. "The Older Volunteer: Social Role Continuity and Development." *The Gerontologist,* 1977, 17(4), pp. 355-361.

Presents a theoretical model of new social role reconstructuring. The model is illustrated by data from a longitudinal study of the older volunteer.

Peters, George R. "Self-Conceptions of the Aged, Age Identification, and Aging." *The Gerontologist,* 1971, 2(4), pt. 2, pp. 69-73.

Reviews the research on self-conception and age identification among older people and focuses on the differences between those persons with positive and negative conceptions of self.

Phillips, Bernard S. "Role Change, Subjective Age, and Adjustment: A Correlational Analysis." *Journal of Gerontology, 1961, 16(4), pp. 347-352.*

Examines the interrelationships among role changes, subjective age, and the adjustment of a sample of older persons. Results indicate that the relationship between aspects of subjective age and adjustment is the most consistent, followed by the relationship between role changes and adjustment. The results of the relationship between role changes and various aspects of subjective ages are mixed.

Riley, Matilda W., et al. "Socialization for Middle and Later Years." In David A. Goslin (Ed.), *Handbook of Socialization Theory and Research.* Chicago: Rand McNally, 1969, pp. 951-982.

Develops a model of the socialization process as an aid to interpreting some of the relevant empirical data. This model regards socialization as a process which occurs not only within the individual being socialized, but also between the individual and the social systems to which he or she belongs. The discussion emphasizes the importance of society in the socialization process.

Rose, Charles L. "The Measurement of Social Age." *Aging and Human Development,* 1972, 3(2), pp. 153-168.

Presents a technique for the measurement of social age. Demonstrates the usefulness of this concept and presents a specific example.

Rosenberg, George S. "Sociology and Age." *Sociological Focus,* 1971, 5(1), pp. 62-72.

Discusses some of the ways in which increased knowledge of the social aspects of age will contribute to our grasp of the structures and processes which affect the lives of the elderly.

Rosow, Irving. "The Social Context of the Aging Self." *The Gerontologist,* 1973, 13(1), pp. 82-87.

Role loss, according to Rosow, underlies the crises that occur with aging. He views old age as a time of personal stresses and social losses with few compensations.

Rosow, Irving. *Socialization to Old Age.* Berkeley: University of California Press, 1974.

Views socialization to old age as a specific problem in the general theory of adult socialization. Analyzes how people in our society are unsuccessfully socialized to the status of old age. Examines the main variables of socialization and shows how norms for the elderly are weak and roles for them are almost nonexistent.

Rosow, Irving. "Status and Role Change Through the Life Span." In Robert H. Binstock and Ethel Shanas (Eds.), *Handbook of Aging and the Social Sciences.* New York: Van Nostrand Reinhold, 1976, pp. 457-482.

Separates the concepts of status and role and constructs a set of role types based on their independence of one another. Also analyzes some changes in the life cycle in terms of this typology.

Seguin, Mary M. "Opportunity for Peer Socialization in a Retirement Community." *The Gerontologist,* 1973, 13(2), pp. 208-214.

Reveals that there is ample opportunity for peer socialization among the residents of a retirement community. The residents generate both an informal social network and a formal social structure through which they enact expressive and instrumental roles.

Sherwood, Sylvia. "Sociological Aspects of Learning and Memory." *The Gerontologist,* 1967, 7(1), pp. 19-23.

Discusses some of the socio-cultural influences on memory and learning and how they relate to the elderly.

Siegel, Barry, and Lasher, Judith. "Deinstitutionalizing Elderly Patients: A Program of Resocialization." *The Gerontologist,* 1978, 18(3), pp. 293-300.

Three components of a deinstitutionalization program are a proper diagnosis, a change in social structure, and familiarity with the proposed new setting. The results show that efforts to deinstitutionalize patients must be based on changes in expectations of staff and changes in the patients' definition of their own situations.

Strauss, Harold; Aldrich, Bruce W.; and Lipman, Aaron. "Retirement and Perceived Status Loss: An Inquiry into Some Objective and Subjective Problems Produced by Aging." In Jaber F. Gubrium (Ed.), *Time, Roles, and Self in Old Age.* New York: Human Sciences Press, 1976, pp. 220-234.

Studies factors associated with the maintenance of feelings of self-respect and social worth among retirees. Findings suggest that highly educated persons experience the least perceived status loss after retirement. While the association between high educational attainment and the absence of feelings of status loss is more apparent among males, it is statistically significant for both sexes.

Tallmer, Margot, and Kutner, Bernard. "Disengagement and the Stresses of Aging." *Journal of Gerontology,* 1969, 24(1), pp. 70-75.

Concludes that it is not age which produces disengagement but the impact of physical and social stresses such as ill health, widowhood, and retirement. These stresses may be expected to increase with age.

Tissue, Thomas. "Disengagement Potential: Replication and Use as an Explanatory Variable." *Journal of Gerontology,* 1971, 26(1), pp. 76-80.

By applying the scale of Disengagement Potential to a population of aged public assistance recipients, the results reveal that ex-middle-class aged and those in good health are more likely to show a high readiness to withdraw. Unmatched life space and readiness to withdraw is associated with low morale while congruence between life space and disengagement potential is associated with high morale.

Uhlenberg, Peter. "Older Women: The Growing Challenge to Design Constructive Roles." *The Gerontologist,* 1979, 19(3), pp. 236-241.

Indicates that a large majority of the 13 million older women are educated, healthy, not poor, and are capable of making a substantial contribution to society. A critical task is to help direct the resources of these women into socially constructive channels.

Ward, Russell A. "The Impact of Subjective Age and Stigma on Older Persons." *Journal of Gerontology,* 1977, 32(2), pp. 227-232.

Examines the effects of changes in age identification by older people from middle-aged to elderly. Findings indicate that the age identification label is unrelated to attitudes toward old people. Also finds a strong relationship between acceptance of negative attitudes toward old people and self-derogation.

Williams, Richard H. "Changing Status, Roles, and Relationships." In Clark Tibbitts (Ed.), *Handbook of Social Gerontology.* Chicago: The University of Chicago Press, 1960, pp. 261-297.

Discusses the changing statuses and roles to which the elderly are being assigned and the effects of these changes. Suggests that the theory of action is important to an understanding of the problems of aging.

Zola, Irving K. "Feelings about Age among Older People." *Journal of Gerontology,* 1962, 17(1), pp. 65-68.

Reports the sex differences in people's perception of their own aging and its relationship to the perception of one's parents' aging. The findings indicate that chronological age is not related to seeing oneself as elderly while "felt age" is strongly associated with this perception. The variable which seems to have the greatest effect on the perception of aging for both sexes is having seen one's father as "elderly" and is associated with how old the subject felt.

Chapter 5

LIFE SATISFACTION

Adams, David L. "Correlates of Satisfaction among the Elderly." *The Gerontologist,* 1971, 11(4), pt. 2, pp. 64-68.

Reviews the correlates of satisfaction and indicates the consistencies and inconsistencies of findings in the literature.

Alston, Jon P., and Dudley, Charles J. "Age, Occupation, and Life Satisfaction." *The Gerontologist,* 1973, 13(1), pp. 58-61.

Finds that the feeling that life is routine and dull tends to increase with age. People with high incomes feel this routinization less than those with low incomes. Also professional and white-collar workers defined life as routine and/or dull less often than executives, and skilled and unskilled workers.

Anderson, Nancy N. "Effects of Institutionalization on Self-Esteem." *Journal of Gerontology,* 1967, 22(3), pp. 313-317.

Compares institutionalized and non-institutionalized older persons to determine if interaction is more closely associated with self-esteem than institutionalization. Findings reveal that changes in self-esteem are explained by variations in the amount of interaction rather than by institutionalization. Those persons having frequent interactions whether living in the community or an institution are most likely to have high self-esteem.

Bell, Bill D. "Cognitive Dissonance and the Life Satisfaction of Older Adults." *Journal of Gerontology,* 1974, 29(5), pp. 564-571.

Interviews were conducted with 114 older males before and after retirement to test the consistency theory with regard to life satisfaction. The analysis gives little support to the consistency hypothesis except in the area of the family.

Bell, Bill D. "The Limitations of Crisis Theory as an Explanatory Mechanism in Social Gerontology." *International Journal of Aging and Human Development,* 1975, 6(2), pp. 153-168.

Using a longitudinal sample of older persons, this study investigates five assumptions of crisis theory as they relate to the prediction of life satisfaction following retirement from work. The correlation between work commitment and the desire for subsequent employment is negative and significant. It was the only assumption out of the five tested which received support.

Bell, Bill D. "Role Set Orientations and Life Satisfaction: A New Look at an Old Theory." In Jaber F. Gubrium (Ed.), *Time, Roles, and Self in Old Age.* New York: Human Sciences Press, 1976, pp. 148-164.

Examines the assumptions and predictions of the continuity theory with regard to life satisfaction. Finds that the more time invested in the family after retirement, the more negative the life satisfaction. However, interaction in the community and involvement in voluntary associations are found to be positively associated with life satisfaction. Concludes that the findings do not substantiate the continuity hypothesis and sees an activity orientation as a more appropriate explanation.

Bell, Bill D. "Life Satisfaction and Occupational Retirement: Beyond the Impact Year." *International Journal of Aging and Human Development,* 1978-1979, 9(1), pp. 31-50.

Tests hypotheses derived from the crisis, the continuity, and the consistency theories relative to the prediction of life satisfaction following retirement. Of the four crisis theory hypotheses, only one hypothesis, that individuals undergo a decline in satisfaction with retirement, is confirmed. In the case of the continuity theory, the only hypothesis partially confirmed is that a positive association is obtained between satisfaction and orientational change in the voluntary association area. Lastly, of the three consistency theory hypotheses, only the hypothesis that expectational disconfirmations are not productive of lowered satisfaction is partially supported.

Bennett, Ruth, and Nahemow, Lucille. "Institutional Totality and Criteria of Social Adjustment in Residence for the Aged." *Journal of Social Issues,* 1965, 21(4), pp. 44-78.

Examines the relationship between institutional totality, and the clarity and complexity of social adjustment criteria. Shows that in homes for the aged participation in formal and informal activities emerges as a major adjustment criterion. In retirement housing participation in informal social relationships is an important adjustment criterion. Adjustment criteria are the clearest and most complex in settings which are established as permanent and which approximate self-contained communities.

Brand, Frederick N., and Smith, Richard T. "Life Adjustment and Relocation of the Elderly." *Journal of Gerontology,* 1974, 29(3), pp. 336-340.

To determine the relationship between involuntary relocation and the life adjustment and health of older people, interview data were obtained from elderly persons who had experienced enforced relocation and those who had not relocated. Results reveal that the relocated residents show greater life dissatisfaction than the control group who did not move. Elderly blacks seem to adjust better after relocation than whites. Life satisfaction is lower among those persons who were in poor health and forced to relocate.

Britton, Joseph H. "Dimensions of Adjustment of Older Adults." *Journal of Gerontology,* 1963, 18(1), pp. 60-65.

Investigates the problem of measuring adjustment by determining the dimensions which underlie several measures of adjustment. Three dimensions emerge: an activity factor, a sociability factor, and a composure-serenity-integrity factor.

Bull, Neil C., and Aucoin, Jackie B. "Voluntary Association Participation and Life Satisfaction: A Replication Note." *Journal of Gerontology,* 1975, 30(1), pp. 73-76.

Reveals that the positive relationship between participation in voluntary associations and life satisfaction of older persons is due to differences between participants and nonparticipants. With health and socioeconomic status held constant, voluntary association participation of the elderly has no significant relationship to life satisfaction.

Bultena, Gordon L. "Life Continuity and Morale in Old Age." *The Gerontologist,* 1969, 9(4), pt. 1, pp. 251-253.

Indicates that there is a positive relationship between morale and socioeconomic status. Low morale is greater among those who experienced dramatic decremental changes in their life patterns between the preretirement period and the present time.

Bultena, Gordon L., and Oyler, Robert. "Effects of Health on Disengagement and Morale." *Aging and Human Development,* 1971, 2(2), pp. 142-148.

Contrary to the theory of disengagement, the authors find little support for the argument that high morale characterizes the final stages of the disengagement process.

Bultena, Gordon L. "Structural Effects on the Morale of the Aged: A Comparison of Age-Segregated and Age-Integrated Communities." In Jaber F. Gubrium (Ed.), *Late Life: Communities and Environmental Policy.* Springfield, Ill.: Charles C. Thomas, 1974, pp. 18-31.

Based on interview data from three age-integrated communities, this study reveals that residents of planned retirement communities have higher morale than those living in regular communities. Retirement communities also facilitate the adaptations of older migrants to the retirement role.

Bultena, Gordon, and Powers, Edward. "Effects of Age-Grade Comparisons on Adjustment in Later Life." In Jaber F. Gubrium (Ed.), *Time, Roles, and Self in Old Age.* New York: Human Sciences Press, 1976, pp. 165-178.

Using data from a longitudinal study of older persons in Iowa, this study explores the effects of age-grade comparisons on adjustment in later life. Finds that favorable comparative evaluations are associated with high levels of life satisfaction. Also that comparative evaluations are as important to the life satisfaction of respondents as are their actual objective positions.

Carp, Frances M. "Compound Criteria in Gerontological Research." *Journal of Gerontology,* 1969, 24(3), pp. 341-347.

Presents two sets of data analyses, one involving adjustment and the other disengagement. The findings indicate that some inconsistencies from study to study concerning disengagement and adjustment may result from the use of different partial and compound criteria with different elements.

Carp, Frances M. "Impact of Improved Housing on Morale and Life Satisfaction." *The Gerontologist,* 1975, 15(6), pp. 511-515.

Reveals the importance of the living environment upon the morale and life satisfaction of older persons. Tenants of Victoria Plaza, a public housing project, are happier than those elderly with generally unsatisfactory housing arrangements living elsewhere in the community.

Cavan, Ruth S. "Self and Role in Adjustment during Old Age." In Arnold M. Rose (Ed.), *Human Behavior and Social Processes.* Boston: Houghton Mifflin, 1962, pp. 526-536.

Illustrates how the concepts of self-conception, role-taking, and role-playing can be used to analyze adjustment to old age, and suggests how better adjustment can be manipulated.

Chatfield, Walter F. "Economic and Sociological Factors Influencing Life Satisfaction of the Aged." *Journal of Gerontology,* 1977, 32(5), pp. 593-599.

Investigates the importance of income, health, and family to life satisfaction. Findings reveal that the lower life satisfaction of retirees results mainly from the lower income associated with retirement and not from the loss of the worker role. In addition, higher income helps lessen the effect that health problems have on life satisfaction and increases life satisfaction associated with family living.

Clark, Margaret, and Anderson, Barbara G. *Culture and Aging: An Anthropological Study of Older Americans.* Springfield, Ill.: Charles G. Thomas, 1967.

This study is based on a sample of 435 elderly persons in San Francisco. Some of the subjects are considered mentally healthy while others have undergone treatment for mental disorders. The major focus is on the personal and social factors relevant to a good or poor adaptation in old age.

Clemente, Frank, and Auer, William J. "Race and Morale of the Urban Aged." *The Gerontologist,* 1974, 14(4), pp. 342-344.

The hypothesis that aged urban blacks have lower morale than aged urban whites is not supported by the findings of this study. Discusses some possible reasons for the failure of race to emerge as a predictor of morale.

Conner, Karen A., and Powers, Edward A. "Structural Effects and Life Satisfaction among the Aged." *International Journal of Aging and Human Development,* 1975, 6(4), pp. 321-327.

Investigates the effects of community structure on the social interaction and life satisfaction of older persons. Suggests that age-graded interaction is significantly correlated with life satisfaction in large communities. Finds no significant relationship is between community structure and total or age-graded interaction.

Conner, Karen A.; Powers, Edward A.; and Bultena, Gordon L. "Social Interaction and Life Satisfaction: An Empirical Assessment of Late-Life Patterns." *Journal of Gerontology,* 1979, 34(1), pp. 116-121.

Reveals that the number of persons interacted with and the frequency of interaction are of little significance for the adjustment and morale of older persons. Of greater importance is under what conditions, for what purposes, and with what degree of intimacy does interaction take place.

Curry, Timothy J., and Tatliff, Bascom W. "The Effects of Nursing Home Size on Resident Isolation and Life Satisfaction." *The Gerontologist,* 1973, 13(3), pt. 1, pp. 295-298.

Finds that small nursing homes facilitate the development of a greater number of friendships. The majority of nursing home residents in the sample are satisfied with their life, regardless of the size of the home they are living in.

Cutler, Neal E. "Age Variations in the Dimensionality of Life Satisfaction." *Journal of Gerontology,* 1979, 34(4), pp. 573-578.

Shows that different age groups do not have the same patterns of life-satisfaction ratings. The number of factors and their content varies substantially across age groups.

Cutler, Stephen J. "The Availability of Personal Transportation, Residential Location, and Life Satisfaction among the Aged." *Journal of Gerontology,* 1972, 27(3), pp. 383-389.

Finds low life-satisfaction scores among those elderly who do not have personal transportation available to them and who live at greater distances from the community's facilities and services.

Cutler, Stephen J. "Transportation and Changes in Life Satisfaction." *The Gerontologist,* 1975, 15(2), pp. 155-159.

Indicates that the quality of an older person's life is partly dependent upon the availability of personal transportation.

Cutler, Stephen J. "Membership in Different Types of Voluntary Associations and Psychological Well-Being." *The Gerontologist,* 1976, 16(4), pp. 335-339.

Psychological well-being for the elderly does not appear to be related to membership in most kinds of voluntary associations. However, when well-being is related to membership in a particular type of association, this effect appears to be confined mainly to membership in church-affiliated associations.

Dick, Harry R., and Friedsam, Hiram J. "Adjustment of Residents of Two Homes for the Aged." *Social Problems,* 1964, 11(3), pp. 282-290.

Examines the adjustment of residents in two homes for the aged. Morale appears to decline during institutionalization even though some favorable adjustments are made to the home. Although good health is significant for high morale, it is not necessary for a favorable attitude toward the home.

Dobson, Cynthia, et al. "Anomia, Self-Esteem, and Life Satisfaction: Interrelationships among Three Scales of Well-Being." *Journal of Gerontology,* 1979, 34(4), pp. 569-572.

The analysis reveals some overlap among the scales. While Srole's anomia scale and Rosenberg's scale of self-esteem measures distinct dimensions, some of the LSI-Z items combined with the anomia and self-esteem items.

Donnenwerth, Gregory V.; Guy, Rebecca F.; and Norvell, Melissa J. "Life Satisfaction among Older Persons: Rural-Urban and Racial Comparisons." *Social Science Quarterly,* 1978, 59(3), pp. 578-583.

Examines the effect of residence and race upon life satisfaction among rural and urban elderly. Finds that overall rural residents have higher life satisfaction scores than urban residents. Also blacks score higher on life satisfaction than do whites.

Dressler, David M. "Life Adjustment of Retired Couples." *International Journal of Aging and Human Development,* 1973, 4(4), pp. 335-349.

Investigates the marital relationship and retirement experiences of couples living in an urban community. While there was some decrease in their level of social participation since retirement, overall, these couples appear to be satisfied with their marriages and life patterns. Results indicate that continuity of life patterns is an important determinant of successful adjustment to retirement.

Edwards, John N., and Klemmack, David L. "Correlates of Life Satisfaction: A Re-Examination." *Journal of Gerontology,* 1973, 28(4), pp. 497-502.

Examines the relationships between life satisfactions and 22 variables. When socioeconomic status is held constant, observed relationships between life satisfaction and age, marital status, and family size are reduced to a nonsignificant level. The primary determinants of life satisfaction are socioeconomic status, health status, and participation in nonfamilial activities.

Fengler, Alfred P., and Goodrich, Nancy. "Wives of Elderly Disabled Men: The Hidden Patients." *The Gerontologist,* 1979, 19(2), pp. 175-183.

Finds an association between the life satisfaction scores of husbands and wives. Morale of the wives is higher when they perceive their income as adequate and when they are not employed full-time.

Filsinger, Erik, and Sauer, William J. "An Empirical Typology of Adjustment to Aging." *Journal of Gerontology,* 1978, 33(3), pp. 437-445.

Constructs a typology of adjustors to age. Derives three male types of adjustors and two female types through cluster analysis.

George, Linda K., and Maddox, George L. "Subjective Adaptation to Loss of the Work Role: A Longitudinal Study." *Journal of Gerontology,* 1977, 32(4), pp. 456-462.

Examines the relationship between retirement and adaptation in 58 male subjects. Indicates that there are high levels of adaptation in the subjects as reflected in the overwhelming stability of morale over time. In addition, finds marital status, occupational prestige, education, and self-perceived health to be significant predictors of adaptation.

George, Linda K. "The Happiness Syndrome: Methodological and Substantive Issues in the Study of Social Psychological Well-Being in Adulthood." *The Gerontologist,* 1979, 19(2), pp. 210-216.

Advocates the use of available survey data as a starting point for examining life satisfaction and related concepts from the perspective of aging. Describes six major national surveys.

George, Linda K., and Bearon, Lucille B. *Quality of Life in Older Persons: Meaning and Measurement.* New York: Human Sciences Press, 1980. Presents a conceptual context for the accessment of quality of life, introduces a set of criteria to use in selecting a measuring instrument, and then describes 22 measuring instruments in terms of psychometric properties and conceptual and methodogical issues.

George, Linda K. *Role Transitions in Later Life.* Monterey, Calif.: Brooks/Cole, 1980.

The first part of the book is devoted to the development of a model of adjustment to social stress in later life. The second half assesses the utility of the social stress model for increasing our understanding of the nature of role transitions and role changes that usually occur in late adulthood.

Graney, Marshall J., and Graney, Edith E. "Scaling Adjustment in Older Persons." *International Journal of Aging and Human Development,* 1973, 4(4), pp. 351-359.

Discusses the advantages and disadvantages of several scaling procedures. Develops a scaling procedure and uses it to collect data to test the hypothetical relationship between happiness and personal adjustment. The data indicate the two are unrelated.

Graney, Marshall J. "Happiness and Social Participation in Aging." *Journal of Gerontology,* 1975, 30(6), pp. 701-706.

A longitudinal study of 60 older women reveals a positive relationship between happiness and social activity. Most of the activities that are highly associated with happiness involve face-to-face interaction or the potential for it.

Gubrium, Jaber F. "Environmental Effects on Morale in Old Age and the Resources of Health and Solvency." *The Gerontologist,* 1970, 10(4), pt. 1, pp. 294-297.

Indicates that for those elderly with poor behavior resources (health and solvency), an age-concentrated environment is positively associated with morale. Finds no relationship between age-concentration and morale for those elderly with high resources.

Harvey, Carol D., and Bahr, Howard M. "Widowhood, Morale, and Affiliation." *Journal of Marriage and the Family,* 1974, 36(1), pp. 97-106.

Based on data from sample surveys in five countries, morale and organizational ties of widowed and married persons are examined. The major finding is that neither the self-theory nor the role-theory perspective is adequate to explain differences between widowed and married persons in morale or affiliations. This study suggests that widows appear to have more negative attitudes than married persons. These attitudes may be due to other factors besides widowhood per se. For example, widows are poorer than married persons and they may be less affiliated for this reason.

Havens, Betty J. "An Investigation of Activity Patterns and Adjustment in an Aging Population." *The Gerontologist,* 1968, 8(3), pp. 201-206.

Older persons who were involuntarily relocated in a public housing facility have a high level of adjustment when there is a continuity of participation in activities. A low level of adjustment is associated with discontinuity of participation in activities.

Havighurst, Robert J. "Successful Aging." *The Gerontologist,* 1961, 1(1), pp. 8-13.

Describes the various measures of successful aging and their validity and use.

Havighurst, Robert J. "Successful Aging." In Richard H. Williams, Clark Tibbitts, and Wilma Donahue (Eds.). *Processes of Aging: Social and Psychological Perspectives,* vol. 1. New York: Atherton Press, 1963, pp. 299-311.

Discusses the definition of successful aging and a method for measuring it.

Hoyt, Danny R., et al. "Life Satisfaction and Activity Theory: A Multidimensional Approach." *Journal of Gerontology,* 1980, 35(6), pp. 935-941.

Tests hypotheses based upon a multidimensional approach to the Life Satisfaction Index A (LSI-A). Little support is provided for the hypotheses relating activity to life satisfaction dimensions. Reveals the importance of considering the dimensions of the LSI-A independently.

Hutchinson, Ira W., III. "The Significance of Marital Status for Morale and Life Satisfaction among Lower-Income Elderly." *Journal of Marriage and the Family,* 1975, 37(2), pp. 287-293.

Examines differences in life satisfaction as they are affected by income, sex, and the marital status of the elderly. Concludes that sex or marital status differences may have a significant influence on the elderly's life satisfaction above a poverty level, but neither is important below the poverty line.

Jackson, James S.; Bacon, John D.; and Peterson, John. "Life Satisfaction among Black Urban Elderly." *International Journal of Aging and Human Development,* 1977-1978, 8(2), pp. 169-179.

Data from a sample of black, retired persons living in a large urban area reveal that factors such as background characteristics, health, political participation, personality variables, and life perceptions are related to life satisfaction.

Jaslow, Philip. "Employment, Retirement, and Morale among Older Women." *Journal of Gerontology,* 1976, 31(2), pp. 212-218.

Tests the hypothesis that older working women have better morale than those who do not work. With the exception of retired women with annual incomes of $5,000 or more, the study finds that employed women have higher morale than retirees. Those women who never worked have the lowest morale.

Kahana, Eva; Liang, Jersey; and Felton, Barbara J. "Alternative Modes of Person-Environment Fit: Prediction of Morale in Three Homes for the Aged." *Journal of Gerontology,* 1980, 35(4), pp. 584-595.

Presents person-environment fit (P-E Fit) conceptualizations for the elderly and gives different methods for operationalizing them. Findings from a study to test these theoretical models indicate that P-E fit scores along the dimensions of impulse control, congregation, and segregation make a significant contribution to the understanding of the morale of the elderly in homes for the aged.

Kerckhoff, Alan C. "Family Patterns and Morale in Retirement." In Ida H. Simpson and John C. McKinney (Eds.), *Social Aspects of Aging.* Durham, N.C.: Duke University Press, 1966, pp. 173-192.

Examines the relationship between family patterns and morale in retirement. The only variable which is consistently associated with morale for both husband and wife is the level of the husband's participation in household tasks. In households where the husband participates, both the husband's and wife's morale is higher than in those in which the husband does not participate.

Lanzer, Anthony. "Sociocultural Influences on Adjustment to Aging." *Geriatrics,* 1961, 16(12), pp. 631-640.

Discusses the transition to old age, the role of the elderly in our society, and the responses of the elderly to the sociocultural environment.

Larson, Reed. "Thirty Years of Research on the Subjective Well-Being of Older Americans." *Journal of Gerontology,* 1978, 33(1), pp. 109-125.

Reviews the major studies published in the last 30 years on the relationship of well-being to the life situations of the elderly. A summary of the studies shows well-being to be most strongly correlated with health, followed by socioeconomic factors, and social activity.

Lawton, M. Powell, and Cohen, Jacob. "The Generality of Housing Impact on the Well-Being of Older People." *Journal of Gerontology,* 1974, 29(2), pp. 194-204.

Makes a comparison between a group of elderly persons that were rehoused and a group of elderly persons that remained in their own homes in the community to determine the impact of rehousing on the well-being of older persons. Results show that the rehoused persons were higher in morale, more satisfied with their housing, and more involved in external activities, but they were significantly poorer in health.

Lee, Gary R. "Marriage and Morale in Later Life." *Journal of Marriage and the Family,* 1978, 40(1), pp. 131-139.

Analyzes the effect of marital satisfaction on morale. Finds that marital satisfaction is positively related to morale among older people and that this relationship is markedly stronger for women than men.

Lee, Gary, R. "Children and the Elderly: Interaction and Morale." *Research on Aging,* 1979, 1(3), pp. 335-360.

Examines the extent to which the frequency of interaction with adult children contributes to the morale of elderly parents. Reveals that the elderly parents' morale is not significantly affected by frequency of contact with their children.

Lee, Gary R., and Ihinger-Tallman, Marilyn. "Sibling Interaction and Morale: The Effects of Family Relations on Older People." *Research on Aging,* 1980, 2(3), pp. 367-391.

Analyzes the relationship between the elderly's morale and interaction with their siblings. Results indicate that interaction with siblings is unrelated to the morale of the elderly.

Lemon, Bruce W.; Bengtson, Vern L.; and Peterson, James A. "An Exploration of the Activity Theory of Aging: Activity Types and Life Satisfaction among In-Movers to a Retirement Community." *Journal of Gerontology,* 1972, 27(4), 511-523.

Using a sample of residents in a retirement community, this study analyzes the relationship between types of social activity and life satisfaction. The results show that only social activity with friends is related to life satisfaction. The data provide only limited support to some of the propositions of the activity theory of aging.

Liang, Jersey, et al. "Social Integration and Morale: A Re-Examination." *Journal of Gerontology,* 1980, 35(5), pp. 746-757.

Indicates that objective social integration is only indirectly related to morale. Subjective perception of integration is a critical intervening variable between objective social integration and morale.

Lipman, Aaron, and Smith, Kenneth J. "Functionality of Disengagement in Old Age." *Journal of Gerontology,* 1968, 23(4), pp. 517-521.

Tests the hypothesis that disengagement from normal roles is functional for the elderly. Results show that high morale is related to engagement, rather than disengagement, regardless of variations in age, sex, income, health, or race.

Lohmann, Nancy. "Correlations of Life Satisfaction, Morale, and Adjustment Measures." *Journal of Gerontology,* 1977, 32(1), pp. 73-75.

Using Pearson Product Moment correlation coefficients, results show a high level of correlation among several measures of life satisfaction, morale, and adjustment.

Lohmann, Nancy. "A Factor Analysis of Life Satisfaction, Adjustment and Morale Measures with Elderly Adults." *International Journal of Aging and Human Development,* 1980, 11(1), pp. 35-43.

Examines seven frequently used measures of life satisfaction by the technique of construct validation. The results reveal that there is a construct, called "life satisfaction," which is shared by six of the seven measures and that no instrument best encompasses that construct.

Lohmann, Nancy. "Life Satisfaction Research in Aging: Implications for Policy Development." In Nancy Datan and Nancy Lohmann (Eds.), *Transitions of Aging.* New York: Academic Press, 1980, pp. 27-40.

Examines the relationship between life satisfaction and each of the following variables: marital status, retirement, health, housing, and social activity. As yet, no clear-cut answers with regard to the causes or correlates of satisfaction have been found.

Lowenthal, Marjorie F., and Boler, Deetje. "Voluntary vs Involuntary Social Withdrawal." *Journal of Gerontology,* 1965, 20(3), pp. 363-371.

The presence or absence of one or more of the following deprivations: retirement, recent widowhood, or physical illness have a greater bearing on morale than does recent social withdrawal. The voluntarily withdrawn have only slightly lower morale than those not withdrawn or deprived. The involuntarily withdrawn have the lowest morale and the most negative attitudes.

Lowenthal, Marjorie F., and Haven, Clayton. "Interaction and Adaptation: Intimacy as a Critical Variable." *American Sociological Review,* 1968, 33(1), pp. 20-30.

Reveals that the presence of an intimate relationship, such as a confidant, serves as a buffer against gradual role losses and the more traumatic losses accompanying widowhood and retirement.

Maddox, George, and Eisdorfer, Carl. "Some Correlates of Activity and Morale among the Elderly." *Social Forces,* 1962, 40(3), pp. 254-260.

Examines the association between age and activity, and morale and activity. The findings give limited support to the hypothesis that activity tends to decrease with age. Also the positive relationship between morale and activity is supported. According to the authors, these conclusions tend to obscure important antecedent and intervening variables.

Maddox, George L. "Activity and Morale: A Longitudinal Study of Selected Elderly Subjects." *Social Forces,* 1963, 42(2), pp. 195-204.

Analyzes the relationships among activity, morale, and aging. The major finding of this research is that there is a significant, positive relationship between activity and morale.

Mancini, Jay A. "Friend Interaction, Competence, and Morale in Old Age." *Research on Aging,* 1980, 2(4), pp. 416-431.

Examines the importance of friendship to successful aging. The findings indicate that morale is positively associated with friend-role competence. Those with higher morale scores define themselves as more active and competent as friends.

Markides, Kyriakos S., and Martin, Harry W. "A Causal Model of Life Satisfaction among the Elderly." *Journal of Gerontology,* 1979, 34(1), pp. 86-93.

Using a path analysis model of life satisfaction, activity and self-reported health emerge as strong predictors of life satisfaction. Income is found to affect life satisfaction indirectly by means of activity.

Martin, William C. "Activity and Disengagement: Life Satisfaction of In-Movers into a Retirement Community." *The Gerontologist,* 1973, 13(2), pp. 224-227.

Based on a study of in-movers into a retirement community, the author examines the activity and disengagement theories in relation to life satisfaction. He concludes that both theories can correctly describe the socio-psychological process of aging, and that a combination of structural disengagement and age-segregated interpersonal activity may result in high life satisfaction.

Medley, Morris L. "Satisfaction with Life among Persons Sixty-Five Years and Older." *Journal of Gerontology,* 1976, 31(4), pp. 448-455.

Uses a causal model to explain the interrelationships of certain determinants of life satisfaction via path analysis. Findings reveal that the causal model is an effective predictor of life satisfaction for both sexes. The next important variables are health satisfaction for males and satisfaction with standard of living for females.

Medley, Morris L. "Life Satisfaction across Four Stages of Adult Life." *International Journal of Aging and Human Development,* 1980, 11(3), pp. 193-209.

Analyzes the effect of finances, health, standard of living, and family upon life satisfaction at four stages of the life cycle. Men are more likely than women to report a high degree of life satisfaction at late adulthood (ages 65 and over). Both older men and women experienced their greatest satisfaction from family life, but health and standard of living are also important factors.

Morgan, Leslie A. "A Re-Examination of Widowhood and Morale." *Journal of Gerontology,* 1976, 31(6), pp. 687-695.

Examines the relationship between widowhood and morale using analysis of covariance. Results reveal that there are important situational factors that cut across marital status differences in explaining morale scores. The lower morale scores of the widows may be due to other factors associated with the status of widowhood and not to the role of widowhood per se.

Neugarten, Bernice L.; Havighurst, Robert J.; and Tobin, Sheldon S. "Measurement of Life Satisfaction." *Journal of Gerontology,* 1961, 16(2), pp. 134-143.

Provides a set of scales for rating life satisfaction.

Pollak, Otto. "The Shadow of Death over Aging." *The Annals of the American Academy of Political and Social Science,* 1980, 447, pp. 71-77.

Discusses the plight of the elderly in today's society and the successful adaptations they make to various losses.

Phillips, Bernard S. "Role Change, Subjective Age, and Adjustment: A Correlational Analysis." *Journal of Gerontology,* 1961, 16(4), pp. 347-352.

Examines the interrelationships among older persons' role changes, subjective age, and adjustment. Indicates that the relationship between subjective age and adjustment is the most consistent, followed by the relationship between role changes and adjustment. Results are mixed regarding the relationship between role changes and various aspects of subjective ages.

Pihlblad, C.T., and Adams, David L. "Widowhood, Social Participation, and Life Satisfaction." *Aging and Human Development,* 1972, 3(4), pp. 323-330.

Investigates the relationship between widowhood, social participation, and life satisfaction among small town elderly. Findings reveal that no major change occurs in social participation among females after widowhood, while males show a linear decline in most kinds of activity patterns with length of widowhood. It seems that satisfaction among the elderly is most affected by participation in formal organizations, next by friendships, and the least by family contacts.

Poorkaj, Houshang. "Social-Psychological Factors and Successful Aging." *Sociology and Social Research,* 1971, 56(3), pp. 289-300.

Explores the relationship between living arrangements and successful aging as well as the utility of the activity and disengagement theories for interpreting successful aging. The major finding of the study is that those living in an age-integrated community have a higher level of morale than those living in an age-segregated retirement community.

Rosow, Irving. "Adjustment of the Normal Aged." In Richard H. Williams, Clark Tibbitts, and Wilma Donahue (Eds.), *Processes of Aging: Social and Psychological Perspectives,* vol. 2. New York: Atherton Press, 1963, pp. 195-223.

Considers several major problems associated with the concept of adjustment in old age and proposes a sociological approach to these problems.

Sauer, William. "Morale of the Urban Aged: A Regression Analysis by Race." *Journal of Gerontology,* 1977, 32(5), pp. 600-608.

Examines variables associated with morale for aged whites to determine if they are the same for aged blacks. Findings indicate that significant predictors of morale for both blacks and whites are health and participation in solitary activities. Finds that interaction with family and sex are significant predicators only for whites.

Seelbach, Wayne, C., and Sauer, William J. "Filial Responsibility Expectations and Morale among Aged Parents." *The Gerontologist,* 1977, 17(6), pp. 492-499.

Findings reveal that levels of filial responsibility expectancy are inversely associated with levels of parental morale. Discusses implications for social policy regarding filial responsibility.

Smith, Kenneth J., and Lipman, Aaron. "Constraint and Life Satisfaction." *Journal of Gerontology,* 1972, 27(1), pp. 77-82.

Examines factors associated with life satisfaction among the aged living in two housing projects. Some of the findings are that those residents who are free from constraints are more likely to be satisfied than those who are not. Also length of residence in a project is positively related to the rate of peer interaction.

Spreitzer, Elmer, and Snyder, Eldon E. "Correlates of Life Satisfaction among the Aged." *Journal of Gerontology,* 1974, 29(4), pp. 454-458.

The findings regarding correlates of life satisfaction among older persons reveal that after age 65 men were more likely than women to report a high degree of life satisfaction. Finds perceived health and financial adequacy to be predictors of life satisfaction.

Spreitzer, Elmer, and Snyder, Eldon. "The Relative Effects of Health and Income on Life Satisfaction." *International Journal of Aging and Human Development,* 1979-1980, 10(3), pp. 283-288.

The results reveal that among persons under age 65, financial adequacy has a stronger effect on life satisfaction than does physical condition. For persons over age 65, physical condition has the strongest impact on life satisfaction.

Sterne, Richard S.; Phillips, James E.; and Rabushka, Alvin. *The Urban Elderly Poor.* Lexington, Mass.: Lexington Books, 1974.

Deals with the behavior of the elderly poor in the inner city and the effect of the inner-city environment upon the elderly. The major findings are that elderly whites are more affluent, better educated, have better jobs, and live longer than their black counterparts. Most of the elderly poor show little interest in political activity except for voting. Chronological age does not correlate with the psychological and social aspects of advancing age, but is useful only as a predictor of reduced mobility.

Tallmer, Margot, and Kutner, Bernard. "Disengagement and Morale." *The Gerontologist,* 1970, 10(4), pt. 1, pp. 317-320.

The findings of this study are contrary to Cumming and Henry's predictions that disengagement must take place with aging to maintain morale, and that there is an improvement in the morale of those persons who are disengaging.

Teaff, Joseph, et al. "Impact of Age Integration on the Well-Being of the Elderly Tenants in Public Housing." *Journal of Gerontology,* 1978, 33(1), pp. 126-133.

Analyzes the relationship between age-integrated and age-segregated housing and the well-being of elderly tenants. Results show that elderly persons living in age-segregated housing participate more in organized activities and have higher morale and housing satisfaction than those in age-integrated settings.

Thompson, Gayle B. "Work versus Leisure Roles: An Investigation of Morale among Employed and Retired Men." *Journal of Gerontology,* 1973, 28(3), pp. 339-344.

Investigates the variation in the morale of retired men and men still working. The findings reveal that the retirees have lower morale than employed men. The lower morale of retirees cannot be attributed just to the fact that they are retired. Their morale is lower because they have more negative evaluations of their health, are more functionally disabled, and are older and poorer.

Thompson, Wayne E.; Streib, Gordon F.; and Kosa, John. "The Effect of Retirement on Personal Adjustment: A Panel Analysis." *Journal of Gerontology,* 1960, 15(2), pp. 165-169.

Suggests that the negative effects of retirement have been overestimated. In general, retirement has a negative effect on adjustment only when there are feelings of income inadequacy and there is difficulty in keeping occupied. But even under these circumstances, there is no evidence of extreme maladjustment.

Tobin, Sheldon S., and Neugarten, Bernice L. "Life Satisfaction and Social Interaction in the Aging." *Journal of Gerontology,* 1961, 16(4), pp. 344-346.

Results reveal that social interaction is positively related to life satisfaction and this association increases with advanced age. Engagement, rather than disengagement, appears to be more closely related to psychological well-being.

Toseland, Ron, and Rasch, John. "Correlates of Life Satisfaction: An Aid Analysis." *International Journal of Aging and Human Development,* 1979-1980, 10(2), pp. 203-211.

Using Automatic Interaction Detector (AID) analysis to develop a model based on the interaction of predictors of life satisfaction, it was found that there is a complex interaction between predictors of life satisfaction. The important predictors of life satisfaction are satisfaction with family life, personal health, and housing.

Videbeck, Richard, and Knox, Alan B. "Alternative Participatory Responses to Aging." In Arnold M. Rose and Warren A. Peterson (Eds.), *Older People and Their Social World.* Philadelphia: F.A. Davis, 1965, pp. 37-48.

Reports the factors associated with the social adjustment of older persons. Persons with higher scores on the social adjustment scale tend to have a youthful self-conception, good health, and a higher income than do those persons with lower scores. Also persons who are better adjusted have a higher degree of social participation with friends and neighbors, and are more active in religious, social, and civic groups.

Walsh, James A., and Kiracofe, Norman M. "Changes in Significant Other Relationships and Life Satisfaction in the Aged." *International*

Journal of Aging and Human Development, 1979-1980, 10(3), pp. 273-288.

Investigates the relationship between life satisfaction and the changes in the choice of an elderly person's significant others before and after entering a retirement home. Finds changes in reported preferences from relatives to friends only in the group with the longest residence in the home. Concludes that this change may be an important factor in the successful adjustment to a retirement home.

Williams, Richard H. "Styles of Life and Successful Aging." In Richard H. Williams, Clark Tibbitts and Wilma Donahue (Eds.), *Processes of Aging: Social and Psychological Perspectives,* vol. 1. New York: Atherton Press, 1963, pp. 335-371.

Analyzes data on 20 older persons in an attempt to delineate their lifestyles and to make some judgments about their successful aging.

Wood, Vivan, and Robertson, Joan F. "Friendship and Kinship Interaction: Differential Effect on the Morale of the Elderly." *Journal of Marriage and the Family,* 1978, 40(2), pp. 367-375.

Focuses on the differential effect of kinship and friendship relationships on the morale of older people. The findings reveal that friends are more important than grandchildren for maintaining morale in the later years.

Wylie, Mary L. "Life Satisfaction as Program Impact Criterion." *Journal of Gerontology,* 1970, 25(1), pp. 36-40.

The Life Satisfaction Index Z (LSI-Z) morale index was successfully used as an impact criterion for assessing the effects of a demonstration program upon a sample of older persons living in the community. Although the LSI-Z was administered only to the elderly, it reflects the effects of the program on the well-being of many younger persons in the community.

Chapter 6

GROUPS AND ORGANIZATIONS

Babchuk, Nicholas. "Aging and Primary Relations." *International Journal of Aging and Human Development,* 1978-1979, 9(2), pp. 137-151.

Documents the fact that few middle-aged and older persons are isolated. A substantial number of the respondents had a large number of primary resources and extensive ties. Those with extensive ties were more likely to be women than men, married rather than single, younger rather than older, and in high-status rather than in low-status occupations.

Babchuk, Nicholas, et al. "The Voluntary Associations of the Aged." *Journal of Gerontology,* 1979, 34(4), pp. 579-587.

Finds that the elderly have a high rate of participation in organizations. No sharp drop in affiliations occurs, not even for those persons 80 years or older. The aged tend to concentrate their membership in organizations that are expressive or expressive-instrumental in function. Women are just as likely as men to be members and hold multiple memberships.

Back, Kurt W. "Social Systems and Social Facts." In Ethel Shanas and Marvin B. Sussman (Eds.), *Family, Bureaucracy and the Elderly.* Durham, N.C.: Duke University Press, 1977, pp. 196-203.

Analyzes the family and bureaucracy not only as systems, but as social facts which occur in society. Discusses the problems encountered by the bureaucracy in taking on family functions and suggests further research to determine the capacity of the family to take on bureaucratic functions.

Bell, Bill D. "The Family Cycle, Primary Relationships, and Social Participation Patterns." *The Gerontologist,* 1973, 13(1), pp. 78-81.

Finds no significant differences between the family life-cycle stages in terms of the number of informal social contacts and the number of memberships and frequency of participation in formal organizations.

Buck, Charles F. "The Older Person, the Family and Church: Selected References." *The Family Life Coordinator,* 1960, 8(4), pp. 71-77.

Provides a bibliography dealing with older persons and their position in the family, and ways in which community agencies and organizations, specifically religious groups and churches, can help the elderly.

Bull, Neil C., and Aucoin, Jackie B. "Voluntary Association Participation and Life Satisfaction: A Replication Note." *Journal of Gerontology,* 1975, 30(1), pp. 73-76.

Finds that the positive relationship between participation in voluntary associations and life satisfaction of older persons is due to differences between participants and nonparticipants. With health and socioeconomic status held constant, voluntary association participation of the elderly has no significant relationship to life satisfaction.

Bultena, Gordon L., and Powers, Edward A. "Denial of Aging: Age Identification and Reference Group Orientations." *Journal of Gerontology,* 1978, 33(5), pp. 748-754.

Data from a 10-year longitudinal study (1960 to 1970) reveal that few subjects viewed themselves as old in 1960, and most thought of themselves as middle-aged. One-third of the subjects, despite their being over 70, continue to think of themselves as middle-aged in 1970. Favorable self-evaluations, which result from reference group comparisons, are positively associated with younger self-images.

Cantor, Marjorie H. "The Informal Support System: Its Relevance in the Lives of the Elderly." In Edgar F. Borgatta and Neil G. McCluskey (Eds.), *Aging and Society: Current Research and Policy Perspectives,* Beverly Hills, Calif.: Sage Publications, 1980.

Discusses the role of the informal network in providing assistance to the elderly. Also considers the interface of formal and informal networks.

Clemente, Frank; Rexroad, Patricia A.; and Hirsch, Carl. "The Participation of the Black Aged in Voluntary Associations." *Journal of Gerontology,* 1975, 30(4), pp. 469-472.

Results demonstrate that aged blacks belong to more voluntary associations than aged whites and have higher attendance rates.

Cutler, Stephen J. "Voluntary Association Participation and Life Satisfaction: A Cautionary Research Note." *Journal of Gerontology,* 1973, 28(1), pp. 96-100.

Although the data show a positive relationship between the extent of participation in voluntary associations and life satisfaction, this relationship is due to the way in which participants differ from nonparticipants. Voluntary associations self-select members who are more satisfied with their lives because of their health and socioeconomic status.

Cutler, Stephen J. "The Effects of Transportation and Distance on Voluntary Association Participation among the Aged." *International Journal of Aging and Human Development,* 1974, 5(1), pp. 81-93.

Finds that in a community in which public and commercial modes of transportation are not available, the absence of personal transportation is related to lower levels of voluntary association participation among the elderly. Also the role of transportation in facilitating voluntary association participation of the elderly increases both as distance of residence from the sites of associations increase, and as the analytical focus shifts from the number of memberships to frequency of attendance at meetings.

Cutler, Stephen J. "Age Profiles of Membership in Sixteen Types of Voluntary Associations." *Journal of Gerontology,* 1976, 31(4), pp. 462-470.

Uses data from the 1974 and 1975 NORC General Social Surveys to study the patterns in age differences of persons belonging to voluntary associations. Findings reveal that older persons are more likely to belong to fraternal and church-affiliated groups, and younger persons are more likely to belong to sports groups. Also the types of associations that were the most attractive to older persons in 1955 continue to be the most attractive in 1974 and 1975.

Cutler, Stephen J. "Membership in Different Types of Voluntary Associations and Psychological Well-Being." *The Gerontologist,* 1976, 16(4), pp. 335-339.

Psychological well-being for the elderly does not appear to be related to membership in most kinds of voluntary associations. However, when well-being is related to membership in a particular type of association, this effect appears to be confined mainly to membership in church-affiliated associations.

Cutler, Stephen J. "Age Differences in Voluntary Association Memberships." *Social Forces,* 1976, 55(1), pp. 43-58.

Previous studies have found that age differences in voluntary association membership are curvilinear in that middle-aged persons have higher rates than younger and older persons. This study finds that the lower membership levels of the older age groups appear to be largely attributable to their socioeconomic characteristics.

Cutler, Stephen J. "Aging and Voluntary Association Participation." *Journal of Gerontology,* 1977, 32(4), pp. 470-479.

Studies a sample of middle-aged persons and a sample of older persons over time to investigate changes in voluntary association participation levels. The results show high levels of voluntary association participation for both samples. As one ages the modal pattern appears to be one of continuity and stability and not withdrawal from social participation.

Dono, John, E., et al. "Primary Groups in Old Age: Structure and Function." *Research on Aging,* 1979, 1(4), pp. 403-433.

Discusses the effects of age on primary groups and factors that influence primary group structure and function in old age.

Estes, Carroll L. "Community Planning for the Elderly: A Study of Goal Displacement." *Journal of Gerontology,* 1974, 29(6), pp. 684-689.

Studies three planning organizations that claim to deal specifically with the problems of the elderly in the community. Results indicate that the planning activities of the organizations are more symbolic than instrumental, and more oriented toward legitimation of their work with the elderly than actual accomplishment. The planning participants try to attain expert status and claim to control decision-making activities in aging as a means of dealing with the survival needs of their organizations.

Estes, Carroll L. "Constructions of Reality." *Journal of Social Issues,* 1980, 36(2), pp. 117-132.

Focuses on the different approaches to working with the elderly that are held and practiced by professionals in local policymaking and service delivery. The major findings are that the organizations that have been developed to plan for the elderly exclude this group from their activities and from influence on planning outcomes. The most influential leaders of planning organizations are professionals whose orientation toward working with the elderly is basically accommodative.

Hampe, Gary D., and Blevins, Audie L. "Primary Group Interaction of Residents in a Retirement Hotel." *International Journal of Aging and Human Development,* 1975, 6(4), pp. 309-320.

Data from residents living in a retirement hotel reveal that the residents have a high level of satisfaction with their housing arrangements. Suggests that this satisfaction is due to better living conditions and the involvement of the individual in primary groups.

Harvey, Carol D., and Bahr, Howard M. "Widowhood, Morale, and Affiliation." *Journal of Marriage and the Family,* 1974, 36(1), pp. 97-106.

Based on data from sample surveys in five countries, the morale and organizational ties of widowed and married persons are examined. The major finding is that neither the self-theory nor the role-theory perspective is adequate to explain differences between widowed and married persons in morale or affiliations. This study suggests that widows appear to have more negative attitudes than married persons. These attitudes may be due to other factors besides widowhood per se. For example, widows are poorer than married persons and they may be less affiliated for this reason.

Jacobs, Ruth H. "The Friendship Club: A Case Study of the Segregated Aged." *The Gerontologist,* 1969, 9(4), pt. 1, pp. 276-280.

Reports that there is a sense of community among the residents of a senior citizens housing project, but at the same time the residents feel rejected and alienated by the larger society.

Kaplan, Jerome. "Voluntary Organizations." In Adeline M. Hoffman (Ed.), *The Daily Needs and Interests of Older People.* Springfield, Ill.: Charles C. Thomas, 1970, pp. 327-346.

Defines and classifies voluntary organizations and describes special volunteer organizations of older people.

McKain, Walter C., Jr. "Community Roles and Activities of Older Rural Persons." In E. Grant Youmans (Ed.), *Older Rural Americans.* Lexington: University of Kentucky Press, 1967, pp. 75-96.

Discusses some of the formal and informal social participation of older people and examines some factors associated with their participation.

Monk, Abraham, and Cryns, Arthur G. "Predicators of Voluntaristic Intent among the Aged: An Area Study." *The Gerontologist,* 1974, 14(5), pt. 1, pp. 425-429.

Identifies six variables that correlate with the older person's attitude toward participation in volunteer activities: (1) age; (2) education; (3) belief in being able to make a contribution; (4) interest in senior citizen activity; (5) range of social interest; and (6) home ownership.

Pihlblad, C.T., and Adams, David L. "Widowhood, Social Participation, and Life Satisfaction." *Aging and Human Development,* 1972, 3(4), pp. 323-330.

Investigates the relationship between widowhood, social participation, and life satisfaction among small town elderly. Findings reveal that no major change occurs in social participation among females after widowhood, while males show a linear decline in most kinds of activity patterns with length of widowhood. It seems that satisfaction among the elderly is most affected by participation in formal organizations, next by friendships, and the least by family contacts.

Rose, Arnold M. "The Impact of Aging on Voluntary Associations." In Clark Tibbitts (Ed.), *Handbook of Social Gerontology.* Chicago: The University of Chicago Press, 1960, pp. 666-697.

Considers the functions and problems of voluntary associations for the elderly and the participation of the elderly in voluntary associations.

Rose, Arnold M. "Group Consciousness among the Aging." In Arnold M. Rose and Warren A. Peterson (Eds.), *Older People and Their Social World.* Philadelphia: F.A. Davis, 1965, pp. 19-36.

Delineates the social characteristics of aging-group consciousness by comparing a sample of persons who are aging-group conscious and a sample of those who are not. Finds that persons who are aging-group conscious are distinguished by their participation in organizations, by their relationships with others, and by certain attitudes.

Shanas, Ethel, and Sussman, Marvin B. (Eds.). *Family, Bureaucracy, and the Elderly.* Durham N.C.: Duke University Press, 1977.

Focuses on the linkage of older persons and their families to bureaucratic systems. The underlying theme is that the elderly are part of a family and kin network that performs a mediating and supportive role for them in their dealings with bureaucracies.

Shanas, Ethel, and Sussman, Marvin B. "Family and Bureaucracy: Comparative Analyzes and Problematics." In Ethel Shanas and Marvin B. Sussman (Eds.), *Family, Bureaucracy and the Elderly.* Durham, N.C.: Duke University Press, 1977, pp. 215-225.

Discusses some of the material in previous chapters and indicates the need for corrective influences on the isolation and exercise of power in the linkages of bureaucracies and families.

Smith, Joel. "The Group Status of the Aged in an Urban Social Structure." In Ida H. Simpson and John C. McKinney (Eds.), *Social Aspects of Aging.* Durham, N.C.: Duke University Press, 1966, pp. 210-225.

Contends that although the aged in the southern city of Dunholme do not constitute a real group in the community, they are members of an emergent group.

Streib, Gordon F. "Bureaucracies and Families: Common Themes and Directions for Further Study." In Ethel Shanas and Marvin B. Sussman (Eds.), *Family, Bureaucracy and the Elderly.* Durham, N.C.: Duke University Press, 1977, pp. 204-214.

Comments upon the descriptions of family-bureaucracy relationships in six cultures. Notes that as societies move from an underdeveloped economic state to one of modernization, they face similar problems concerning the family and bureaucracy.

Sussman, Marvin B. "Family, Bureaucracy, and the Elderly Individual: An Organizational/ Linkage Perspective." In Ethel Shanas and Marvin B. Sussman (Eds.), *Family, Bureaucracy, and the Elderly,* Durham, N.C.: Duke University Press, 1977, pp. 2-20.

Uses the conceptual framework of the exchange theory to analyze the facilitating roles the family and kin networks perform for the elderly in dealing with bureaucratic organizations.

Taietz, Philip. "Two Conceptual Models of the Senior Center." *Journal of Gerontology,* 1976, 31(2), pp. 219-222.

Analyzes whether a senior center best fits the model of a social agency or a voluntary organization. Findings support the voluntary organization model because members of a senior center tend to have a stronger attachment to the community and a lifestyle of organizational participation more often than those elderly who do not belong to the center.

Tissue, Thomas. "Social Class and the Senior Citizen Center." *The Gerontologist,* 1971, 11(3), pt. 1, pp. 196-200.

Finds that those who participate in a local senior citizen center are typically members of the middle class. Low rates of center participation characterize the Old-Age-Assistance recipients who have working-class backgrounds.

Trela, James E. "Age Structure of Voluntary Associations and Political Self-Interest among the Aged." *The Sociological Quarterly,* 1972, 13(2), pp. 244-258.

Examines whether or not there is a relationship between the age structure of voluntary-association ties and sentiments of political self-interest among the elderly. Indicates that the desire for political changes to benefit the elderly and willingness to engage in behavior to secure these changes are greatest among members of age-graded associations, and lowest among the elderly with mixed-generational memberships.

Trela, James E. "Social Class and Association Membership: Analysis of Age-Graded and Non-Age-Graded Voluntary Participation." *Journal of Gerontology,* 1976, 31(2), pp. 198-203.

Using a sample of suburban retirees, the relationship between social class and age-graded and non-age-graded voluntary association membership was studied. The data show that persons in the higher classes are more likely to belong to age-graded associations. However, when there was a recruitment campaign to expand the membership of a senior center, no significant class differences are found between joiners and nonjoiners.

Trela, James E. "Social Class and Political Involvement in Age-Graded and Non-Age Graded Associations." *International Journal of Aging and Human Development,* 1977-1978, 8(4), pp. 301-309.

Examines the relationship between social and political activity among retired persons with different age-related patterns of association membership. Findings reveal that for individuals who belong to non-age-graded associations, there are smaller class differences in political involvement. Also class differences disappear among members of age-graded associations exclusively.

Trela, James E., and Jackson, David J. "Family Life and Community Participation in Old Age." *Research on Aging,* 1979, 1(2), pp. 233-251.

Investigates the relationship between family role-playing opportunities and community participation. Suggests that in some cases we can conceive of community roles as substituting for family roles. Also the loss of the role of spouse appears to restructure the value of the family and community roles.

Trela, James E., and Simmons, Lee W. "Health and Other Factors Affecting Membership and Attrition in a Senior Center." *Journal of Gerontology,* 1971, 26(1), pp. 46-51.

The major reasons given by individuals for joining a senior center are the utilization of leisure time, companionship, and the urging of the member volunteers. The main reasons for not becoming a member, as well as the termination of membership, are competing activities and ambivalence toward exclusive associations with age peers or organizational activity in general.

Ward, Russell A. "Aging-Group Consciousness: Implications in an Older Sample." *Sociology and Social Research,* 1977, 61(4), pp. 496-519.

Focuses on two questions concerning the subculture of aging: when does such a subculture develop and what are the implications of such a subculture? Finds a positive relationship between aging-group consciousness and self-esteem for those who considered themselves as elderly. Feelings of aging-group consciousness are not widespread and are related to group interaction with age peers.

Wilensky, Harold L. "Life Cycle, Work Situation, and Participation in Formal Associations." In Robert W. Kleemeier, (Ed.), *Aging and Leisure.* New York: Oxford University Press, 1961, pp. 213-242.

Focuses on the sources and effects of variations in formal organizational ties among the elderly.

Zborowski, Mark, and Eyde, Lorraine D. "Aging and Social Participation." *Journal of Gerontology,* 1962, 17(4), pp. 424-430.

Suggests that with age there is little change in social participation. Most persons in the sample maintain their social contacts at the same level as they did in the past, and expect to continue to do so in the future.

Chapter 7

CRIME AND DEVIANCE

A. CRIME

Adams, Mark E., and Vedder, Clyde B. "Age and Crime." *Geriatrics,* 1961, 16(4), pp. 177-181.

Analyzes the relationship of age and crime using data collected from prisoners aged 50 years and over at the time of commitment. The older prisoners show a high incidence of convictions for embezzlement, forgery, and gambling. Also their incidence of crimes of violence is about twice that of the general prison population.

Antunes, George, et al. "Patterns of Personal Crime against the Elderly: Findings from a National Survey." *The Gerontologist,* 1977, 17(4), pp. 321-327.

In comparison with other age groups the elderly are less likely to be victimized. Attacks on the elderly which involve violence are more likely to occur in or near the home than for other age groups. Also the elderly are more likely than younger persons to have been attacked by black youths acting alone who were strangers to them. Discusses several solutions to prevent the elderly from being victimized.

Clemente, Frank, and Kleiman, Michael B. "The Fear of Crime among the Aged." *The Gerontologist,* 1976, 16(3), pp. 207-210.

Reveals that race, sex, and city size are important factors in determining the relationship between the elderly and fear of crime. Blacks are more afraid of crime than whites, women are more fearful than men, and residents of large cities are more afraid than those who live in small towns.

Conklin, John E. "Robbery, the Elderly and Fear: An Urban Problem in Search of Solution." In Jack Goldsmith and Sharon S. Goldsmith (Eds.), *Crime and the Elderly.* Lexington, Mass.: Lexington Books, 1976, pp. 99-110.

Deals with robbery of older persons, their reactions to it, and the consequences of their reactions. Offers some suggestions for reducing the risk of robbery among the elderly.

Cook, Fay L., et al. "Criminal Victimization of the Elderly: The Physical and Economic Consequences." *The Gerontologist,* 1978, 18(4), pp. 338-349.

Using data from national surveys, this study finds that the elderly are no more likely than other age groups to suffer severe physical injuries or economic losses. However, consequences of crime against the elderly are most serious when losses by the elderly are examined relative to their incomes, and not by absolute measurements of loss.

Cutler, Stephen J. "Safety in the Streets: Cohort Changes in Fear." *International Journal of Aging and Human Development,* 1979-1980, 10(4), pp. 373-384.

Using data from a 1965 Gallup Poll and 1976 NORC Survey, the findings reveal that older cohorts were more likely than younger cohorts to express fear for their safety on the streets in both 1965 and 1976. Although fear increased for all cohorts during this 11 year period, the rate of increase in fear was lower for the younger cohorts and higher for the older cohorts.

Gillespie, Michael W., and Galliher, John F. "Age, Anomie, and the Inmate's Definition of Aging in Prison: An Exploratory Study." In Donald P. Kent, Robert Kastenbaum, and Sylvia Sherwood (Eds.), *Research Planning and Action for the Elderly: The Power and Potential of Social Science.* New York: Behavioral Publications, 1972, pp. 465-483.

Interviews with inmates of a midwestern state penitentiary reveal that the younger inmates tend to give an optimistic view of aging in prison, while the older inmates have a more pessimistic view. The older inmates believe that prison has made them age faster than normal.

Goldsmith, Jack, and Goldsmith, Sharon S. *Crime and the Elderly.* Lexington, Mass.: Lexington Books, 1976.

Contains papers from a conference on the problem of criminal victimization of the elderly. Discusses patterns of victimization, the plight of the older victim, and responses to victimization.

Gubrium, Jaber F. "Victimization in Old Age - Available Evidence and Three Hypotheses." *Crime and Delinquency,* 1974, 20(3), pp. 245-250.

Survey data does not support the belief that the aged as a group are the greatest victims of crimes. Offers three hypotheses regarding the impact of protectiveness of the environment and the social effects of age-concentration on victimization, and concern about crime and fear.

Hahn, Paul H. *Crimes Against the Elderly: A Study in Victimology.* Santa Cruz, Calif.: Davis, 1976.

Describes the vulnerability of the elderly as victims of crime and the effects of crimes against them.

Kahana, Eva, et al. "Perspectives of Aged on Victimization, Ageism, and Their Problems in Urban Society." *The Gerontologist,* 1977, 17(2), pp. 121-129.

Reveals that elderly persons do not perceive ageism to be an important influence on their personal lives. They report relatively few instances of discrimination. Neighborhood problems, including fear of crime, appear to be the primary concern of elderly persons.

Keller, Oliver J., and Vedder, Clyde B. "The Crimes that Old Persons Commit." *The Gerontologist,* 1968, 8(1), pt. 1, pp. 43-50.

Based on an examination of the 1964 *Uniform Crime Reports,* this article lists and compares the "Top 20" crimes for younger and older age groups. Arrests for drunkeness rank first on the list for all age groups.

Laufer, Robert S., and Bengtson, Vern L. "Generations, Aging, and Social Stratification: On the Development of Generational Units." *Journal of Social Issues,* 1974, 30(3), pp. 181-205.

Explores the construction of generations as sources of social change. Describes four types of generation units of youth, and discusses the prospects for generational units among the elderly.

Lawton, M. Powell, and Yaffee, Silvia. "Victimization and Fear of Crime in Elderly Public Housing Tenants." *Journal of Gerontology,* 1980, 35(5), pp. 768-779.

Indicates that as far as well-being is concerned, fear of crime is the strongest of the crime variables. Fear of crime is higher in age-integrated settings, high-crime areas, in larger communities, and among those who have been victimized.

Ragan, Pauline K. "Crimes against the Elderly: Findings from Interviews with Blacks, Mexican-Americans, and Whites." In Marlene A.Y. Rifai (Ed.), *Justice and Older Americans.* Lexington, Mass.: Lexington Books, 1977, pp. 25-36.

Findings from a community survey indicate that most older persons do not perceive crime to be one of their most serious problems. Also racial minorities bear the greatest burden of crime in the community; blacks report greater problems than Mexican Americans.

Reed, Monika B., and Glamser, Francis D. "Aging in a Total Institution: The Case of Older Prisoners." *The Gerontologist,* 1979, 19(4), pp. 354-360.

Aging in a prison setting differs from normal aging in the community in that prisoners are less aware of chronological age. Also productivity, occupation, income level, and retirement are not important issues.

Rifai, Marlene A.Y. (Ed.). *Justice and Older Americans,* Lexington, Mass.: Lexington Books, 1977.

Deals with the victimization of older persons and society's response to this victimization.

Shichor, David, and Kobrin, Solomon. "Note: Criminal Behavior among the Elderly." *The Gerontologist,* 1978, 18(2), pp. 213-218.

From an examination of the national arrest data, the authors note the following trends concerning the elderly and crime: (1) the arrests for this group in all crimes show a gradual decline while their share in arrests for index crimes has risen; (2) aggravated assault, followed by murder are the largest categories among the index offenses for which the elderly are arrested; and (3) most of the arrests for misdemeanor offenses are related to alcohol consumption.

Sundeen, Richard A., and Mathieu, James T. "The Urban Elderly: Environments of Fear." In Jack Goldsmith and Sharon S. Goldsmith (Eds.), *Crime and the Elderly.* Lexington, Mass.: Lexington Books, 1976, pp. 51-66.

Explores some of the factors that increase or lessen the fear of victimization among the elderly in three types of communities: a central city, an urban municipality, and a retirement community. The findings show that within the central city social support is the most important factor in diffusing the fear of crime. In the urban municipality, a feeling of belonging to the community and perceived safety of the neighborhood at night helped to decrease the fear of robbery and burglary. Finally, the number of persons in one's residence does not appear to be as important as other factors in reducing the fear of crime.

Sundeen, Richard A., and Mathieu, James T. "The Fear of Crime and Its Consequences among Elderly in Three Urban Communities." *The Gerontologist,* 1976, 16(3), pp. 211-219.

Deals with the fear of crime among three groups of elderly persons who differ in the extent to which they live in a protected environment and possess social and economic resources. While all three groups have high level of fear, those in the central city manifest the most fear. The residents in the retirement community tend to have the least fear because of their greater sense of social support, perceptions of higher safety, and higher evaluation of the police.

Sundeen, Richard A. "The Fear of Crime and Urban Elderly." In Marlene A.Y. Rifai (Ed.), *Justice and Older Americans.* Lexington, Mass.: Lexington Books, 1977, pp. 13-24.

Discusses the relationship between the fear of crime and factors which represent life circumstances among urban elderly. High levels of fear of burglary are related to a low sense of participation in one's community, while high levels of fear of robbery are related to a low level of self-perceived health. Also perception of less security in one's neighborhood during the day is related to being female.

B. Deviance

English, Clifford, and Joyce Stephens. "On Being Excluded: An Analysis of Elderly and Adolescent Street Hustlers." *Urban Life,* 1975, 4(2), pp. 201-212.

Compares a group of very young and very old street hustlers. The youth are found to be optimistic and aspire to upward mobility within the street culture, whereas the elderly are resigned to their fate and hope only to preserve their present level of autonomy.

Kelly, Jim. "The Aging Homosexual: Myth and Reality." *The Gerontologist,* 1977, 17(4), pp. 328-332.

Finds that there is little evidence to indicate that being gay causes problems in old age, but there is much evidence to suggest that societal stigma causes problems for aging gays.

Kimmel, Douglas C. "Life-History Interviews of Aging Gay Men." *International Journal of Aging and Human Development,* 1979-1980, 10(3), pp. 239-248.

Focusing on the lifestyles and aging experiences of a sample of gay men over the age of 55, this study shows that growing old as a gay does not necessarily lead to loneliness or isolation. Although many of the respondents have created a satisfying social and physical environment, the social stigma of homosexuality still has an effect on their lives.

Laner, Mary R. "Growing Older Male: Heterosexual and Homosexual." *The Gerontologist,* 1978, 18(5), pt. 1, pp. 496-501.

According to this study which is based on newspaper "personals" advertisements, it appears that when homosexual men reach middle age, they are like their heterosexual counterparts in some ways, and both better and less well adjusted than heterosexual males.

Miller, Leo. "Toward a Classification of Aging Behaviors." *The Gerontologist,* 1979, 19(3), pp. 283-289.

Attempts to classify 18 types of deviance related to aging based on the dimensions of legitimacy and seriousness and three indices of social functioning. The author feels that this classification should be helpful in predicting how others may respond to the aging person to whom deviance has been imputed.

Rooney, James F. "Friendship and Disaffiliation among Skid Row Population." *Journal of Gerontology,* 1976, 31(1), pp. 82-88.

Interview data from 304 skid row men shows that old friends are replaced by new friends chosen from skid row. After the age of 70, there is a decline in the number of friendships one has, but this is associated more with length of skid row residence than with age.

Stephens, Joyce. "Carnies and Marks: The Sociology of Elderly Street Peddlers." *Sociological Symposium,* 1974, No. 11, pp. 25-41.

Using the theoretical framework developed by Howard S. Becker (1963) in his research on dance musicians, the author describes the prevalence of peddling among elderly SRO (single-room occupancy) tenants.

Stephens, Joyce. "Romance in the SRO: Relationships of Elderly Men and Women in a Slum Hotel." *The Gerontologist,* 1974, 14(4), pp. 279-282.

Mutual suspicion and avoidance tend to characterize the relationships between elderly men and women living in a SRO (single-room occupancy) slum hotel. For the men, the seeking out of female company usually means the services of a prostitute. The women do not relate well to each other because of the competition, hostility, and jealousy that exists between them.

Stephens, Joyce. "Society of the Alone: Freedom, Privacy, and Utilitarianism as Dominant Norms in the SRO." *Journal of Gerontology,* 1975, 30(2), pp. 230-235.

This study finds that the majority of elderly tenants in a SRO (single-room occupancy) hotel are lifelong social isolates. The impersonal world of the SRO allows them to live a lifestyle of their own choosing and encourages freedom, privacy, and utilitarianism to extreme degrees.

Stephens, Joyce. *Loners, Losers, and Lovers: Elderly Tenants in a Slum Hotel.* Seattle: University of Washington Press, 1976.

Using the technique of participant observation, the author gives a descriptive analysis of the social world of the elderly tenant living in a SRO (single-room occupancy) slum hotel. She describes the roles and role patterns found within the SRO society, the norms and values that serve to maintain relationships, and the nature of the relationships between the tenants and the outside world.

Stephens, Joyce. "Elderly People as Hustlers: Observations on the Free Deviant Work Situations of SRO Tenants." *Sociological Symposium,* 1979, no. 26, pp. 102-115.

Discusses some types of deviant occupations of elderly SRO (single-room occupancy) tenants. These occupations include conning, shoplifting, peddling, and pimping.

PART 3

SOCIAL INEQUALITY

Chapter 8

CLASS and AGE STRATIFICATION

Adams, Bert N. "The Middle-Class Adult and His Widowed or Still-Married Mother." *Social Problems,* 16(1), pp. 50-59.

Compares the relations of middle-class adults and their widowed mothers to a similar group of adults whose mothers are still married. The results show that the most satisfactory relations between a son and widowed mother are those in which the mother is independent. The most satisfactory relations between a daughter and widowed mother are those in which there is reciprocal help.

Bloom, Martin. "Measurement of the Socioeconomic Status of the Aged: New Thoughts on an Old Subject." *The Gerontologist,* 1972, 12(4), pp. 375-378.

Attempts to clarify the meaning of socioeconomic status for the elderly and offers a procedure for measuring it.

Cowgill, Donald O., and Holmes, Lowell D. (Eds.). *Aging and Modernization.* New York: Appleton-Century-Crofts, 1972.

Contains eighteen papers that deal with aging in various societies and settings, ranging from primitive to highly modern. These papers provide the basis for the testing of a number of hypotheses. The general conclusion is that the status of the aged is inversely associated with modernization.

Cowgill, Donald O. "Aging and Modernization: A Revision of the Theory." In Jaber F. Gubrium, *Late Life: Communities and Environmental Policy.* Springfield, Ill.: Charles C. Thomas, 1974, pp. 123-146.

Extends the theory of aging and modernization. New evidence suggests that in advanced stages of modernization the trend toward a decline in the relative status of the elderly may "bottom out" and at some point begin to improve.

Cutler, Stephen J. "An Approach to the Measurement of Prestige Loss among the Aged." *Aging and Human Development,* 1972, 3(3), pp. 285-292.

Suggests a method for measuring the status of the elderly in industrial societies. By employing this method, tentative findings indicate the existence and recognition of prestige loss among the aged.

Dowd, James J. *Stratification Among the Aged.* Monterey, Calif.: Brooks/Cole, 1980.

Offers a new perspective to the study of the problems of the elderly by drawing on the social exchange theory. Dowd examines the relationship between the aging process and social class membership.

He maintains that the degree of control persons have over their lives is in proportion to the social class that they belong to and other measures of status.

Elder, Glen H., Jr. "Age Differentiation and the Life Course." In Alex Inkeles (Ed.), *Annual Review of Sociology,* vol. 1. Palo Alto, Calif.: Annual Reviews, Inc., 1975, pp. 165-190.

Focuses on social change in the life course. Draws mainly upon the age stratification perspective (cohort-historical) found in the work of Riley and associates and from the age-status system and age-norms perspective (sociocultural) found in the work of Neugarten.

Foner, Anne. "Age Stratification and Age Conflict in Political Life." *American Sociological Review,* 1974, 39(2), pp. 187-196.

Discusses age as a basis for political conflict in modern society and suggests that the understanding of such conflict requires a theory about the processes operating to stratify society by age.

Foner, Anne. "Age in Society: Structure and Change." *American Behavioral Scientist,* 1975, 19(2), pp. 144-165.

Examines the stratification approach as it relates to age. This approach, according to Foner, advances a theoretical perspective for studying age in society and suggests a way of interpreting and organizing information about it.

Foner, Anne. "Age Stratification and the Changing Family." In John Demos and Sarane S. Boocock (Eds.), *Turning Points: Historical and Sociological Essays on the Family.* Chicago: The University of Chicago Press, 1978, pp. 340-365.

Deals with the importance of the age structure of a family at a given time, changing family patterns over the family cycle, and the impact of the succession of cohorts of families.

Goldstein, Sidney. "Socio-Economic and Migration Differentials between the Aged in the Labor Force and in the Labor Reserve." *The Gerontologist,* 1967, 7(1), pp. 31-40 and p. 79.

Indicates that older persons in high white-collar positions display the greatest tendency toward continued labor force participation. Also higher proportions of those with a college education continue to work. But regardless of labor force status, the aged manifest a high degree of residential stability.

Henretta, John C., and Campbell, Richard T. "Status Attainment and Status Maintenance: A Study of Stratification in Old Age." *American Sociological Review,* 1976, 41(6), pp. 981-992.

Using a comparison of status attainment models for a cohort before and after most of its members have retired, the effect of aging on the relation of status variables to income was analyzed. The findings show little change in the pattern of effects and suggest that the factors which determine income in retirement are the same ones that determine income before retirement.

Henretta, John C. "Using Survey Data in the Study of Social Stratification in Late Life." *The Gerontologist,* 1979, 19(2), pp. 197-201.

The most commonly used measure of economic status is yearly income. Henretta proposes that the broader concept of net worth provides a more powerful predictor and he presents a well-established way of measuring it.

Hirsch, Carl; Kent, Donald P.; and Silverman, Suzanne L. "Homogeneity and Heterogeneity among Low-Income Negro and White Aged." In Donald P. Kent, Robert Kastenbaum, and Sylvia Sherwood (Eds.), *Research Planning and Action for the Elderly: The Power and Potential of Social Science.* New York: Behavioral Publications, 1972, pp. 484-500.

Provides a descriptive report of the characteristics of family structure, group affiliations, housing and mobility, income, health, and religious affiliation among the low-income black and white elderly.

Hutchinson, Ira W., III. "The Significance of Marital Status for Morale and Life Satisfaction among Lower-Income Elderly." *Journal of Marriage and the Family,* 1975, 37(2), pp. 287-293.

Examines the differences in life satisfaction as they are affected by income, sex, and the marital status of the elderly. Concludes that sex or marital-status differences may have a significant influence on the elderly's life satisfaction above the poverty level, but neither is important below the poverty line.

Jackson, Jacquelyne J. "Sex and Social Class Variations in Black Aged Parent-Adult Child Relationships." *Aging and Human Development,* 1971, 2(2), pp. 96-107.

Indicates that black parents engaged in nonmanual occupations are more likely to receive instrumental aid from their adult children than those parents in manual occupations. Daughters are more likely to provide instrumental aid to their parents than sons. Most children of parents in manual occupations do not receive instrumental assistance from their parents, while the opposite is true of children of nonmanual workers. Daughters are more frequent recipients of aid than sons in both cases.

Neugarten, Bernice L., and Hagestad, Gunhild O. "Age and the Life Course." In Robert H. Binstock and Ethel Shanas (Eds.), *Handbook of*

Aging and the Social Sciences. New York: Van Nostrand Reinhold, 1976, pp. 35-55.

Uses the age organization of society as a context for studying the life course of individuals.

Palmore, Erdman B., and Whittington, Frank. "Trends in the Relative Status of the Aged." *Social Forces,* 1971, 50(1), pp. 84-91.

The comparison of similarity indexes from 1940 through 1969 supports the theory that the relative status of the elderly tends to decline in an industrial society. The evidence shows that gaps are steadily increasing in the areas of income, employment, and education between the older and younger population.

Palmore, Erdman B., and Manton, Kenneth. "Modernization and Status of the Aged: International Correlations." *Journal of Gerontology,* 1974, 29(2), pp. 205-210.

Examines aspects of modernization which are related to the status of the elderly in 31 countries. The analysis reveals that the occupational and educational status of the aged decline in the advanced stages of modernization. However, after an initial period of rapid modernization, these aspects of status may begin to rise and the discrepancies between the elderly and other age groups decrease.

Parelius, Ann P. "Lifelong Education and Age Stratification: Some Unexplored Relationships." *American Behavioral Scientist,* 1975, 19(2), pp. 206-223.

Discusses the potential impact of lifelong education from the perspective of age stratification theory.

Patten, Thomas H., Jr. "Social Class and the 'Old Soldier'." *Social Problems,* 1960-1961, 8(3), pp. 263-271.

This exploratory study of veterans in domiciliaries finds that the social and economic characteristics of "old soldiers" are sufficiently similar to constitute a social class in our society.

Riley, Matilda W. "Social Gerontology and the Age Stratification of Society." *The Gerontologist,* 1971, 2(1), pt. 1, pp. 79-87.

Riley makes an analogy between class stratification and age stratification. She discusses how the forces of social change are affecting the aging process and bringing new influences to bear on the older and younger age stratas.

Riley, Matilda W.; Johnson, Marilyn; and Foner, Anne. *Aging and Society: A Sociology of Age Stratification,* vol. 3. New York: Russell Sage Foundation, 1972.

Presents a theory of age stratification. The first part of the book contains a sociological view of age which is examined in later chapters with reference to society and some selected social institutions.

Riley, Matilda W., and Waring, Joan. "Age and Aging." In Robert K. Merton and Robert Nisbet (Eds.), *Contemporary Social Problems,* 4th ed. New York: Harcourt Brace Jovanovich, 1976, pp. 355-410.

Examines the problems of aging and age-stratification and explores some ways for correcting them.

Riley, Matilda W. "Age Strata in Social Systems." In Robert H.Binstock and Ethel Shanas (Eds.), *Handbook of Aging and the Social Sciences.* New York: Van Nostrand Reinhold, 1976, pp. 189-217.

Deals with how people and roles are stratified by age at certain periods of time, and how these strata are interrelated and change across time. Also discusses the ways people relate to one another according to their ages, and how age norms and roles come to be defined and institutionalized.

Rose, Arnold. "Class Differences among the Elderly: A Research Report." *Sociology and Social Research,* 1966, 50(3), pp. 356-360.

Data from a sample of elderly persons who identified themselves as either middle class or lower class reveal that the middle-class respondents are more likely to think of themselves as being in better health and happier, and less likely to have a problem with interpersonal relationships.

Rosenberg, George S. "Age, Poverty, and Isolation from Friends in the Urban Working Class." *Journal of Gerontology,* 1968, 23(4), pp. 533-538.

Investigates the relationship between poverty, aging, and isolation from friends. The findings indicate that men over 65, whether poor or solvent, living in neighborhoods where their wealth, occupation, or race differs from that of their neighbors tend to be isolated from friends.

Rosenberg, George S. *The Worker Grows Old.* San Francisco: Jossey-Bass, 1970.

Based on a sample of white working-class persons between the ages of 45 to 79, this study examines the relationships between poverty, old age, and social isolation from friends and kin. Finds that age and poverty as well as widowhood and retirement are unrelated to kin contact. A larger proportion of younger than of older workers report that there is a closed-class system. Also older men who live in the poorest neighborhoods are more likely to have a conception of a closed-class system.

Rosow, Irving. *Social Integration of the Aged.* New York: The Free Press, 1967.

This study of older middle-class and working-class residents living in apartment buildings in Cleveland deals with friendship and social class. Findings show that the number of older people's local friends varies with the proportion of older neighbors. The friends of older persons consist disproportionately of older rather than younger neighbors. Also middle-class persons have more friends than those in the working class; there is a greater local dependency for friendships in the working class than in the middle class.

Shanas, Ethel. "Family Help Patterns and Social Class in Three Countries." *Journal of Marriage and the Family,* 1967, 29(2), pp. 257-286.

Reports that family help patterns in Denmark, Britain, and the United States vary by the social class of the older person. In Britain and the United States, old people of white-collar backgrounds are the most likely to help their children while old people of working-class backgrounds need help from their children.

Shanas, Ethel, et al. *Old People in Three Industrial Societies.* New York: Atherton Press, 1968.

Provides information on the social class of the aged in Denmark, Great Britain, and the United States.

Shanas, Ethel. "The Family and Social Class." In Ethel Shanas, et al., *Old People in Three Industrial Societies.* New York: Atherton Press, 1968, pp. 227-256.

The analysis of social class and family life in Denmark, Britain, and the United States indicates that in Britain and the United States the family life of old people differs by whether they are of white-collar or blue-collar backgrounds. Middle-class, white-collar persons in Britain and the United States are more likely than working-class, blue-collar persons to have only a few children and to live at a greater distance from their children. In Denmark old people of white-collar and those of blue-collar backgrounds show no marked differences in family life.

Sheppard, Harold L. "The Poverty of Aging." In Ben B. Seligman (Ed.), *Poverty as a Public Issue.* New York: The Free Press, 1965, pp. 85-101.

Discusses some of the sources of poverty among the aged and some solutions for it.

Simpson, Ansel P. "Social Class Correlates of Old Age." *Sociology and Social Research,* 1961, 45(2), pp. 131-139.

Using existing research findings, this paper discusses the differences between social classes with respect to old age.

Sterne, Richard S.; Phillips, James E.; and Rabushka, Alvin. *The Urban Elderly Poor.* Lexington, Mass.: Lexington Books, 1974.

Deals with the behavior of the elderly poor in the inner city and the effect of the inner-city environment upon the elderly. The major findings are that the elderly whites are more affluent, better educated, have better jobs, and live longer than their black counterparts. Most of the elderly poor show little interest in political activity except for voting. Chronological age does not correlate with the psychological and social aspects of advancing age, but is useful only as a predictor of reduced mobility.

Streib, Gordon F. "Social Stratification and Aging." In Robert H. Binstock and Ethel Shanas (Eds.), *Handbook of Aging and the Social Sciences.* New York: Van Nostrand Reinhold, 1976, pp. 160-185.

Discusses some of the major dimensions of the interrelationships of aging and stratification along with the concept of age consciousness. Reviews stratification and aging in the United States and also from a cross-national perspective.

Tissue, Thomas. "Downward Mobility in Old Age." *Social Problems,* 1970, 18(1), pp. 67-77.

Examines some of the consequences of downward mobility in old age of ex-middle-class poor and those persons of working-class origins. Findings reveal that downward mobility in old age is associated with social isolation and low morale. In comparison with the elderly poor in the working class, the ex-middle-class aged maintain lower levels of interaction and more frequently describe themselves as being dissatisfied with their present lives.

Tissue, Thomas. "Social Class and the Senior Citizen Center." *The Gerontologist,* 1971, 2(3), pt. 1, pp. 196-200.

Finds that those who participate in a local senior citizen center are typically members of the middle class. A low rate of center participation characterizes the Old Age Assistance recipient who has a working-class background.

Trela, James E. "Social Class and Association Membership: Analysis of Age-Graded and Non-Age-Graded Voluntary Participation." *Journal of Gerontology,* 1976, 31(2), pp. 198-203.

Using a sample of suburban retirees, the relationship between social class and age-graded and non-age-graded voluntary association membership was studied. The data show that persons in the higher classes are more likely to belong to age-graded associations. However, when there was a recruitment campaign to expand the membership of a senior center, no significant class differences were found between joiners and nonjoiners.

Trela, James E. "Social Class and Political Involvement in Age-graded and Non-Age-Graded Associations." *International Journal of Aging and Human Development*, 1977-1978, 8(4), pp. 301-310.

Examines the relationship between social and political activity among retired persons with different age-related patterns of association membership. Findings reveal that for individuals who belong to non-age-graded associations, there are smaller class differences in political involvement. Also class differences disappear among members of age-graded associations exclusively.

Youmans, Grant E. "Age Stratification and Value Orientations." *International Journal of Aging and Human Development*, 1973, 4(1), pp. 53-65.

Compares value orientations of younger and older adults in a rural and metropolitan area. Finds show significant differences between the two age groups in both geographical areas on such values as authoritarianism, dependency, achievement, religiosity, and anomia.

Chapter 9

RACIAL and ETHNIC GROUPS

Bengtson, Vern L. "Ethnicity and Aging: Problems and Issues in Current Social Science Inquiry." In Donald Gelfand and Alfred Kutzik (Eds.), *Ethnicity and Aging.* New York: Springer Publishing Co., 1979, pp. 9-31.

Provides a survey of the research in the area of ethnicity and aging and discusses some of the problems that have made research in this area difficult.

Bengtson, Vern L.; Cuellar, Jose B.; and Ragan, Pauline K. "Stratum Contrasts and Similarities in Attitudes toward Death." *Journal of Gerontology,* 1977, 32(1), pp. 76-88.

Examines differences between blacks, Mexican-Americans, and whites in their attitudes toward death. Analysis by age and race reveals that middle-aged persons express the greatest fear of death and the elderly express the least. Blacks expect to live the longest and Mexican-Americans expect to die at earlier ages.

Carp, Frances M. "Housing and Minority-Group Elderly." *The Gerontologist,* 1969, 9(1), pp. 20-24.

Reports that despite poor housing, the Mexican-American elderly are satisfied with their living conditions and do not want to move to a new public-housing facility. Reasons for not moving are pride in home ownership and interpersonal bonds with relatives and friends.

Bremer, Teresa H., and Ragan, Pauline K. "The Empty Nest: A Comparison Between Older Mexican-American and White Women." *Sociological Symposium,* 1979, no. 26, pp. 64-82.

Investigates the responses of Mexican-American women to the empty nest in comparison with that of white women. Few older white women experience feelings of low morale regarding the empty nest. The highest percentage of women reporting low morale occur among the Mexican-American women having a "full-nest" (some 18 or under in the home).

Clemente, Frank, and Auer, William J. "Race and Morale of the Urban Aged." *The Gerontologist,* 1974, 14(4), pp. 342-344.

The hypothesis that aged urban blacks have lower morale than aged urban whites is not supported by the findings of this study. Discusses some possible reasons for the failure of race to emerge as a predictor of morale.

Clemente, Frank; Rexroad, Patricia; and Hirsch, Carl. "The Participation of the Black Aged in Voluntary Associations." *Journal of Gerontology,* 1975, 30(4), pp. 469-472.

Results reveal that aged blacks belong to more voluntary associations than aged whites and have higher attendance rates.

Crouch, Ben M. "Age and Institutional Support: Perceptions of Older Mexican-Americans." *Journal of Gerontology,* 1972, 27(4), pp. 524-529.

Investigates how older Mexican-Americans view old age and how they regard the family, church, and government as sources of support for the elderly. They view old age negatively and as beginning at 60 years or below. The subjects expect less aid from the family than they do from the church or government. Very little difference is found between older Mexican-Americans and other older persons in these areas.

Carp, Frances M. "Communicating with the Elderly Mexican-Americans." *The Gerontologist,* 1970, 10(2), pp. 126-134.

Older Mexican-Americans pose a difficult problem in communication in that the usual techniques for dissemination of information to them are ineffective. They obtain most of their information about the broader society from family and friends and not the mass media.

Carp, Frances M., and Eunice Kataoka. "Health Care Problems of the Elderly of San Francisco's Chinatown." *The Gerontologist,* 1976, 16(1), pt. 1, pp. 30-38.

The elderly residents of Chinatown have a great need for health care services and inadequate personal resources for obtaining them. Solutions to their problems involve an effort on the part of the broader society.

Dowd, James J., and Bengtson, Vern L. "Aging in Minority Populations: An Examination of the Double Jeopardy Hypothesis." *Journal of Gerontology,* 1978, 33(3), pp. 427-436.

Analyzes status indicators and primary group interaction to determine variations among middle-aged and aged blacks, Mexican-Americans, and Anglos. Marked differences in income and self-assessed health constitute a case of double jeopardy for the blacks and Mexican-Americans. Ethnic variation in frequency of interaction with relatives and life satisfaction declines across age strata.

Dowd, James J. "Prejudice and Proximity: An Analysis of Age Differences." *Research on Aging,* 1980, 2(1), pp. 23-48.

Focuses on racial prejudice as it varies by age and residential contact. Results reveal that residential contact does not uniformly affect racial prejudice but interacts with age to produce variations depending on educational level and region.

Eribes, Richard A., and Bradley-Rawls, Martha. "The Underutilization of Nursing Home Facilities by Mexican-American Elderly in the Southwest." *The Gerontologist,* 1978, 18(4), pp. 363-371.

Mexican-Americans view the nursing home not as a culturally viable alternative but only as a last resort. Mexican-American families try to keep their elderly out of institutionalized facilities and prefer to handle the medical care of their elderly in other ways.

Fujii, Sharon. "Minority Group Elderly: Demographic Characteristics and Implications for Public Policy." In C. Eisdorfer (Ed.), *Annual Review of Gerontology and Geriatrics.* New York: Springer, vol. 1, 1980, pp. 261-284.

Provides a description in terms of demographic characteristics and policy issues for the aged in the following minority groups: the blacks, Hispanic/Latinos, American Indians, and Pacific/Asians.

Gelfand, Donald E. "Ethnicity, Aging and Mental Health." *International Journal of Aging and Human Development,* 1979-1980, 10(3), pp. 289-298.

Discusses the relationship of ethnicity to the mental health problems of the elderly in our society and offers recommendations for research and training in this area.

Gelfand, Donald E., and Fandetti, Donald V. "Suburban and Urban White Ethnics: Attitudes towards Care of the Aged." *The Gerontologist,* 1980, pp. 588-594.

Compares a sample of Italian-American suburban residents and a sample of Italian and Polish inner-city residents regarding attitudes toward their continued use of traditional structures for the care of aged family members. The suburban group is more likely than the inner-city group to turn to purchasing care for the bedridden elderly in the private sector. Both groups show continued respect for services under church auspices.

Gelfand, Donald E., and Kutzik, Alfred A. (Eds.). *Ethnicity and Aging.* New York: Springer, 1979.

Contains a series of papers from a variety of disciplines that relate to ethnicity and aging. The first part of this volume provides an overview of important issues in the area of ethnicity and aging, the second deals with ethnic families and the aged, and the last part focuses on research related to ethnicity and aging. Gives major attention to the white-ethnic aged of European descent.

Golden, Herbert M. "Black Ageism." *Social Policy,* 1976, 7(3), pp. 40-42.

Argues that the black elderly should be studied as a group without necessarily making comparisons to the larger white elderly population. Only then can the unique problems that this minority group membership imposes on one's adaptation to aging be attacked.

Goldstein, Sidney. "Negro-White Differentials in Consumer Patterns of the Aged, 1960-1961." *The Gerontologist,* 1971, 2(3), pt. 1, pp. 242-249.

In comparing the income, expenditure, and savings patterns of aged white and black consumers, this study documents the disadvantaged position of the black aged. Important differences characterize the expenditure dimension of the consumer behavior of the two groups.

Heyman, Dorothy K., and Jeffers, Frances C. "Study of the Relative Influence of Race and Socio-Economic Status upon the Activities and Attitudes of a Southern Aged Population." *Journal of Gerontology,* 1964, 19(2), pp. 225-229.

Finds that differences in activity patterns between the white and black populations are socio-economic rather than racial. Attitudes show a socio-economic difference only within the black group.

Harper, D. Wood, Jr., and Garza, Joseph M. "Ethnicity, Family Generational Structure, and Intergenerational Solidarity." *Sociological Symposium,* no. 2, Spring 1969, pp. 75-82.

Reveals that the relationship between family generational structure and family solidarity are better understood when the influence of ethnic group identification is considered.

Hirsch, Carl; Kent, Donald P.; and Silverman, Suzanne L. "Homogeneity and Heterogeneity among Low-Income Negro and White Aged." In Donald P. Kent, Robert Kastenbaum, and Sylvia Sherwood (Eds.), *Research Planning and Action for the Elderly: The Power and Potential of SocialScience.* New York: Behavioral Publications, 1972, pp. 484-500.

Provides a descriptive report of the characteristics of family structure, group affiliations, housing and mobility, income, health, and religious affiliation among the low-income black and white elderly.

Jackson, Jacquelyne J. "Social Gerontology and the Negro: A Review." *The Gerontologist,* 1967, 7(3), pp. 168-178.

This review paper on the aged black points up some of the emergent issues in this area and makes suggestions for further research.

Jackson, Jacquelyne J. "Aged Negroes: Their Cultural Departures from Statistical Stereotypes and Rural-Urban Differences." *The Gerontologist,* 1970, 10(2), pp. 140-145.

Finds that many of the commonly held stereotypes about aged blacks are invalid. The author notes that the family is the primary source of assistance for aged blacks and that older blacks are no more religious than aged whites. Also the organizational participation of elderly blacks may be somewhat higher than for whites, and the health of aged blacks is no better or worse than their white counterparts.

Jackson, Jacquelyne J. "The Blacklands of Gerontology." *Aging and Human Development,* 1971, 2(3), pp. 156-171.

Reviews the literature and trends in research on the black aged from 1950 to 1971 and focuses on social patterns, policies, and resources. Provides an extensive bibliography.

Jackson, Jacquelyne J. "Sex and Social Class Variations in Black Aged Parent-Adult Child Relationships." *Aging and Human Development,* 1971, 2(2), pp. 96-107.

Indicates that black parents engaged in nonmanual occupations are more likely to receive instrumental aid from their adult children than parents in manual occupations. Daughters are more likely to provide instrumental aid to their parents than sons. Most children of parents in manual occupations do not receive instrumental assistance from their parents, while the opposite is true of children of nonmanual workers. Daughters are more frequent recipients of aid than sons in both cases.

Jackson, Jacquelyne J. "Negro Aged: Toward Needed Research in Social Gerontology." *The Gerontologist,* 1971, 2(1), pt. 2, pp. 52-57.

Surveys the gerontological literature concerning the black elderly and provides a selected bibliography of research that is presently available on aged blacks. Provides some research suggestions for the coming decade.

Jackson, Jacquelyne J. "Marital Life among Aging Blacks." *The Family Coordinator,* 1972, 21(1), pp. 21-27.

Examines dominance patterns among a sample of older, urban, married blacks. Finds that matriarchy is not the dominant pattern among them.

Jackson, Jacquelyne J. "Social Impacts of Housing Relocation Upon Urban Low-Income Black Aged." *The Gerontologist,* 1972, 12(1), pp. 32-37.

Black aged applicants who were accepted for a public housing project and those who were not accepted are compared. The results indicate that those who were accepted tend to be males, married, and more sociable. Also those who describe themselves as being dependent and pessimistic were admitted more often than those who are not.

Jackson, Jacquelyne J. "Aged Blacks: A Potpourri in the Direction of the Reduction of Inequalities." In Bess B. Hess (Ed.), *Growing Old in America.* New Brunswick, N.J.: Transaction Books, 1976, pp. 390-416.

Discusses the grandparental roles of southern urban blacks, the National Caucus of the Black Aged, and a proposal for reducing racial inequalities in eligibility requirements for social security.

Jackson, Jacquelyne J. *Minorities and Aging.* Belmont, Calif.: Wadsworth, 1980.

Focuses on the issues and problems associated with minority aging and the various federal programs that are helping to solve and reduce some of these problems. To examine how minority groups are affected by the aging process, the author singles out nine minorities for study: (1) Black American women; (2) Black American men; (3) American Indian women; (4) American Indian men; (5) Asian-American women; (6) Asian-American men; (7) Hispanic American women; (8) Hispanic American men; and (9) Anglo-American women.

Jackson, James S.; Bacon, John D.; and Peterson, John. "Life Satisfaction among Black Urban Elderly." *International Journal of Aging and Human Development,* 1977-1978, 8(2), pp. 169-179.

Data from a sample of black retired persons living in a large urban area reveals that factors such as background characteristics, health, political participation, personality variables, and life perceptions are related to life satisfaction.

Kalish, Richard A., and Yuen, Sam. "Americans of East Asian Ancestry: Aging and the Aged." *The Gerontologist,* 1971, 2(1), pt. 2, pp. 36-47.

Gives statistical data for three Asian groups: the elderly Chinese-American,Japanese-American, and Filipino-American. Stresses program evaluation and suggests directions for future research.

Kalish, Richard A., and Moriwaki, Sharon. "The World of the Elderly Asian American." *Journal of Social Issues,* 1973, 29(2), pp. 187-209.

Stresses how the understanding of elderly Asian Americans requires some knowledge regarding the effects of their early socialization, their cultural origins, as well as their history in this country.

Kasschau, Patricia L. "Age and Race Discrimination Reported by Middle-Aged and Older Persons." *Social Forces,* 1977, 55(3), pp. 728-742.

Surveys blacks, Mexican-Americans, and whites aged 45 to 74 about their experiences with race and age discrimination in finding or staying on a job. The majority of the respondents state that race and age discrimination are common in this country today. Blacks are more likely to report the existence of race discrimination than are Mexican-Americans, while Mexican-Americans are more likely to report race discrimination than whites. Blacks tend to note a greater exposure to age discrimination than either Mexican-Americans or whites.

Kent, Donald P. "The Negro Aged." *The Gerontologist,* 1971, 2(1), pt. 2, pp. 48-51.

Suggests the need for demographic research to provide base-line data for program planning.

Lawton, M. Powell; Kleban, Morton H.; and Singer, Maurice. "The Aged Jewish Person and the Slum Environment." *Journal of Gerontology,* 1971, 26(2), pp. 231-239.

Elderly Jewish slum residents when compared to several groups of other older people were found to be worse off financially, in poorer health, and less mobile. In addition, the Jewish elderly interacted less with their peers, their morale was lower, and they were less satisfied with their housing.

Leonard, Olen E. "The Older Rural Spanish-Speaking People of the Southwest." In E. Grant Youmans (Ed.), *Older Rural Americans.* Lexington: University of Kentucky Press, 1967, pp. 239-261.

Deals with older rural Spanish-speaking people of the Southwest. Discusses their socioeconomic and health status as well as their family system and participation in community activities.

Levin, Jack, and Levin, William C. *Ageism: Prejudice and Discrimination against the Elderly.* Belmont, Calif.: Wadsworth, 1980.

Approaches stereotyping, prejudice and discrimination, and minority-group status from the perspective of race and ethnic relations. The authors argue that the aged constitute an important minority group. Compares the reactions of the aged to their status and treatment in society with those of other minorities.

Levy, Jerrold E. "The Older American Indian." In E. Grant Youmans (Ed.), *Older Rural Americans.* Lexington: University of Kentucky Press, 1967, pp. 221-238.

Discusses the aboriginal period of Indian life and then examines the present conditions and problems of the aged Navaho.

Markson, Elizabeth W. "Ethnicity as a Factor in the Institutionalization of the Ethnic Elderly." In Donald Gelfand and Alfred Kutzik (Eds.), *Ethnicity and Aging.* New York: Springer Publishing Co., 1979, pp. 341-356.

Finds that placing the aged of different ethnic groups into the same mental institution produces discontent and often open confrontation.

Messer, Mark. "Race Differences in Selected Attitudinal Dimensions of the Elderly." *The Gerontologist,* 1968, 8(4), pp. 245-249.

Reveals that the elderly blacks have higher morale, less of a feeling of integration with the overall society, and are less likely to deny their actual age status than their white counterparts.

Moore, Joan W. "Mexican-Americans." *The Gerontologist,* 1971, 2(1), pt. 2, pp. 30-35.

Gives a 1960 profile of the Mexican-American elderly and suggests some areas for future research.

Moore, Joan W. "Situational Factors Affecting Minority Aging." *The Gerontologist,* 1971, 2(1), pt. 2, pp. 88-93.

Outlines five characteristics of minority groups and discusses their relevance for general issues in the study of aging.

Murdock, Steve H., and Schwartz, Donald F. "Family Structure and the Use of Agency Services: An Examination of Patterns among Elderly Native Americans." *The Gerontologist,* 1978, 18(5), pt. 1, pp. 475-501.

Findings from a survey of elderly Indians living on reservations in North and South Dakota reveal that those who live in households with their children are more aware of their needs and have greater levels of service usage. This may be due to the fact that extended families serve to increase the mechanisms for service usage and sources of information concerning services.

Osako, Masako M. "Aging and Family among Japanese Americans: The Role of Ethnic Tradition in the Adjustment to Old Age." *The Gerontologist,* 1979, 19(5), pp. 448-455.

Takes the position that the continuity between rural Japanese filial norms and contemporary American norms has aided the Japanese Americans' adjustment to old age. Furthermore, the Japanese emphasis on group orientation and acceptance of dependence which is not shared by American culture, helps alleviate the strains between the Japanese elderly and their adult children.

Palmore, Erdman B., and Manton, Kennth. "Ageism Compared to Racism and Sexism." *Journal of Gerontology,* 1973, 28(3), pp. 363-369.

The Equality Index was used to measure the equality of income, occupation, weeks worked, and education by age, race, and sex groups. Among the findings are that age inequality is highest in education and weeks worked and is greater among men and nonwhites than among women and whites. Changes since 1950 reveal that the aged are losing ground in income and education.

Reynolds, David K., and Kalish, Richard A. "Anticipation of Futurity as a Function of Ethnicity and Age." *The Journal of Gerontology,* 1974, 29(2), pp. 224-231.

Respondents in a community sample composed of four ethnic groups and three age groups were asked how long they expected to live and how long they wished to live. Results show that the elderly anticipate living longer than the younger age groups, but younger persons expect to live the most additional years. Black respondents expect to live longer and wanted to live longer than Japanese Americans, Mexican-Americans, or white Americans.

Rogers, C. Jean, and Gallion, Teresa E. "Characteristics of Elderly Pueblo Indians in New Mexico." *The Gerontologist,* 1978, 18(5), pp. 482-487.

Barriers to service delivery for this group include the difficulty in obtaining accurate statistical data, the lack of transportation, and language problems. Many programs are designed for the elderly Pueblo who lack the support of a family. When such a program is imposed on the Pueblo elderly who have strong family ties, it is ineffective and disruptive.

Rubenstein, Daniel I. "An Examination of Social Participation Found among a National Sample of Black and White Elderly." *Aging and Human Development,* 1971, 2(3), pp. 172-188.

Finds that the black elderly are not as alone or isolated as commonly assumed. Also they are not as limited as the white elderly in the opportunity for social participation in their household.

Sauer, William. "Morale of the Urban Aged: A Regression Analysis by Race." *Journal of Gerontology,* 1977, 32(5), pp. 600-608.

Examines variables which have been shown to be associated with morale for aged whites to determine if they are the same for aged blacks. Results indicate that significant predictors of morale for both blacks and whites are health and participation in solitary activities. Interaction with family and sex are significant predictors only for whites.

Streib, Gordon F. "Are the Aged a Minority Group?" In Alvin W. Gouldner and S.M. Miller (Eds.), *Applied Sociology.* New York: Free Press, 1965, pp. 311-328.

Discusses the evidence for viewing the aged as a minority group. Streib concludes that the notion of the aged having minority status does not clarify their social role in society, but only obscures it.

Thune, Jeanne M. "Racial Attitudes of Older Adults." *The Gerontologist,* 1967, 7(3), pp. 179-182.

Reports the results of the first year of a three-year study of the racial attitudes of aged blacks and whites. The findings indicate that older blacks are less prejudiced than older whites. Older blacks in comparison with older whites feel they have less personal control over their environment and are controlled more by outside forces.

Thune, Jeanne M.; Webb, Celia R.; and Thune, Leland E. "Interracial Attitudes of Younger and Older Adults in a Biracial Population." *The Gerontologist,* 1971, 2(4), pt. 1, pp. 305-309.

Indicates that race affects racial attitudes more than age. The differences between whites and blacks in the degree of prejudice increases across age groups as a result of the greater prejudice of older whites.

Torres-Gil, Fernando, and Becerra, Rosina M. "The Political Behavior of the Mexican-American Elderly." *The Gerontologist,* 1977, 17(5), pp. 392-399.

Finds the older Mexican-American's political activity to be low and it appears to be reflected in their low sense of efficacy. This lack of political participation is attributed, in part, to their low socioeconomic status, and language and cultural barriers.

Trela, James E., and Sokolovsky, Jay H. "Culture, Ethnicity, and Policy for the Aged." In Donald Gelfand and Alfred Kutzik (Eds.), *Ethnicity and Aging.* New York: Springer Publishing Co., 1979, pp. 341-356.

Discusses the complexity of the relationship between aging and ethnicity. The authors identify those factors in both traditional and modern societies which affect the aging experience and explore the possibilities for an ethnically conscious social policy toward aging.

Weinstock, Comilda, and Bennett, Ruth. "Problems in Communication to Nurses among Residents of a Racially Heterogeneous Nursing Home." *The Gerontologist,* 1968, 8(2), pp. 72-75.

Strained interaction is reflected mainly in the negative attitudes of the white patients toward the black staff, and not from the staff members having negative attitudes toward the elderly.

Wu, Frances Y.T. "Mandarin-Speaking Aged Chinese in the Los Angeles Area." *The Gerontologist,* 1975, 15(3), pp. 271-275.

Language barriers separate the elderly Chinese from the mainstream of American society and exclude them from receiving the services they need.

Zola, Irving K. "Oh Where, Oh Where Has Ethnicity Gone?" In Donald Gelfand and Alfred Kutzik (Eds.), *Ethnicity and Aging.* New York: Springer Publishing Co., 1979, pp. 66-80.

Reviews and interprets the development of ethnic and cultural research in the field of health care.

PART 4

SOCIAL INSTITUTIONS

Chapter 10

FAMILY and FRIENDSHIP

A. Family

Adams, Bert N. "Structural Factors Affecting Parental Aid to Married Children." *Journal of Marriage and the Family,* 1964, 26(3), pp. 327-331.

Examines the effect of residence, length of child's marriage, occupational level, and the sex of the child upon parental aid. The findings reveal that receiving aid is greatest during the young couple's first ten years of marriage. Financial help is given more frequently to middle-class children than to those in the working class. In addition, in both classes, the wife's parents help more often than do the husband's parents.

Adams, Bert N. "The Middle-Class Adult and His Widowed or Still-Married Mother." *Social Problems,* 1968, 16(1), pp. 50-59.

Compares the relations of middle-class adults and their widowed mothers with a similar group whose mothers are still married. The results show that the most satisfactory relations between a son and widowed mother are those in which the mother is independent. The most satisfactory relations between a daughter and widowed mother are those in which there is reciprocal help.

Albrecht, Ruth. "The Role of Older People in Family Rituals." In Clark Tibbitts and Wilma Donahue (Eds.), *Social and Psychological Aspects of Aging.* New York: Columbia University Press, 1962, pp. 486-489.

Examines the extent to which older people continue to participate in family rituals and what roles they play in them. Three distinct patterns of roles emerge. First are rituals with younger children, usually grandchildren. Next are rituals that older people started many years ago and continue because they are meaningful to the family members. Lastly, are rituals started by the younger generation to honor and show respect for their elders.

Albrecht, Ruth. "The Family and Aging Seen Cross-Culturally." In Rosamonde R. Boyd and Charles G. Oakes (Eds.), *Foundations of Practical Gerontology,* 2d ed., Columbia, South Carolina: University of South Carolina Press, 1973, pp. 27-34.

Deals with the meaning of age and the family relationships of the elderly in the United States and other countries.

Aldous, Joan. "The Consequences of Intergenerational Continuity." *Journal of Marriage and the Family,* 1965, 27(4), pp. 462-468.

Based on a three-generation sample, this study examines the consequences of intergenerational continuity for members of the youngest generation. The findings indicate that white-collar workers following the family-occupational tradition appear to have higher incomes than white-collar workers lacking such a tradition. Also continuity in religious affiliation over three generations is associated with less marital tension for the youngest generation.

Arling, Greg. "The Elderly Widow and Her Family, Neighbors and Friends." *Journal of Marriage and the Family,* 1976, 38(4), pp. 757-768.

Compares the family involvement of elderly widows with friendship and neighboring to determine which has a greater effect on their morale. Results indicate that friendships and neighboring are more satisfying to the elderly widow because these relationships are based on common interests and lifestyles. Family involvement is less meaningful because of differences in interests and lifestyles between the widow and her children.

Arling, Greg. "Resistance to Isolation among Elderly Widows." *International Journal of Aging and Human Development,* 1976, 7(1), pp. 67-86.

Finds that the social involvement of elderly widows with family and neighbors, and their participation in daily activities is facilitated by their being in good health and having adequate economic resources.

Atchley, Robert C. "Dimensions of Widowhood in Later Life." *The Gerontologist,* 1975, 15(2), pp. 176-178.

Indicates that widowhood among working-class women produces income inadequacy. Insufficient income affects car driving and social participation which results in social isolation and loneliness.

Atchley, Robert C., and Miller, Sheila J. "Older People and Their Families." In C. Eisdorfer (Ed.), *Annual Review of Gerontology and Geriatrics,* vol. 1. New York: Springer, 1980, pp. 337-369.

Provides a 23-year review of the literature on living arrangements, family structure, and relationships of older persons. Family relationships within and outside the household are considered as well as the relationships of those elderly who live with relatives, nonrelatives, or alone.

Atchley, Robert C.; Pignatiello, Linda; and Shaw, Ellen C. "Interactions with Family and Friends: Marital Status and Occupational Differences among Older Women." *Research on Aging,* 1979, 1(1), pp. 83-85.

Examines differences in the levels of interaction for married, widowed, and never-married older women who retired from professional or clerical employment. The findings reveal that widows from both occupational groups have the highest levels of interaction with family and friends. Professional women tend to interact more with primary relatives and friends, and less with extended kin than do women who were employed in clerical jobs.

Bachrach, Christine A. "Childlessness and Social Isolation among the Elderly." *Journal of Marriage and the Family,* 1980, 42(3), pp. 627-637.

Using data from a national sample of persons aged 65 and over, this study examines the relationship between isolation and the number of living children. Results indicate a strong association between childlessness and the probability of social isolation in old age. Health and occupational class conditions the effect of childlessness on the probability of social isolation among persons living alone.

Back, Kurt W. "Social Systems and Social Facts." In Ethel Shanas and Marvin B. Sussman (Eds.), *Family, Bureaucracy and the Elderly.* Durham, N.C.: Duke University Press, 1977, pp. 196-203.

Analyzes the family and bureaucracy not only as systems, but as social facts which occur in society. Discusses the problems encountered by bureaucracies in taking over family functions and suggests further research to determine the capacity of the family to undertake bureaucratic functions.

Ballweg, John A. "Resolution of Conjugal Role Adjustment after Retirement." *Journal of Marriage and the Family,* 1967, 29(2), pp. 277-281.

Reveals that retired husbands participate in more household tasks than do men in the same category still working.

Beard, Belle B. "Longevity and the Never-Married." In Clark Tibbitts and Wilma Donahue (Eds.), *Social and Psychological Aspects of Aging.* New York: Columbia University Press, 1962, pp. 36-50.

Investigates singleness in relation to longevity. Finds that single persons in their later years outlive those who have married.

Beeson, Diane. "Women in Studies of Aging: A Critique and Suggestion." *Social Problems,* 1975, 23(1), pp. 52-59.

Contends that gerontologists often dismiss the problems of aging that women experience and overestimate the problematic nature of the male experience.

Bekker, L. DeMoyne, and Taylor, Charles. "Attitudes toward the Aged in a Multi-generational Sample." *Journal of Gerontology,* 1966, 21(1), pp. 115-118.

Reveals that students who have living great-grandparents perceive their grandparents as having fewer characteristics of old age than those students who have no living great-grandparents.

Bell, Bill D. "The Family Cycle, Primary Relationships, and Social Participation Patterns." *The Gerontologist,* 1973, 13(1), pp. 78-81.

Finds no significant differences between the family-cycle stages in terms of the number of informal social contacts, the number of memberships, and the frequency of participation in formal organizations.

Bell, Inge P. "The Double Standard." *Trans-Action,* 1970, 8(1-2), pp. 75-80.

Discusses how the differential definition of age in men and women gives men a decided advantage by increasing their options for emotional satisfaction, and raising their prestige and self-esteem.

Bengtson, Vern L. "Inter-Age Perceptions and the Generation Gap." *The Gerontologist,* 1971, 2(4), pt. 2, pp. 85-89.

Indicates that the youngest age group sees a greater generation gap than the middle or oldest groups. Also the generation gap is perceived of as being much larger for "people in general" than for persons in one's own family.

Bengtson, Vern L. "Generation and Family Effects in Value Socialization." *American Sociological Review,* 1975, 40(3), pp. 358-371.

Tests several propositions concerning generational contrasts and within-family similarities in value orientations. The findings indicate neither marked generational differences, nor strong familial similarity in value orientations.

Bengtson, Vern L., and Cutler, Neal E. "Generations and Intergenerational Relations: Perspectives on Age Groups and Social Change." In Robert H. Binstock and Ethel Shanas (Eds.), *Handbook of Aging and the Social Sciences,* New York: Van Nostrand Reinhold, 1976, pp. 130-159.

Discusses major issues in generational analysis. Explores the ways that groups, which are identified by generation membership, differ with respect to attitudes and behavior, and examines the patterns of interaction that are observable between generations, especially those regarding older family members.

Bengtson, Vern L.; Olander, Edward B.; and Haddad, Anees A. "The 'Generation Gap' and Aging Family Members: Toward a Conceptual Model." In Jaber F. Gubrium (Ed.), *Roles, and Self in Old Age.* New York: Human Sciences Press, 1976, pp. 237-263.

Presents a model for research studies in the measurement of intergenerational solidarity.

Berardo, Felix M. "Widowhood Status in the United States: Perspective on a Neglected Aspect of the Family Life-Cycle." *The Family Coordinator,* 1968, 17(3), pp. 191-203.

Highlights the problems associated with widowhood status and points out some needed areas of research concerning the phenomenon of widowhood.

Berardo, Felix M. "Survivorship and Social Isolation: The Case of the Aged Widower." *The Family Coordinator,* 1970, 19(1), pp. 11-25.

Examines the environmental conditions surrounding the aged male survivor. Indicates that the aged widower encounters severe difficulty in adapting to the single status.

Bock, E. Wilbur. "Aging and Suicide: The Significance of Marital Kinship, and Alternative Relations." *The Family Coordinator,* 1972, 21(1), pp. 71-79.

Investigates elderly suicides and the circumstances surrounding them. Finds that social involvement such as marriage, kin networks, and organizational membership provides meaningful interaction and helps prevent suicide. Also various kinds of relationships tend to reinforce each other in preventing suicide. The highest suicide rate is among the lower-class levels.

Bremer, Teresa H., and Ragan, Pauline K. "The Empty Nest: A Comparison between Older Mexican-American and White Women." *Sociological Symposium,* 1979, no. 26, pp. 64-82.

Investigates the responses of Mexican-American women to the empty nest in comparison with that of white women. Few older white women experience feelings of low morale regarding the empty nest. The highest percentage of women reporting low morale occur among the Mexican-American women having a "full-nest" (someone 18 or under in the home).

Britton, John H., and Britton, Jean O. "The Middle-Aged and Older Rural Person and His Family." In E. Grant Youmans (Ed.), *Older Rural Americans.* Lexington, Ky.: University of Kentucky Press, 1967, pp. 44-74.

Reviews the research literature on living arrangements of older persons, relationships of the elderly with their families, and family norms for aging in rural communities.

Brody, Elaine M. "The Aging of the Family." *The Annals of the Academy of Political and Social Science,* 1978, 438, pp. 13-26.

Discusses the behavior of the modern family in response to the needs of its older members.

Brown, Arnold S. "Satisfying Relationships for the Elderly and Their Patterns of Disengagement." *The Gerontologist,* 1974, 14(3), pp. 258-262.

Reveals that when older persons are dissatisfied with relationships outside their immediate family, they withdraw and substitute other contacts. However, when they are dissatisfied with relationships within their immediate family, they do not withdraw but choose to remain engaged if possible.

Brown, Robert G. "Family Structure and Social Isolation of Older Persons." *Journal of Gerontology,* 1960, 15(2), pp. 170-174.

The majority of the subjects did not appear to live in social isolation from their children and saw them weekly or oftener. This high rate of parent-child interaction was associated with a low prevalence of reported feelings of neglect.

Buck, Charles F. "The Older Persons, the Family and Church: Selected References." *The Family Life Coordinator,* 1960, 8(4), pp. 71-77.

Presents a bibliography dealing with older persons and their position in the family, and ways in which community agencies and organizations, specifically religious groups and churches, can help the elderly.

Bultena, Gordon L., and Marshall, Douglas G. "Family Patterns of Migrant and Nonmigrant Retirees." *Journal of Marriage and the Family,* 1970, 32(1), pp. 89-92.

Compares older persons who have retired in their home communities and those who moved to Florida or Arizona upon retirement. Results indicate that the migrants tend to be more isolated from their children than nonmigrants. This isolation is more of a function of the residential mobility of children than the migration of their parents after retirement.

Burgess, Ernest W. "Family Structure and Relationships." In Ernest W. Burgess(Ed.), *Aging in Western Societies,* Chicago: The University of Chicago Press, 1960, pp. 271-298.

Discusses the family structure and relationships of the elderly in various Western societies in the context of social and economic change.

Cain, Leonard D. "The Young and the Old: Coalition or Conflict Ahead?" *Behavioral Scientist,* 1975, 19(2), pp. 166-175.

Discusses the two-generation interpretation of power relations among age categories, and considers the prospects for coalition and conflict between the old and the young.

Carp, Frances M. "Some Components of Disengagement." *Journal of Gerontology,* 1968, 23(3), pp. 382-386.

Suggests that as participation in activities and involvement with friends declines, the parental role becomes more important to the older person.

Cavan, Ruth S. "The Couple in Old Age." In Arnold M. Rose (Ed.), *Human Behavior and Social Processes.* Boston: Houghton Mifflin, 1962, pp. 526-535.

Demonstrates the way in which the concepts of role taking, role playing, and self-conception can be used to analyze certain types of adjustment in old age.

Cavan, Ruth S. "Speculations on Innovations to Conventional Marriage in Old Age." *The Gerontologist,* 1973, 13(4), pp. 409-411.

Lists the following unmet needs of older persons: (1) intimacy and sexual needs; (2) desire for a dependency relationship with younger kin; (3) for a peer group; and (4) for family life with peers. Considers some innovations to meet these needs.

Chappell, Neena L., and Havens, Betty. "Old and Female: Testing the Double-Jeopardy Hypothesis." *The Sociological Quarterly,* 1980, 21(2), pp. 157-171.

Provides an empirical test of the double-jeopardy hypothesis on the combined negative effects of being female and old. The findings reveal support of the double-jeopardy hypothesis for the mental health status of the elderly women, but not for their perceived well-being.

Chevan, Albert, and Korson, J. Henry. "The Widowed Who Live Alone: An Examination of Social and Demographic Factors." *Social Forces,* 1972, 51(1), pp. 45-53.

Examines various demographic and social factors to determine their influence on the living arrangements of the widowed. Reveals that the percentage of the widowed living alone peaks at ages 65 to 69 and then declines at ages 80 and over. The groups least disposed to living alone include American Indians, Asians, and whites with Spanish surnames. The widowed with six years of education or less are found living alone less often than those with more education.

Clavan, Sylvia, and Vatter, Ethel. "The Affiliated Family: A Device for Integrating Old and Young." *The Gerontologist,* 1972, 12(4), pp. 407-411.

As an alternative to the traditional nuclear family structure, the authors propose a family of affiliation. This family would consist of any combination of husband/father, wife/mother and their children, plus one or more older persons who are part of the kin network. The basic criterion would be voluntary commitment and responsibility for one another within the unit.

Croog, Sydney H., and Kong-Ming New, Peter. "Knowledge of Grandfather's Occupation: Clues to American Kinship Structure." *Journal of Marriage and the Family,* 1965, 27(1), pp. 69-77.

In a study of newly inducted soldiers, respondents were found to differ in their knowledge of their grandfather's occupation according to their education, their father's social class and occupation, their own mobility aspirations, and their parent's immigration status.

Dahlin, Michel. "Perspectives on the Family Life of the Elderly in 1900." *The Gerontologist,* 1980, 20(1), pp. 99-107.

Outlines some of the major facets of the family life of older persons at the turn of the century. Dispels many of the popular notions of what old age was like in the past.

Dressler, David M. "Life Adjustment of Retired Couples." *International Journal of Aging and Human Development,* 1973, 4(4), pp. 335-349.

Investigates the marital relationship and retirement experiences of a sample of couples living in an urban community. Although there is some decrease in their level of social participation since retirement, overall, these couples appear to be satisfied with their marriages and life patterns. Results indicate that continuity of life patterns is an important determinant of successful adjustment to retirement.

Fengler, Alfred P., and Goodrich, Nancy. "Wives of Elderly Disabled Men: The Hidden Patients." *The Gerontologist,* 1979, 19(2), pp. 175-183.

Finds an association between the life satisfaction scores of husbands and wives. Morale of the wives is higher when they perceive their income as adequate and they are not employed full-time.

Fengler, Alfred P., and Wood, Vivian. "The Generation Gap: An Analysis of Attitudes on Contemporary Issues." *The Gerontologist,* 1972, 12(2), pt. 1, pp. 124-128.

Studies attitude differences among three generations: a college student, his two parents, and one grandparent. Age provides the most consistent explanation for the generational differences in their values and attitudes.

Foner, Anne. "Age Stratification and the Changing Family." In John Demos and Sarane S. Boocock (Eds.), *Turning Points: Historical and Sociological Essays on the Family.* Chicago: The University of Chicago Press, 1978, pp. 340-365.

Deals with the importance of the age structure of a family at a given time, changing family patterns over the family cycle, and the impact of the succession of cohorts of families.

Friedman, Edward P. "Spatial Proximity and Social Interaction in a Home for the Aged." *Journal of Gerontology,* 1966, 21(4), pp. 566-670.

Indicates that spatial proximity is the most important single variable in explaining friendship formation among elderly women in a home for the aged. Although living on the same floor of the home is an important factor in friendship choice, friendship choice and the relationship between proximity does not decline as the length of residence of the person making the choice increases. Also proximity is a more important factor in those choices in which reciprocity is present than in those in which it is absent.

Glasser, Paul H., and Glasser, Lois N. "Role Reversal and Conflict between Aged Parents and Their Children." *Marriage and Family Living,* 1962, 24(1), pp. 46-51.

Explores the problems that arise between aged parents and their adult children. The authors suggest that some of these problems might stem from a gap between expectation and reality which leads to role conflict between parents and children. Also changing societal norms push many of the aged into dependency roles resulting in a reversal of the roles they played with their own children. Finds social class differences between children and parents have no bearing on their problems.

Gubrium, Jaber F. "Marital Desolation and the Evaluation of Everyday Life in Old Age." *Journal of Marriage and the Family,* 1974, 36(1), pp. 107-113.

Indicates that the single and married (categorized as nondesolate) tend to be less negative in their evaluations of everyday life in old age than widowed and divorced persons (categorized as desolate). The desolate are also more likely than the nondesolate to say that their personal feelings have changed since age 45.

Gubrium, Jaber F. "Being Single in Old Age." *International Journal of Aging and Human Development,* 1975, 6(1), pp. 29-41.

Suggests that single elderly persons constitute a distinct type of social personality and have certain social characteristics in common. These characteristics include personal independence and minimal social involvements.

Harper, D. Wood, Jr., and Garza, Joseph M. "Ethnicity, Family Generational Structure, and Intergenerational Solidarity." *Sociological Symposium,* no. 2, Spring 1969, pp. 75-82.

Reveals that the relationship between family generational structure and family solidarity are better understood when the influence of ethnic group identification is considered.

Harvey, Carol D., and Bahr, Howard M. "Widowhood, Morale, and Affiliation." *Journal of Marriage and the Family,* 1974, 36(1), pp. 97-106.

Based on data from sample surveys in five countries, morale and organizational ties of widowed and married persons were examined. The major finding is that neither the self-theory nor the role-theory perspective is adequate to explain differences between widowed and married persons in morale or affiliations. This study suggests that the widowed appear to have more negative attitudes than married persons. These attitudes may be due to other factors besides widowhood per se. For example, widows are poorer than married persons and they may be less affiliated for this reason.

Hawkinson, William P. "Wish, Expectancy, and Practice in the Interaction of Generations." In Arnold M. Rose and Warren A. Peterson (Eds.), *Older People and Their Social World.* Philadelphia: F.A. Davis, 1965, pp. 181-190.

Focuses on beliefs of elderly parents regarding the obligations of their adult children to them. Reveals that the aged parents wish for more frequent and intimate contact with their children. Also there is a preference for financial support from government or some other agency rather than from one's own children.

Heltsley, Mary E., and Powers, Ronald C. "Social Interaction and Perceived Adequacy of Interaction of the Rural Aged." *The Gerontologist,* 1975, 15(6), pp. 533-536.

Results reveal that proximity leads to more intensive and extensive interaction between aged parents and their daughters, but it is not related to the amount of interaction for sons. Also age, health, and economic status have little influence on the reported contacts of older persons with children and friends.

Hess, Beth B., and Waring, Joan M. "Parent and Child in Later Life: Rethinking the Relationship." In Richard M. Lerner and Graham B. Spanier (Eds.), *Child Influences on Marital and Family Interaction: A Life-Span Perspective.* New York: Academic Press, 1978, pp. 241-273.

Focuses on the nature of intergenerational relations in later life. Discusses the ways in which these relations differ from those at earlier stages in family development, and the factors that undermine and strengthen them.

Hill, Reuben. "Decision Making and the Family Life Cycle." In Ethel Shanas and Gordon F. Streib (Eds.), *Social Structure and the Family:*

Generational Relations. Englewood Cliffs, N.J.: Prentice-Hall, 1965, pp. 113-139.

Uses interview data from a sample of grandparent families, parent families, and married children to examine the extent of planning and decision making over the life cycle. Indicates that the married child generation does the most planning in every area of activity studied, and the grandparent generation does the least. As far as the outcome of decisions is concerned, the parent generation is the most likely to be completely satisfied, the grandparent generation next, and the married child generation the least.

Hoffman, Edward. "Young Adults' Relations with Their Grandparents: An Exploratory Study." *International Journal of Aging and Human Development,* 1979-1980, 10(3), pp. 299-310.

Finds that the grandparents' kin position relative to the grandchild affects the intensity of the bond. Adult grandchildren tend to be closer to maternal grandparents than to paternal grandparents. The findings also reveal a wide variability among young adults on frequency of direct involvement and emotional attachment to their grandparents.

Hutchinson, Ira W., III. "The Significance of Marital Status for Morale and Life Satisfaction among Lower-Income Elderly." *Journal of Marriage and the Family,* 1975, 37(2), pp. 287-293.

Examines the differences in life satisfaction as they are affected by income, sex, and the marital status of the elderly. Concludes that sex or marital status differences may have a significant influence on the elderly's life satisfaction above a poverty level, but that neither is important below the poverty line.

Jackson, Jacquelyne J. "Sex and Social Class Variations in Black Aged Parent-Adult Child Relationships." *Aging and Human Development,* 1971, 2(2), pp. 96-107.

Indicates that black parents engaged in nonmanual occupations are more likely to receive instrumental aid from their adult children than those parents in manual occupations. Daughters are more likely to provide instrumental aid to their parents than sons. Most children of parents in manual occupations do not receive instrumental assistance from their parents, while the opposite is true of children of nonmanual workers. Daughters are more frequent recipients of aid than sons in both cases.

Jackson, Jacquelyne J. "Marital Life among Aging Blacks." *The Family Coordinator,* 1972, 21(1), pp. 21-27.

Examines spouse dominance patterns among a sample of older, urban, married blacks. Finds that matriarchy is not the dominant pattern among them.

Jacobs, Ruth H. "A Typology of Older American Women." *Social Policy,* 1976, 7(3), pp. 34-39.

Jacobs delineates 13 types of older women. These include nurturers, careerists, advocates, escapists, and isolates.

Johnson, Elizabeth S. "'Good' Relationships between Older Mothers and Their Daughters: A Causal Model." *The Gerontologist,* 1978, 18(3), pp. 301-306.

Indicates that the strongest direct predictor of the quality of the relationship between mothers and their adult daughters is the mother's attitude toward aging, followed by satisfaction with her living environment. Health and finances had an indirect impact on the relationship in that they affected the mother's attitude toward aging and her living environment.

Johnson, Elizabeth S., and Bursk, Barbara J. "Relationships between the Elderly and Their Adult Children." *The Gerontologist,* 1977, 17(1), pp. 90-96.

Suggests that good health for older persons can be an important variable in how elderly parents and their adult children view their relationships.

Kahana, Eva, and Kahana, Boaz. "Theoretical and Research Perspectives on Grandparenthood." *Aging and Human Development,* 1971, 2(4), pp. 261-268.

Based on a review of the literature and several exploratory studies, the authors summarize some of the issues and problems relating to research on grandparenthood. They propose a scheme for sorting out some of the findings about grandparents and grandchildren.

Kalish, Richard A. "The Old and the New as Generation Gap Allies." *the Gerontologist,* 1969, 9(2), pt. 2, pp. 83-89.

Kalish presents a theory of generation gap problems followed by a discussion of the ways in which the youth and the elderly are similar.

Kalish, Richard A., and Johnson, Ann I. "Value Similarities and Differences in Three Generations of Women." *Journal of Marriage and the Family,* 1972, 34(1), pp. 49-54.

Using a sample of young women, their mothers, and maternal grandmothers, a Likert-type questionnaire composed of six scales was employed to investigate similarities and differences in values and attitudes between generations. The results show that mother-daughter correlations are higher than mother-grandmother or daughter-grandmother correlations on some scales but lower on others. Grandmothers and mothers seem farthest apart and daughters and mothers the closest.

Kassel, Victor. "Polygyny after 60." *Geriatrics,* 1966, 21(1), pp. 214-218.

Polygyny after 60 is suggested as a solution to some of the problems of the elderly.

Keating, Norah C., and Cole, Priscilla. "What Do I Do with Him 24 Hours a Day? Changes in the Housewife Role After Retirement." *The Gerontologist,* 1980, 20(1), pp. 84-89.

A study of 400 retired teachers and wives reveals no significant male-female differences with levels of communication in retirement and in satisfaction with division of household tasks. Women are significantly happier than men with the retirement stage of the life cycle in that it gives them a new sense of being needed.

Kent, Donald P., and Matson, Margaret B. "The Impact of Health on the Aged Family." *the Family Coordinator,* 1972, 21(1), pp. 29-36.

Tensions arising from the cost of illness, psychological stress, and role disruptions are frequent reactions to health problems. These reactions have important implications for family relations. The authors suggest that policy makers should concentrate on the family as the central unit around which to build health services for the elderly.

Kerckhoff, Alan C. "Husband-Wife Expectations and Reactions to Retirement." *Journal of Gerontology,* 1964, 19(4), pp. 510-516.

Wives seem to be less deeply involved than husbands in expectations of and reactions to retirement. The husbands tend to have higher expectations of retirement and soon after retiring they have a greater sense of improvement and satisfaction than their wives. However, after about 5 years, husbands became less satisfied and they respond more negatively to retirement than their wives. In addition, upper-level couples respond the most favorably to retirement, followed by middle-level couples. Lower-level couples tend to be the least favorable in their reactions to the experience and do not regard retirement as a particularly pleasant change in their lives.

Kerckhoff, Alan C. "Nuclear and Extended Family Relationships: A Normative and Behavioral Analysis." In Ethel Shanas and Gordon F. Streib (Eds.), *Social Structure and the Family: Generational Relations.* Englewood Cliffs, N.J.: Prentice-Hall, 1965, pp. 93-112.

Based on data obtained from interviews with older couples having adult children, Kerckhoff analyzed the normative and behavioral aspects of extended family relationships. He found that there is considerable deviation between normative definitions and actual behavior in the families studied.

Kerckhoff, Alan C. "Family Patterns and Morale in Retirement." In Ida H. Simpson and John C. McKinney (Eds.), *Social Aspects of Aging.* Durham,N.C.: Duke University Press, 1966, pp. 173-192.

Examines the relationship between family patterns and morale in retirement. The only variable which is consistently associated with morale for both husband and wife is the level of the husband's participation in household tasks. In households where the husband participates, both the husband's and wife's morale is higher than those in which the husband does not participate.

Kerckhoff, Alan C. "Husband-Wife Expectations and Reactions to Retirement." In Ida H. Simpson and John C. McKinney (Eds.), *Social Aspects of Aging.* Durham, N.C.: Duke university Press, 1966, pp. 160-172.

Compares the responses of husbands and wives before, soon after, and well after retirement. Pre-retired husbands look forward to retirement, and retired husbands show a greater sense of satisfaction in retirement than do their wives. Men who are retired less than five years show the greatest satisfaction. Couples in which the husband was in a professional or managerial category did not welcome retirement, but their reactions to the experience are generally positive while those in the lower-level occupations do not find the retirement experience pleasant and tend to respond more negatively.

Kerckhoff, Alan C. "Norm-Value Clusters and the 'Strain toward Consistency' among Older Married Couples." In Ida H. Simpson and John C. McKinney (Eds.), *Social Aspects of Aging.* Durham, N.C.: Duke University Press, 1966, pp. 138-159.

Finds that among older married couples there is a strain toward consistency in the following measures: parent-child norms, normative definitions of husband-wife division of labor, the degree of acceptance of the value of changes, and the degree to which there is a conflict between children's mobility and family values.

Kivett, Vira R., and Learner, R. Max. "Perspectives on the Childless Rural Elderly: A Comparative Analysis." *The Gerontologist,* 1980, 20(6), pp. 708-715.

There are few significant differences between the childless rural elderly and the general population of rural elderly in terms of needs and resources. However, the childless rural elderly in this study are at high risk for certain kinds of dependency.

Laufer, Robert S., and Bengtson, Vern L. "Generations, Aging, and Social Stratification: On the Development of Generational Units." *Journal of Social Issues,* 1974, 30(3), pp. 181-205.

Explores the construction of generations as sources of social change. Describes four types of generation units of youth and discusses the prospects for generational units among the elderly.

Lee, Gary R. "Marriage and Morale in Later Life." *Journal of Marriage and the Family,* 1978, 40(1), pp. 131-139.

Analyzes the effect of marital satisfaction on morale. The findings reveal that marital satisfaction is positively related to morale among older people and that this relationship is markedly stronger for women than men.

Lee, Gary R. "Children and the Elderly: Interaction and Morale." *Research on Aging,* 1979, 1(3), pp. 335-360.

Examines the extent to which the frequency of interaction with adult children contributes to the morale of their elderly parents. Results reveal that the elderly parents' morale is not significantly affected by frequency of contact with their children.

Lee, Gary R., and Ihinger-Tallman, Marilyn. "Sibling Interaction and Morale: The Effects of Family Relations on Older People." *Research on Aging,* 1980, 2(3), pp. 367-391.

Analyzes the relationship between the elderly's morale and interaction with their siblings. Results indicate that interaction with siblings is unrelated to the morale of the elderly.

Lipman, Aaron. "Role Conceptions and Morale of Couples in Retirement." *Journal of Gerontology,* 1961, 16(3), pp. 267-271.

At retirement role differentiation by sex is reduced. The preretirement roles of the couple that were mainly of an instrumental nature shift to supportive roles after retirement which require expressive qualities such as sharing, cooperation, love, and companionship.

Lipman, Aaron. "Role Conceptions of Couples in Retirement." In Clark Tibbitts and Wilma Donahue (Eds.), *Social and Psychological Aspects of Aging.* New York: Comumbia University Press, 1962, pp. 475-485.

Analyzes preretirement role orientations and new role conceptions emerging as a result of retirement. Concludes that retirement brings a definite change in the traditional activities of the male which alters the preretirement division of males and females. It appears that role differentiation by sex is reduced with increased age and retirement. Because non-sex differentiated roles demand expressive rather than instrumental qualities, they tend to be well-adapted for the personality system of both husband and wife in retirement.

Lopata, Helena Z. "Loneliness: Forms and Components." *Social Problems,* 1969, 17(2), pp. 248-262.

Describes the various types of loneliness experienced by widows and the ways in which they deal with it.

Lopata, Helena Z. "The Social Involvement of American Widows." *American Behavioral Scientist,* 1970, 14(1), pp. 41-57.

Some reasons widows may be socially isolated in that they have not been socialized to analyze the resources of their environment, to choose desired social roles, and generally to rebuild their lives.

Lopata, Helena Z. "Living Arrangements of American Urban Widows." *Sociological Focus,* 1971, 5(1), pp. 41-61.

Examines the attitudes expressed by older widows in the metropolitan Chicago area toward living with their married children. Finds that older widows enjoy the ease and independence of living alone and believe that there would be problems in living with their married children.

Lopata, Helena Z. "Widows as a Minority Group." *The Gerontologist,* 1971, 2(1), pt. 2, pp. 67-77.

Discusses five reasons why widows could be classified as a minority group, summarizes some facts about widows, and suggests areas for research.

Lopata, Helena Z. "Social Relations of Widows in Urbanizing Societies." *The Sociological Quarterly,* 1972, 13(2), pp. 259-271.

Urbanization and increasing societal complexity are modifying the lifestyles of widows in various communities of the world. Many widows are living in situations which do not permit them to utilize the emerging social resources.

Lopata, Helena Z. "Role Changes in Widowhood: A World Perspective." In Donald O. Cowgill and Lowell D. Holmes (Eds.), *Aging and Modernization.* New York: Appleton-Century-Crofts, 1972, pp. 275-303.

Examines role shifts in the lives of widows in different societies and the types of lifestyles or alternatives which are available to them.

Lopata, Helena Z. *Widowhood in an American City.* Cambridge: Schenkman Publishing, 1973.

Examines the lifestyles and social roles of American urban widows fifty years of age or older. A major finding of the study is that the way in which different kinds of women re-engage in society following their husband's death reflects their location in the social system.

Lopata, Helena Z. "Self-Identity in Marriage and Widowhood." *The Sociological Quarterly,* 1973, 14(3), pp. 407-418.

Deals primarily with the relationship between education and identity reformulation among widows. Results reveal that widowhood is less disorganizing to the identities of lower-class women than those of upper-class women. Lower-class women are less affected in their conscious identities by the world-view constructs and presence of their husbands.

Lopata, Helena Z. "Widowhood: Societal Factors in Life-Span Diruptions and Alternatives." In Nancy Datan and Leon Ginsberg (Eds.), *Life-Span Developmental Psychology: Normative Life Crises.* New York: Academic Press, 1975, pp. 217-234.

Deals with the death of a spouse and the effects and the changes that take place over time upon the survivor.

Lopata, Helena Z. "Contributions of Extended Families to the Support Systems of Metropolitan Area Widows: Limitations of the Modified Kin Network." *Journal of Marriage and the Family,* 1978, 40(2), pp. 355-364.

Examines the economic, service, social, and emotional support systems of widows in the Chicago area. The findings indicate that extended kin make infrequent contributions to these support systems, while children and parents are frequent contributors.

Lopata, Helena Z. *Women as Widows.* New York: Elsevier, 1979.

Deals with the social integration and support system of widows in metropolitan Chicago. Finds that while friends tend to supply self-feelings of importance and usefulness, it is the children, especially the daughters, that take over the emotional support system for their mothers. One of the more dramatic findings is the absence of the "helping professions and groups" during the husband's illness and immediately after his death. Community resources are seldom used to help the widow solve problems or to help in her re-engagement.

Lopata, Helena Z. "The Widowed Family Member." In Nancy Datan and Nancy Lohmann (Eds.), *Transitions of Aging.* New York: Academic Press, 1980, pp. 93-115.

The support systems and lifestyles of widows and widowers reveal many common problems from the immediate effects of a spouse's death. The same factors operate to isolate both widows and widowers.

McKain, Walter C. "A New Look at Older Marriages." *The Family Coordinator,* 1972, 21(1), pp. 61-69.

Research on remarriage of elderly widows and widowers finds that success in remarriages tends to be related to a number of factors. These factors include knowing each other well before marriage, having the approval of friends and relatives, and having sufficient incomes.

Martin, William C.; Bengtson, Vern L.; and Adcock, Alan C. "Alienation and Age: A Context-Specific Approach." *Social Forces,* 1974, 53(2), pp. 266-274.

Finds consistent age differences in alienation. Youth are the most alienated, the middle generation the least alienated, and the older generation is in between.

Matthews, Sarah H. *The Social World of Old Women: Management of Self-Identity.* Beverly Hills, Calif.: Sage Publications, 1979.

Attempts to give a better understanding of what being old is like by clarifying the social forces or rules of the "game" that impinge on the worlds of old women and the way actors mediate these forces.

Medley, Morris L. "Marital Adjustment in the Post-Retirement Years." *The Family Coordinator,* 1977, 26(1), pp. 5-11.

Presents a comprehensive, theoretical framework in which to analyze marital adjustment in the post-retirement years.

Messer, Mark. "Age Grouping and the Family Status of the Elderly." *Sociology and Social Research,* 1968, 52(3), pp. 271-279.

Investigates the possibility of age grouping among the elderly as an alternative to the family for consummatory needs. Tentative findings suggest that age grouping is associated with less dependence on the family for morale and that it is not accompanied by feelings of familial neglect. Also age grouping acts as a mediator between the older person and the overall society.

Mindel, Charles H. "Multi-generational Family Households: Recent Trends and Implications for the Future." *The Gerontologist,* 1979, 19(5), pp. 456-463.

Despite the fact that the prevalence of multi-generational households has been relatively low in the past, there has been an even greater decrease in their number and proportion in recent years. Multi-generational households are more common among those "single" elderly 75 and older than those younger.

Moore, Wilbert E. "Aging and the Social System." In John C. McKinney and Frank de Vyver (Eds.), *Aging and Social Policy.* New York: Appleton-Century-Crofts, 1966, pp. 23-41.

Deals with continuities and discontinuities in the life cycle, intergenerational reciprocity, and the strains that arise in the modernized kinship system.

Morgan, Leslie A. "A Re-Examination of Widowhood Morale." *Journal of Gerontology,* 1976, 31(6), pp. 687-695.

Examines the relationship between widowhood and morale using analysis of covariance. The results reveal that there are important situational factors that cut across marital status differences in explaining morale scores. The lower morale scores of the widows may be due to other factors associated with the status of widowhood, and not to the role of widowhood in itself.

Morgan, Leslie A. "Work in Widowhood: A Viable Option?" *The Gerontologist,* 1980, 20(5), pp. 581-587.

Finds little evidence to suggest that women widowed in mid-life turn to work as a substitute for the role of wife. In the future women who are widowed and not already in the labor force will face many obstacles to employment, and work as a role substitute will be even less of an option.

Neugarten, Bernice L., and Weinstein, Karol K. "The Changing American Grandparent." *Journal of Marriage and Family Living,* 1964, 26(2), pp. 199-204.

Differentiates five styles of grandparenting: The Formal, the Fun Seeker, the Surrogate Parent, the Reservoir of Family Wisdom, and the Distant Figure. The Fun Seeker and Distant Figure are the most frequent patterns adopted and are found in half of all the cases in the sample.

Nimkoff, Meyer F. "The Changing Family Relationship of Older People in the United States during the Last Fifty Years." *The Gerontologist,* 1961, pp. 92-97.

Compares family relationships of the elderly in 1900 to those in the 1950s and the 1960s. Nimkoff concludes that the aged's loss of economic power, authority, and deferences within the family is the most important change in the family situation in the past fifty years. He sees this loss being offset by growing public benefits for the elderly.

Nimkoff, Meyer F. "Changing Family Relationships of Older People in the United States during the Last Forty Years." *The Gerontologist,* 1961, 1(1), pp. 92-97.

Discusses the changing relationships of older people with their spouses, children, grandchildren, siblings, and other kin.

Osako, Masako M. "Aging and Family among Japanese Americans: The Role of Ethnic Tradition in the Adjustment to Old Age." *The Gerontologist,* 1979, 19(5), pp. 448-455.

Maintains that the continuity between rural Japanese filial norms and contemporary American norms has aided the Japanese Americans' adjustment to old age. Furthermore, the Japanese emphasis on group orientation and aceptance of dependence, which is not shared by American culture, helps alleviate the strains between the Japanese elderly and their adult children.

Petrowsky, Marc. "Marital Status, Sex, and the Social Networks of the Elderly." *Journal of Marriage and the Family,* 1976, 38(4), pp. 749-756.

Indicates that the widowed may not be as isolated as past research has suggested. Also interaction in religious organizations, especially for widows, is pronounced and may serve as a surrogate family for them.

Pihlblad, C.T., and Adams, David L. "Widowhood, Social Participation, and Life Satisfaction." *Aging and Human Development,* 1972, 3(4), pp. 323-330.

Investigates the relationship between widowhood, social participation, and life satisfaction among small town elderly. Findings reveal that no major change occurs in social participation among females after widowhood. Males show a linear decline in most kinds of activity patterns with length of widowhood. Satisfaction among the elderly is most affected by participation in formal organizations, next by friendships, and the least by family contacts.

Pihlblad, C.T., and Habenstein, Robert. "Social Factors in Grandparent Orientation of High School Youth." In Arnold M. Rose and Warren A. Peterson (Eds.), *Older People and Their Social World.* Philadelphia: F.A. Davis, 1965, pp. 163-179.

Based on the assumption that kinship ties in the family are directly related to the degree of knowledge held by grandchildren of their grandparents, this paper offers some tentative conclusions. First, as compared to blacks, twice as many whites knew the occupations of both grandfathers. Second, knowledge of grandfathers' occupations was positively associated with a higher occupational and educational status of both parents, and a higher social class status of the father.

Powers, Edward A. "The Effect of the Wife's Employment on Household Tasks among Postparental Couples: A Research Note." *Aging and Human Development,* 1971, 2(4), pp. 284-287.

In postparental families where the wife works, husbands are more likely to perform nearly all the household chores. However, the traditional sex-linked division of labor still persists between postparental couples whether the wife works or not.

Robertson, Joan F. "Interaction in Three Generation Families, Parents as Mediators: Toward A Theoretical Perspective." *International Journal of Aging and Human Development,* 1975, 6(2), pp. 103-110.

Reports the development of a theoretical perspective for describing the dimensions of parental mediation in interactions between grandparents and grandchildren. Identifies eight dimensions of parental mediation.

Robertson, Joan F. "Significance of Grandparents: Perceptions of Young Adult Grandchildren." *The Gerontologist,* 1976, 16(2), pp. 137-140.

Negates the functionality of grandparents to young adult grandchildren except as gift-givers, bearers of family history, and emotional gratification. Finds that grandchildren's responsibilities toward their grandparents include giving them emotional support, helping them when possible, and visiting them.

Robertson, Joan F. "Grandmotherhood: A Study of Role Conceptions." *Journal of Marriage and the Family,* 1977, 39(1), pp. 165-174.

Predicts grandparenting types by lifestyle. The grandmother role, enjoyed by 80 percent of the respondents, involves babysitting, home recreation, and drop-in visits.

Seelbach, Wayne C. "Gender Differences in Expectations for Filial Responsibility." *The Gerontologist,* 1977, 17(5), pp. 421-425.

Finds elderly women have greater filial responsibility expectancies than elderly men. Women are more likely than men to think that old people who do not wish to live alone should live with their children. Also women are more apt than men to believe that old people who are unable to care for themselves should live with their children.

Seelbach, Wayne C., and Hansen, Charles J. "Satisfaction with Family Relations among the Elderly." *Family Relations,* 1980, 29(1), pp. 91-106.

Examines data from both institutionalized and noninstitutionalized elderly regarding their satisfaction with the quality of their family relationships. Finds that overall older persons are satisfied with their family relationships and they do not feel abandoned or neglected. However, there is a significant difference between the "young-old" and the "old-old" in that the older respondents are more likely to report "perfect satisfaction."

Seelbach, Wayne C., and Sauer, William J. "Filial Responsibility Expectations and Morale among Aged Parents." *The Gerontologist,* 1977, 17(6), pp. 492-499.

Reveals that levels of filial responsibility expectancy are inversely associated with levels of parental morale. Discusses implications for social policy regarding filial responsibility.

Seltzer, Mildred M. "The Older Woman: Facts, Fantasies, and Fiction." *Research on Aging,* 1979, 1(2), pp. 139-151.

The research and literature about older women is discussed from a sociology of knowledge perspective and then it is classified into seven categories. Content analysis is suggested as a technique for examining behavior, belief systems, and values pertaining to older women.

Shanas, Ethel. "Family Responsibility and the Health of Older People." *Journal of Gerontology,* 1960, 15(4), pp. 408-411.

Indicates that most older people live close to at least one child and see him or her often. Also the poorer the health of the older person, the more likely he or she is to be living in the same household with an adult child. When faced with parental health problems, children tend to assume their obligations and responsibilities.

Shanas, Ethel. *Family Relationships of Older People.* New York: Health Information Foundation, 1961.

This is a partial report of a National Opinion Research Center survey. Discusses how the closeness of family ties of the elderly affect their health and finances. Also the report contains opinions concerning the health of the elderly expressed by near relatives or friends to whom older persons said they would turn to in a health crisis.

Shanas, Ethel. "Family and Household Characteristics of Older People in the United States." In P. From Hansen (Ed.), *Age With a Future.* Philadelphia: F.A. Davis, 1964, pp. 449-454.

The findings reported here were part of a survey made in Denmark, Great Britain and the United States on the health, economic status, and family structure of the elderly. The emerging pattern for the elderly in the United States is to maintain separate households from their children but to live near at least one child. The proximity of older people and their adult children make it possible for extended family relationships to flourish despite the growth of independent households.

Shanas, Ethel, and Streib, Gordon F. (Eds.). *Social Structure and the Family: Generational Relations.* Englewood Cliffs, N.J.: Prentice-Hall, 1965.

A collection of papers written from the perspective of several disciplines about the family, its intergenerational relations, and social structure.

Shanas, Ethel. "Family Help Patterns and Social Class in Three Countries." *Journal of Marriage and the Family,* 1967, 29(2), pp. 257-286.

Reports that family help patterns in Denmark, Britain, and the United States vary by the social class of the older person. In Britain and the United States, old people of white-collar backgrounds are the most likely to help their children, while old people of working-class backgrounds need help from their children.

Shanas, Ethel. "The Family and Social Class." In Ethel Shanas, et al., *Old People in Three Industrial Societies.* New York: Atherton Press, 1968, pp. 227-256.

The analysis of social class and family life in Denmark, Britain, and the United States indicates that in Britain and the United States the family life of old people differ by whether they are of white-collar or blue-collar backgrounds. Middle class, white-collar persons in Britain and the United States are more likely than working-class, blue-collar persons to have only a few children and to live at a greater distance from their children. In Denmark old people of white-collar and those of blue-collar backgrounds show no marked differences in family life.

Shanas, Ethel. "The Family and the Aged in Western Societies." *Sociological Symposium,* no. 2, Spring 1969, pp. 147-152.

Findings about the elderly and their families in five countries reveal that old persons with children maintain close contact with at least one child, and that persons with no children substitute interaction with siblings and relatives.

Shanas, Ethel. "The Family as a Social Support System in Old Age." *The Gerontologist,* 1979, 19(2), pp. 169-174.

Reports that the immediate family of the old person (husband, wife, and children) is the major social support of the elderly in times of illness.

Shanas, Ethel. "Older People and Their Families: The New Pioneers." *Journal of Marriage and the Family,* 1980, 42(1), pp. 9-15.

Considers the relationship of older people and their families in our society. Discusses the physical proximity of older persons to their families, family help patterns, and four-generation families.

Shanas, Ethel, and Sussman, Marvin B. (Eds.). *Family, Bureaucracy, and the Elderly.* Durham, N.C.: Duke University Press, 1977.

Focuses on the linkage of older persons and their families to bureaucratic systems. The underlying theme is that the elderly are part of a family and kin network that performs a mediating and supportive role for them in their dealings with bureaucracies.

Shanas, Ethel, and Sussman, Marvin B. "Family and Bureaucracy: Comparative Analyzes and Problematics." In Ethel Shanas and Marvin B. Sussman (Eds.), *Family, Bureaucracy and the Elderly.* Durham, N.C.: Duke University Press, 1977, pp. 215-225.

Discusses some of the material in previous chapters and indicates the need for corrective influences on the isolation and exercise of power in the linkages of bureaucracies and families.

Sheehan, Robert. "Young Children's Contact with the Elderly." *Journal of Gerontology,* 1978, 33(4), pp. 567-574.

Examines the frequency of contact between young children and the elderly as well as the children's ability to identify older persons. Demonstrates that a significant proportion of the children interact with older persons, mainly grandparents and great-grandparents at least 52 times a year. This frequency of contact is related to the children's ability to identify older persons.

Sherman, Susan R. "Mutual Assistance and Support in Retirement Housing." *Journal of Gerontology,* 1975, 30(4), pp. 479-483.

Compared networks of mutual assistance for the elderly living in retirement housing with those elderly living in conventional housing. Retirement housing residents do not suffer from a lack of assistance from children but neither do they benefit overall from greater assistance from neighbors.

Smith, Harold E. "Family Interaction Patterns of the Aged: A Review." In Arnold M. Rose and Warren A. Peterson (Eds.), *Older People and Their Social World.* Philadelphia: F.A. Davis, 1965, pp. 143-161.

Provides a summary of some of the hypotheses, generalizations, and conclusions relating to the kinship-family structure.

Smith, Kristen F., and Bengtson, Vern L. "Positive Consequences of Institutionalization: Solidarity between Elderly Parents and Their Middle-Aged Children." *The Gerontologist,* 1979, 19(5), pp. 438-447.

Based on interviews with institutionalized elderly parents and their adult children, this study indicates that in only about 10 percent of parent-child combinations does institutionalization have a negative effect on their relationship. Finds that in the majority of families the elderly parents' institutionalization strengthens ties and renews closeness between parent and child.

Stinnett, Nick; Collins, Janet; and Montgomery, James E. "Marital Need Satisfaction of Older Husbands and Wives." *Journal of Marriage and the Family,* 1970, 32(3), pp. 428-434.

Deals with the measurement of marital satisfaction of older husbands and wives. Using the Marital Need Satisfaction Scale, this study finds that marital need satisfaction is associated with sex, amount of contact with children, perceived happiness of marriage, and the perception of whether the marriage has improved or declined over time.

Stone, Carol. "Three-Generation Influences on Teen-Agers Conceptions of Family Culture Patterns and Parent-Child Relationships." *Marriage and Family Living,* 1962, 24(3), pp. 287-293.

Focuses on the family interaction patterns and social adjustment of teen-agers living in families containing both parents and grandparents. The findings indicate no consistent differences in patterns of family interaction between three- and two-generation families. The teen-agers in three-generation families appear to be slightly more socially active than those in two-generation families.

Streib, Gordon F., and Thompson, Wayne E. "The Older Person in a Family Context." In Clark Tibbitts (Ed.), *Handbook of Social Gerontology.* Chicago: The University of Chicago Press, 1960, pp. 447-488.

Deals primarily with the older person's role in the family and the perspective of the older generation.

Streib, Gordon F. "Intergenerational Relations: Perspectives of the Two Generations on the Older Parent." *Journal of Marriage and the Family,* 1965, 27(4), pp. 469-476.

Finds there is a tendency for retirees to place more emphasis on the ties of affection between themselves and their adult children than the children do. Also financial assistance tends to flow from the parent to the child. Lastly, the data indicate that retirement may not necesarily have a deleterious effect on family relations.

Streib, Gordon F. "Old Age and the Family: Facts and Forecasts." *American Behavioral Scientist,* 1970, 14(1), pp. 25-39.

Points to three problem areas in which the elderly have little or no control: inflation, declining health, and for the women, widowhood. In the future Streib sees more old people living apart from children and relatives, and more living in age-segregated communities.

Streib, Gordon F. "Older Families and Their Troubles: Familial and Social Responses." *The Family Coordinator,* 1972, 21(1), pp. 5-19.

Examines some of the ways in which primary groups and bureaucratic organizations may share functions in meeting family problems.

Streib, Gordon F. "Bureaucracies and Families: Common Themes and Directions for Further Study." In Ethel Shanas and Marvin B. Sussman (Eds.), *Family, Bureaucracy and the Elderly.* Durham, N.C.: Duke University Press, 1977, pp. 204-214.

Comments upon the descriptions of family-bureaucracy relationships in six cultures. Notes that as societies move from an underdeveloped economic state to one of modernization, they face similar problems concerning the family and bureaucracy.

Streib, Gordon F., and Beck, Rubye W. "Older Families: A Decade Review." *Journal of Marriage and the Family,* 1980, 42(4), pp. 937-956.

Reviews the literature on older families in the decade of the seventies and includes some newer areas of research such as older ethnic families, and law and the older family. According to the authors, the area of family-bureaucratic linkages will provide some of the most challenging research opportunities in the future.

Sussman, Marvin B. "Relationships of Adult Children with Their Parents in the United States." In Ethel Shanas and Gordon F. Streib (Eds.), *Social Structure and the Family: Generational Relations.* Englewood Cliffs, N.J.: Prentice-Hall, 1965, pp. 62-92.

Demonstrates that adult children have important social relationships with their aged parents. Kin networks in urban society are widespread and are important for the provision of material and nonmaterial mutual aid. Studies reveal that the flow of aid tends to be mainly from parents to children.

Sussman, Marvin B. "Family Relations and the Aged." In Adeline M.Hoffman (Ed.), *The Daily Needs and Interests of Older People.* Springfield, Ill.: Charles C. Thomas, 1970, pp. 300-324.

Emphasizes the importance of the family as a viable structure in which the elderly members can find support and participate in useful and satisfying ways. In addition, the family-kin network can serve as a mediator between the aged person and other societal institutions.

Sussman, Marvin B. "The Family Life of Old People." In Robert H. Binstock and Ethel Shanas (Eds.), *Handbook of Aging and the Social Sciences.* New York: Van Nostrand Reinhold, 1976, pp. 218-243.

The family life of the elderly is explained in terms of historic and ongoing changes in family structure, the behavior of family members, and the factors which have an impact on the quality of life of older persons.

Sussman, Marvin B. "Family, Bureaucracy, and the Elderly Individual: An Organizational/Linkage Perspective." In Ethel Shanas and Marvin B. Sussman (Eds.), *Family, Bureaucracy, and the Elderly.* Durham, N.C.: Duke University Press, 1977, pp. 2-20.

Uses the conceptual framework of the exchange theory to analyze the facilitating roles the family and kin networks perform for the elderly members in dealings with bureaucratic organizations.

Sussman, Marvin B., and Burchinal, Lee. "Kin Network: Unheralded Structure in Current Conceptualizations of Family Functioning." *Marriage and Family Living,* 1962, 24(3), pp. 231-240.

Reviews theory and conclusions derived from research on kin family networks. Gives suggestions for modifications of existing theory on the isolated nuclear family.

Sussman, Marvin B., and Burchinal, Lee. "Parental Aid to Married Children: Implications for Family Functioning." *Marriage and Family Living,* 1962, 24(4), pp. 320-332.

Examines financial aid exchanged between parents and their married children. In the early years of the child's marriage, the flow of aid is from parents to children. As children become middle-aged, the flow of aid may be reversed. Also middle-class, middle-aged children may be helping young, married children and aged parents at the same time.

Thompson, Wayne E., and Streib, Gordon F. "Meaningful Activity in a Family Context." In Robert W. Kleemeier (Ed.), *Aging and Leisure,* New York: Oxford University Press, 1961, pp. 177-211.

Describes the family of the later years and its relevance to the question of how people use their leisure time.

Thompson, Wayne E., and Streib, Gordon F. "Meaningful Activity in a Family Context." In Clark Tibbitts and Wilma Donahue (Eds.), *Social and Psychological Aspects of Aging.* New York: Columbia University Press, 1962, pp. 905-912.

Describes the varying family contexts at different stages of the family cycle.

Treas, Judith. "Aging and the Family." In Diana S. Woodruff and James E. Birren (Eds.), *Aging: Scientific Perspectives and Social Issues.* New York: D. Van Nostrand Co., 1975, pp. 92-108.

Discusses the relationship of older persons to their extended kin network and the conjugal family of parents and dependent children sharing a common household.

Treas, Judith. "Family Support Systems for the Aged: Some Social and Demographic Considerations." *The Gerontologist,* 1977, 17(6), pp. 486-491.

Financial support of the aged no longer rests solely with younger family members but has shifted to a broader societal base. As a result, this shift reduces the dependence of the old on the family support systems. Also discusses the future of the family support systems for the elderly.

Treas, Judith, and Vanhilst Anke. "Marriage and Remarriage Rates among Older Americans." *The Gerontologist,* 1976, 16(2), pp. 132-136.

The low rates for marriages in late life have not changed over the last decade and are not expected to change in the future. Old age poses many limitations to marriage. Not only is there a scarcity of older men which limits the older woman's choice of a partner, but our society discourages late-life marriages and remarriages.

Trela, James E., and Jackson, David J. "Family Life and Community Participation in Old Age." *Research on Aging,* 1979, 1(2), pp. 233-251.

Investigates the relationship between family role-playing opportunities and community participation. The results suggest that in some cases we can conceive of community roles as substitutions for family roles. Also loss of the role of spouse appears to restructure the value of the family and community roles.

Troll, Lillian E. "Issues in the Study of Generations." *Aging and Human Development,* 1970, 1(3), pp. 199-218.

Discusses concepts of generation and related general issues. The author stresses the need for the study of generations not only to be focused on social change, but on development over the entire life span.

Troll, Lillian E. "The Family of Later Life: A Decade Review." *Journal of Marriage and the Family,* 1971, 33(2), pp. 263-290.

Reviews the literature on the family which has appeared mainly in the 1960s in the areas of sociology and social psychology.

Troll, Lillian E. "The 'Generation Gap' in Later Life: An Introductory Discussion and Some Preliminary Findings." *Sociological Focus,* 1971, 5(1), pp. 18-28.

Deals with generational similarities that exist in later life with an emphasis on the family. Some preliminary findings on a three-generation sample indicate that older people are more conventionally moral than younger people. Husbands and wives are most alike, but their children are more like them than their peers. Finally, the greatest similarity was between the grandparent and middle-aged parent.

Troll, Lillian E. "Intergenerational Relations in Later Life: A Family Systems Approach." In Nancy Datan and Nancy Lohmann (Eds.), *Transitions of Aging.* New York: Academic Press, 1980, pp. 75-91.

Since all generations in a family share perceptions of how aging should go, which is based upon models presented by previous family members who grew old, Troll points to some of the advantages in applying a system approach to the study of intergenerational relations.

Troll, Lillian E., and Bengtson, Vern L. "Generations in the Family." In Wesley R. Burr, et al. (Eds.), *Contemporary Theories about the Family,* vol. 1. New York: The Free Press, 1979, pp. 127-161.

Evaluates the findings about generations from the perspective of the family. Suggests some propositions which are supported by existing research for use in research and theory building.

Troll, Lillian E.; Miller, Shelia J.; and Atchley, Robert C. *Families in Later Life.* Belmont, Calif.: Wadsworth, 1979.

Provides both a synthesis and review of the literature and research pertaining to the family of later life. It deals with a variety of family relationships including older couples, being unmarried in later life, parents and their adult children, and being a grandparent or a great-grandparent.

Turner, Joseph G. "Patterns of Intergeneration Exchange: A Developmental Approach." *International Journal of Aging and Human Development,* 1975, 6(2), pp. 111-115.

Discusses the existence of definitive patterns of intergenerational exchange and how they operate between generations.

Wake, Sandra B., and Sporakowski, Michael J. "An Intergenerational Comparison of Attitudes towards Supporting Aged Parents." *Journal of Marriage and the Family,* 1972, 34(1), pp. 42-48.

Studies generational differences between students and their parents regarding filial responsibilities. The findings reveal that students show more willingness to support aged parents than their parents. Also there are greater differences in religious affiliation within-generations for parents than for students or between generations.

Ward, Russell A. "The Never-Married in Later Life." *Journal of Gerontology,* 1979, 34(6), pp. 861-869.

Examines the consequences of lifelong singlehood for 162 persons aged 50 and over. The findings indicate that education beyond high school for females is associated with being single. Also the loss of the work role is more consequential for the never-married who lack family to fall back on. Compared to married older persons, those that remain single do not belong to more organizations, and do not see friends and neighbors much more often. The never-married are less happy and more vulnerable than the married, and in some ways seem to be better off than the widowed or divorced.

Wood, Vivan, and Robertson, Joan F. "The Significance of Grandparenthood." In Jaber F. Gubrium (Ed.), *Time, Roles, and Self in Old Age.* New York: Human Sciences Press, 1976, pp. 278-304.

Suggests that grandchildren appear to be significant to older persons because they provide a primary group reference. Also grandparents do not seem to expect tangible commitments from their grandchildren, and appear to be content with only a small amount of interest and concern from them.

Youmans, Grant E. "Family Disengagement among Older Urban and Rural Women." *Journal of Gerontology,* 1967, 22(2), pp. 209-211.

Compares samples of older and younger urban women, and older and younger rural women to determine the extent of disengagement in their family life. The findings reveal evidence of disengagement but only in the rural areas. Older rural women visit less often than younger women with their children, and give less help to their brothers and sisters.

B. Friendship

Arth, Malcolm J. "American Culture and the Phenomenon of Friendship in the Aged." *The Gerontologist,* 1961, 1(4), pp. 168-170.

Men seem to have fewer close friendships than women. Men often name their wives as their best friends, but wives seldom designate their husbands.

Arth, Malcolm J. "American Culture and the Phenomenon of Friendship in the Aged." In Clark Tibbitts and Wilma Donahue (Eds.), *Social and Psychological Aspects of Aging.* New York: Columbia University Press, 1962, pp. 529-534.

Deals with the depth or limits of close friendships among the elderly. Describes three such studies by the author and discusses some implications.

Blau, Zena Smith. "Structural Constraints on Friendships in Old Age." *American Sociological Review,* 1961, 26(3), pp. 429-439.

Examines how widowhood and retirement affect the friendships of older people. Results reveal that in those groups in which being widowed or retired is a relatively rare status, the person who is widowed or retired is placed in a deviant position among his or her peers which has an adverse effect on friendships. But in those contexts in which being widowed or retired is a fairly common status, then those persons who are still married or working occupy a deviant position and see less of old friends.

Cantor, Marjorie H. "Neighbors and Friends: An Overlooked Resource in the Informal Support System." *Research on Aging,* 1979, 1(4), pp. 434-463.

Examines the extent to which the elderly of the inner-city neighborhoods of New York City have an informal network of neighbors and friends, and the type of interactions which occur. Kin are considered the primary source of help, regardless of the task. Only when family are not available do friends, neighbors, and formal organizations become important in the provision of informal social supports.

Dowd, James J. "Exchange Rates and Old People." *Journal of Gerontology,* 1980, 35(4), pp. 596-602.

Reviews and applies some concepts derived from exchange theory. Indicates some ways in which these concepts can increase our understanding of the elderly's social behavior, especially as their behavior relates to age-conscious social movements and age-segregated friendship patterns.

Hess, Beth. "Friendship." In Matilda W. Riley, Marilyn Johnson, and Anne Foner, *Aging and Society: A Sociology of Age Stratification,* vol. 3. New York: Russell Sage Foundation, 1972, pp. 357-393.

Describes how the ages of individuals can have an important bearing on their friendships. Discusses how age can affect the choice of friends, the kinds of relationships between friends at various ages, and the conditions under which friendships are formed or dissolved.

Hess, Beth B. "Sex Roles, Friendship, and the Life Course." *Research on Aging,* 1979, 1(4), pp. 494-515.

Reviews the research on friendship and aging and discusses the nature of friendship in old age as it differs by sex.

Lowenthal, Marjorie F., and Haven, Clayton. "Interaction and Adaptation: Intimacy As a Critical Variable." *American Sociological Review,* 1968, 33(1), pp. 20-30.

Reveals that the presence of an intimate relationship, such as a confidant, serves as a buffer against gradual role losses, and against the more traumatic losses accompanying widowhood and retirement.

Mancini, Jay A. "Friend Interaction, Competence, and Morale in Old Age." *Research on Aging,* 1980, 2(4), pp. 416-431.

Examines the importance of friendship to successful aging. The findings indicate that morale is positively associated with friend-role competence. Those with higher morale scores define themselves as more active and competent as friends.

Powers, Edward A., and Bultena, Gordon L. "Sex Differences in Intimate Friendships of Old Age." *Journal of Marriage and the Family,* 1976, 38(4), pp. 739-746.

Indicates that the social contacts of older men and women differ in that men are less likely than women to have intimate friends, and are less likely to replace lost friends. Men limit their interaction to family and friends, whereas women have a more diverse social world.

Rooney, James F. "Friendship and Disaffilitation among the Skid Row Population." *Journal of Gerontology,* 1976, 31(1), pp. 82-88.

Interview data from 304 skid row men shows that old friends are replaced by new friends chosen from skid row. After the age of 70, there is a decline in the number of friendships one has, but this is associated more with length of skid row residence than with age.

Rosenberg, George S. "Age, Poverty, and Isolation from Friends in the Urban Working Class." *Journal of Gerontology,* 1968, 23(4), pp. 533-538.

Investigates the relationship between poverty, aging, and isolation from friends. The findings indicate that men over 65, whether poor or solvent, living in neighborhoods where their wealth, occupation, or race differs from that of their neighbors, tend to be isolated from friends.

Wood, Vivan, and Robertson, Joan F. "Friendship and Kinship Interaction: Differential Effect on the Morale of the Elderly." *Journal of Marriage and the Family,* 1978, 40(2), pp. 367-375.

Focuses on the differential effect of kinship and friendship relationships on the morale of older people. The findings reveal that friends are more important than grandchildren for maintaining morale in the later years.

Rosow, Irving. "Old People: Their Friends and Neighbors." *American Behavioral Scientist,* 1970, 14(1), pp. 59-69.

Reviews some of the major features of the elderly's relations with their friends and neighbors. Shows that residential segregation increases the social integration of the elderly.

Rosow, Irving. *Social Integration of the Aged.* New York: The Free Press, 1967.

This study of older middle-class and working-class residents living in apartment buildings in Cleveland deals with friendship and social class. Findings show that the number of older people's local friends varies with the proportion of older neighbors. The friends of older persons consist disproportionately of older rather than younger neighbors. Also middle-class persons have more friends than those in the working class; there is a greater local dependency for friendships in the working class than in the middle class.

Chapter 11

RELIGION AND EDUCATION

A. Religion

Bahr, Howard. "Aging and Religious Disaffiliation." *Social Forces,* 1970, 49(1), pp. 59-71.

Based on samples from skid row, the urban-lower class, and the upper-middle class, this paper investigates the relation between aging, church attendance, and affiliation in voluntary associations. The findings indicate that substantial religious disaffiliation occurs during later adult life. With age church attendance becomes less important as a source of voluntary affiliation among both the well-to-do and the poor.

Blazer, Dan, and Palmore, Erdman B. "Religion and Aging in a Longitudinal Panel." *The Gerontologist,* 1976, 16(1), pt. 1, pp. 82-85.

Reveals that religious activities such as church attendance tend to decline in late old age, while religious attitudes tend to remain fairly stable.

Buck, Charles F. "The Older Person, the Family, and Church: Selected References." *The Family Life Coordinator,* 1960, 8(4), pp. 71-77.

Provides a bibliography dealing with older persons' position in the family and ways in which community agencies and organizations, specifically religious groups and churches, can help the elderly.

Hickey, Thomas, and Kalish, Richard A. "The New Old Nuns: The Changing Life Patterns of Catholic Sisters." *The Gerontologist,* 1969, 9(3), pt. 1, pp. 170-178.

Explores the changes occurring among the different Catholic orders and the impact of these changes on elderly nuns.

Longino, Charles F., Jr., and Kitson, Gay C. "Parish Clergy and the Aged: Examining Stereotypes." *Journal of Gerontology,* 1976, 31(3), pp. 340-345.

Although clergy enjoy ministering to the elderly, they would rather teach adults and young people. Ministers who prefer expressive over instrumental role activities tend to find their contacts with the elderly more enjoyable.

Mindel, Charles H., and Vaughan, C. Edwin. "A Multidimensional Approach to Religiosity and Disengagement." *Journal of Gerontology,* 1978, 33(1), pp. 103-108.

Examines religious disaffiliation as an expression of disengagement. Analyzes religiosity in a subjective and non-organizational sense and as organized religious behavior. Findings reveal that the elderly might have disengaged from religion as a formal organizational activity, but that they continue to retain a meaningful relationship with religion in a more subjective and personal way.

Moberg, David O. "The Integration of Older Members in the Church Congregation." In Arnold M. Rose and Warren A. Peterson (Eds.), *Older People and Their Social World.* Philadelphia: F.A. Davis, 1965, pp. 125-140.

In two similar congregations, which have different programs for older members, only slight differences are found regarding elderly members. Reveals that transportation to church is a significant problem for many older people. Also more visitation by lay or professional church leaders is desired by many of the elderly, especially the shut-ins.

Moberg, David O. "Religiosity in Old Age." *The Gerontologist,* 1965, 5(2), pp. 78-87.

Indicates that in old age religious rituals outside the home tend to decrease, whereas religious feelings and attitudes apparently increase among religious people.

Moberg, David O. "Religion in the Later Years." In Adeline M. Hoffman (Ed.), *The Daily Needs and Interests of Older People.* Springfield, Ill.: Charles C. Thomas, 1970, pp. 175-191.

Discusses the functions and dysfunctions of religion and its major dimensions. Also how religious institutions serve older people as well as how older people can serve their church.

Moberg, David O. "Religion and the Aging Family." *The Family Coordinator,* 1972, 21(1), pp. 47-60.

Although church attendance tends to decrease during the later years, internalized religious attitudes tend to increase among those persons who acknowledge having a religion. Churches perform many functions such as family integration, the satisfaction of needs, and opportunities for service. However, churches can be dysfunctional at times.

Moberg, David O. "Spiritual Well-Being in Late Life." In Jaber F. Gubrium (Ed.), *Late Life: Communities and Environmental Policy.* Springfield, Ill.: Charles C. Thomas, 1974, pp. 256-279.

Discusses the nature and indicators of spiritual well-being, spiritual needs in later life, and some of the research findings on religion and aging.

Moberg, David O., and Taves, Marvin J. "Church Participation and Adjustment in Old Age." In Arnold M. Rose and Warren A. Peterson

(Eds.), *Older People and Their Social World.* Philadelphia: F.A. Davis, 1965, pp. 113-124.

Compares the adjustment of church leaders, other church members, and non-church members in four states. Indicates that church members have higher adjustment scores than non-members, and that lay leaders in the church have higher scores than other members.

Orbach, Harold L. "Aging and Religion." *Geriatrics,* 1961, 16(10), pp. 530-540.

Examines the relationship of religion and aging. Results do not support the view that people become more religious as they age.

Wingrove, C. Ray and Alston, John P. "Age, Aging, and Church Attendance." *The Gerontologist,* 1971, 2(4), pt. 1, pp. 356-358.

Although variations in church attendance are related to age, other additional factors should be considered. These include sex, specific cohort membership, and general societal environment.

Wingrove, C. Ray,and Alston, Jon P. "Cohort Analysis of Church Attendance, 1939-69." *Social Forces,* 1974, 53(2), pp. 324-331.

Presents a cohort analysis of church attendance which spans a 30-year. Indicates that while church attendance varies somewhat by age, many other factors must be taken into account.

B. Education

Bynum, Jack E.; Cooper, B.L.; and Acuff, F. Gene. "Retirement Reorientation: Senior Adult Education." *Journal of Gerontology,* 1978, 33(2), pp. 253-261.

Evaluates an educational program at a junior college which was designed to meet the needs and interests of older persons. The program appears to function successfully in easing the role transition from employment to retirement.

Covey, Herbert C. "An Exploratory Study of the Acquisition of a College Student Role by Older People." *The Gerontologist,* 1980, 20(2), pp. 173-181.

The better educated older persons have higher rates of college participation than those with less education. Reveals that special courses are not necessary for older people as they seem pleased with what is available.

Parelius, Ann P. "Lifelong Education and Age Stratification: Some Unexplored Relationships." *American Behavioral Scientist,* 1975, 19(2), pp. 206-223.

Discusses the potential impact of lifelong education from the perspective of age stratification theory.

Chapter 12

POLITICS AND THE ECONOMY

A. Politics

Agnello, Thomas J., Jr. "Aging and the Sense of Political Powerlessness." *Public Opinion Quarterly,* 1973, 37(2), pp. 251-259.

Suggests that the political powerlessness that the young feel is not only a deterrent to their voting, but may motivate them to seek new channels of influence which tend to reduce their sense of powerlessness. In contrast, the elderly having experienced the rewards of conventional political behavior in middle age, are more reluctant to seek such alternatives. Therefore, their sense of powerlessness is the highest of the other age groups despite their continued high level of voting.

Anderson, William A., and Anderson, Norma D. "The Politics of Age Exclusion: The Adult Only Movement in Arizona." *The Gerontologist,* 1978, 18(1), pp. 6-12.

As a result of the concentration of adult communities in Arizona, the authors argue that a subculture of aging is emerging in Arizona. The Adults Only Movement in Arizona, facilitated by the age consciousness of adult community residents, had sufficient strength to lobby successfully for the legislation it desired.

Bengtson, Vern L. "Comparative Perspectives on the Microsociology of Politics and Aging." In Marlene A.Y. Rifai (Ed.). *Justice and Older Americans.* Lexington, Mass.: Lexington Books, 1977, pp. 177-193.

Reports three conclusions related to ethnicity, aging and politics. First, in contrast to a homogeneous Anglo majority, Mexican-Americans and blacks do not constitute a homogeneous minority. Next, decision makers are dependent on information which is often inaccurate or very selective. Lastly, regarding the politics of aging, it is evident that the issue of responsibility and accountability is one which researchers will have to face in the future.

Binstock, Robert H. "Interest-Group Liberalism and the Politics of Aging." *The Gerontologist,* 1972, 12(3), pt. 1, pp. 265-280.

Based on Lowi's characterization of American politics, this article focuses on the ways in which the politics of aging may increase the understanding of American politics. Although the aged voter and the aging organizations have access to power and political equality with other groups, this does little to further the economic and social situation of the disadvantaged aged.

Binstock, Robert H. "Aging and the Future of American Politics." *The Annals of the Academy of Political and Social Sciences,* 1974, 415, pp. 199-212.

Through an examination of electoral politics, Binstock finds no evidence of an "aging vote" now and no reason to expect one in the future. He notes that the most likely result for aging-based interest groups in the future is that they will have the credentials to participate in politics of a broader range of forums or arenas.

Brotman, Herman B. "Voter Participation in November, 1976." *The Gerontologist,* 1977, 17(2), pp. 157-159.

Presents data on persons voting in the presidential election of 1976 by sex and age. Older people cast 16% of the votes in this election.

Campbell, Angus. "Social and Psychological Determinants of Voting Behavior." In Wilma Donahue and Clark Tibbitts (Eds.), *Politics of Age.* Ann Arbor: Division of Gerontology, University of Michigan, 1962, pp. 87-100.

Discusses the political interest, partisan attitudes and political ideologies of older persons.

Campbell, Angus. "Politics through the Life Cycle." *The Gerontologist,* 1971, 2(2), pt. 1, pp. 112-117.

Although age is associated with party identification and the party that one chooses, there is no simple relationship between age and political conservatism. At the present time, age is not a strong force in American politics and it is not likely to become such in the near future.

Carlie, Michael K. "The Politics of Age: Interest Group or Social Movement?" *The Gerontologist,* 1969, pt. 1, pp. 259-263.

Concludes that income-maintenance legislation did not stem from old-age political interest groups, but rather from organizations that were not aging-based.

Cottrell, Fred. "Governmental Functions and the Politics of Age." In Clark Tibbitts (Ed.), *Handbook of Social Gerontology.* Chicago: The University of Chicago Press, 1960, pp. 627-665.

Discusses how government has changed and is likely to change in the future in terms of what it is doing for the elderly. Cottrell also examines the ways in which the elderly are likely to modify the government.

Cottrell, Fred. "Aging and the Political System." In John C. McKinney and Frank de Vyver (Eds.), *Aging and Social Policy.* New York: Appleton-Century-Crofts, 1966, pp. 77-113.

According to the author, the aged are pushing for more than has been allotted to them in the past as their fair share. He maintains that they can threaten the balance of political power among minorities and force concessions. As a result, new bases may be emerging upon which to organize various segments of the older voting population.

Cox, Harold. "The Motivation and Political Alienation of Older Americans." *International Journal of Aging and Human Development,* 1980, 11(1), pp. 1-12.

Investigates the relationship between older persons' motivation (internally or externally oriented), and their feelings of estrangement from the political system. A strong relationship is found between external orientation and feelings of political incapability. Those persons who are externally oriented are likely to experience greater feelings of political discontentment and a greater degree of anomie.

Crittenden, John. "Aging and Party Affiliation." *Public Opinion Quarterly,* 1962, 26(1), pp. 648-657.

Shows that the aging process has an effect on party affiliation which is independent of any generational factors. Based on four nationwide surveys that span a twelve year period, the findings reveal that aging seems to produce a shift toward Republicanism in the period from 1946 to 1958.

Crittenden, John. "Aging and Political Participation." *The Western Political Quarterly,* 1963, 16(2), pp. 323-331.

Indicates that political activity and political interest remain very high well into old age. Although the evidence is not conclusive, aging seems to result in greater consistency in political attitudes.

Cutler, Neal E. "The Aging Population and Social Policy." In Richard H. David (Ed.), *Aging: Prospects and Issues,* 3d ed. Los Angeles: Ethel Percy Andrus Gerontology Center, University of Southern California, 1976, pp. 102-126.

Analyzes some of the factors underlying the "aging explosion" in this country. Discusses the fact that chronological age is not the only definition of age and may not be the best one. Considers several possible connections between population changes and social policy planning.

Cutler, Neal E. "Age and the Future of American Politics: From Bicentennial to Millenium 3." In Marlene A.Y. Rifai (Ed.), *Justice and Older Americans.* Lexington, Mass.: Lexington Books, 1977, pp. 163-176.

Discusses past and future population trends, levels of old-age political participation, organizational activity, and the influence of generational trends.

Cutler, Neal E., and Bengtson, Vern L. "Age and Politial Alienation: Maturation, Generation and Period Effects." *The Annals of the American Academy of Political and Social Sciences,* 1974, 415, pp. 160-175.

Using cohort analysis and data from three nationwide attitude surveys, this research examines political alienation from 1952 to 1968. Results reveal that political alienation decreased between 1952 and 1960 and then increased between 1960 and 1968. Period effects, not generational or maturational effects, best explain these changes in political alienation.

Cutler, Neal E., and Schmidhauser, John R. "Age and Political Behavior." In Diana S. Woodruff and James E. Birren (Eds.), *Aging: Scientific Perspectives and Social Issues.* New York: D. Van Nostrand Co., 1975, pp. 374-403.

Discusses age and political attitudes, participation, and leadership as well as the future of age in politics. Proposes two alternatives to the traditional approach in which chronological age is employed as an index of maturational change.

Cutler, Stephen J. "Perceived Prestige Loss and Political Attitudes among the Aged." *The Gerontologist,* 1973, 13(1), pp. 69-75.

The elderly who perceive themselves and other older people as having low prestige tend to support government intervention on their behalf, as well as organized political activity by the elderly to influence national policy decision-making.

Cutler, Stephen J., and Kaufman, Robert L. "Cohort Changes in Political Attitudes: Tolerance of Ideological Nonconformity." *The Public Opinion Quarterly,* 1975, 39(1), pp. 69-81.

This study of cohort changes in political attitudes reveals that although all cohorts have participated in the shift to higher levels of tolerance, this attitudinal change is not uniformly distributed. This change occurs to a greater degree among the younger cohorts than it does among the older cohorts. Therefore, the rate at which tolerant political attitudes are formed in times of increasing tolerance of ideological nonconformity appears to be slower among the older cohorts.

Donahue, Wilma and Tibbitts, Clark (Eds.). *Politics of Age.* Ann Arbor: Division of Gerontology, University of Michigan, 1962.

Contains a compilation of papers from a conference dealing with politics and the elderly.

Douglass, Elizabeth B.; Cleveland, William P.; and Maddox, George L. "Political Attitudes, Age, and Aging: A Cohort Analysis of Archival Data." *Journal of Gerontology,* 1974, 29(6), pp. 666-675.

Addresses a number of conceptual and methodological problems associated with studies of politics and age, and explores the use of archival data for cohort analysis. Suggests that relationships between political attitudes and variables such as age, historical period, and birth cohort are complex and changing.

Estes, Carroll L. "Toward a Sociology of Political Gerontology." *Sociological Symposium,* 1979, no. 26, pp. 1-27.

Examines major themes and perspectives in political gerontology and suggests directions for further research.

Foner, Anne. "The Polity." In Matilda W. Riley, Marilyn Johnson, and Anne Foner, *Aging and Society: A Sociology of Age Stratification,* vol. 3. New York: Russell Sage Foundation, 1972, pp. 115-159.

Analyzes the polity from the perspective of age stratification. Reviews the ways in which age is related to political participation, political attitudes, and the potential for conflict.

Foner, Anne. "Age Stratification and Age Conflict in Political Life." *American Sociological Review,* 1974, 39(2), pp. 187-196.

Discusses age as a basis for political conflict in modern society, and suggests that the understanding of such conflict requires a theory about the processes operating to stratify society by age.

Glenn, Norval D. "Aging, Disengagement, and Opinionation." *The Public Opinion Quarterly,* 1969, 33(1), pp. 17-33.

Tests the hypothesis that as individuals age they become less likely to hold or to express opinions to interviewers. No support for this hypothesis is found. Data from 35 American opinion surveys fail to reveal any evidence that as persons grow older, they become less interested in national and international affairs, or that they become less likely to express their opinions to interviewers for attitudinal surveys.

Glenn, Norval D. "Aging and Conservatism." *The Annals of the American Academy of Political and Social Sciences,* 1974, 415, pp. 176-186.

Cohort analysis of nationwide survey data indicates that in the last 30 years in conformity with societal trends, people have become less, rather than more, conservative as they have aged. But persons who have aged into and beyond middle age during this period have become more conservative relative to the total adult population.

Glenn, Norval D., and Grimes, Michael. "Aging, Voting, and Political Interest." *American SociologicalReview,* 1968, 33(4), pp. 563-575.

Data on political participation and interest reveals that while voter turnout remains almost constant from middle age to old age, political interest tends to increase as people grow older.

Glenn, Norval D., and Hefner, Ted. "Further Evidence on Aging and Party Identification." *Public Opinion Quarterly,* 1972, 36(1), pp. 31-47.

Using cohort analysis spanning a 23-year period, the authors find no evidence for the belief that the aging process has been an important influence of Republicanism. Their findings also cast doubt on the belief that aging individuals tend to become more conservative in their political attitudes and values.

Glenn, Norval D., and Zody, Richard E. "Cohort Analysis with National Survey Data." *The Gerontologist,* 1970, 10(3), pt. 1, pp. 233-240.

Points out how cohort analysis of existing survey sample data can be a valuable resource for social gerontologists. Reviews the procedures that must be followed in this type of analysis and provides an example of a cohort study.

Gubrium, Jaber F. "Continuity in Social Support, Political Interest, and Voting in Old Age." *The Gerontologist,* 1972, 12(4), pp. 421-423.

According to the author, changes in the social support of having or not having a spouse may influence political behavior more than aging itself.

Hudson, Robert B., and Binstock, Robert H. "Political Systems and Aging." In Robert H. Binstock and Ethel Shanas (Eds.), *Handbook of Aging and the Social Sciences.* New York: Van Nostrand Reinhold, 1976, pp. 369-400.

Discusses the political attitudes and behavior of older persons and the politics of aging-based organizations. Also considers the elderly and the future of governmental concerns.

Hudson, Robert B. "Old-Age Politics in a Period of Change." In Edgar F. Borgatta and Neil B. McCluskey (Eds.), *Aging and Society: Current Research and Policy Perspectives.* Beverly Hills, Calif.: Sage Publications, 1980.

Discusses past research in the politics of aging and the areas in need of additional exploration.

Kreps, Juanita M. "Economic Status of the Rural Aged." In E. Grant Youmans (Ed.), *Older Rural Americans.* Lexington: University of Kentucky Press, 1967, pp. 144-168.

Notes that the rural aged are one of the lowest income groups in this country. This is due, in part, to their lower educational level which is less than that of the urban aged. Examines some recent economic trends and their impact on the rural elderly.

Maddox, George L. "Will Senior Power Become a Reality?" In Lissy, Jarvik F. (Ed.). *Aging into the 21st Century: Middle-Agers Today.* New York: Gardner Press, 1978, pp. 185-196.

According to the author, the possibility of "senior power" in a political sense and a self-serving gerontocracy in the future is very low.

Miller, Arthur H.; Gurin, Patricia; and Gurin, Gerald. "Age Consciousness and Political Mobilization of Older Americans." *The Gerontologist,* 1980, 20(6), pp. 691-700.

Finds a negative correlation between age identification and political participation. The lack of resources, especially economic ones, a belief that the groups with which the elderly identify cannot increase their power in society, and a sense of personal powerlessness all tend to deter political participation among the elderly.

Parsons, Talcott. "The Cultural Background of Today's Aged." In Wilma Donahue and Clark Tibbitts (Eds.), *Politics of Age.* Ann Arbor: Division of Gerontology, University of Michigan Press, 1962, pp. 3-15.

Gives some background considerations concerning the problem of the political aspects of aging along with a comparison of some characteristics of our society with those that have existed in other societies.

Pratt, Henry J. *The Gray Lobby.* Chicago: The University of Chicago Press, 1976.

Analyzes the modern senior movement. Describes how aging has emerged as a public-agenda priority and has gained policy-system status.

Ragan, Pauline K. and Dowd, James J. "The Emerging Political Consciousness of the Aged: A Generational Interpretation." *Journal of Social Issues,* 1974, 30(3), pp. 137-158.

Presents a model of participation in political movements. Specifies that a social movement of the elderly will not emerge unless political consciousness among older persons develops. According to the authors, this political consciousness should emerge within the next decade. In comparison with today's elderly, tomorrow's elderly will be a more cohesive and powerful political force.

Rose, Arnold M. "Organizations for the Elderly: Political Implications." In Wilma Donahue and Clark Tibbitts (Eds.), *Politics of Age.* Ann Arbor: Division of Gerontology, University of Michigan, 1962, pp. 135-145.

Rose delineates five forms of political activity among the elderly, and offers some observations to provide a framework for their study.

Rule, Wilma L.B. "Political Alienation and Votiung Attitudes among the Elderly Generation." *The Gerontologist,* 1977, 17(5), pp. 400-404.

Investigates the paradox between high alienation and high voting rates. The analysis shows that alienation is composed of two dimensions--inefficacy and cynicism. The inefficacious elderly are the nonvoters in the sample while the cynical elderly vote. The study concludes that attitudes toward voting mediate between cynicism, inefficacy, and the act of voting.

Schmidhauser, John. "The Political Influence of the Aged." *The Gerontologist,* 1968, 8(1), pt. 2, pp. 44-49.

Provides a discussion of the political role of the elderly and stresses the need for research on the political behavior of older persons.

Schmidhauser, John R. "The Elderly and Politics." In Adeline M. Hoffman (Ed.), *The Daily Needs and Interests of Older People.* Springfield, Ill.: Charles C. Thomas, 1970, pp. 70-82.

Discusses the concentration of the elderly, their sense of political efficacy, and older voter behavior.

Sheppard, Harold L. "Relationship of an Aging Population to Employment and Occupational Structure." *Social Problems,* 1960, 8(2), pp. 159-162.

Examines the problems resulting from the changes in the demographic and employment trends in our society.

Sheppard, Harold L. "Implications of an Aging Population for Political Sociology." In Wilma Donahue and Clark Tibbitts (Eds.), *Politics of Age.* Ann Arbor: Division of Gerontology, University of Michigan, 1962, pp. 3-15.

The primary purpose of this paper is to stimulate an interest in studies of relevant demographic trends among the elderly.

Tissue, Thomas. "Old Age and the Perception of Poverty." *Sociology and Social Research,* 1971, 56(3), pp. 331-344.

Based on a sample of aged welfare recipients, the subjective responses to poverty are studied. Results suggest that there is considerable dissatisfaction with the welfare standard of living. Finds a significant relationship between morale and the perception of money problems.

Torres-Gil, Fernando, and Becarra, Rosina M. "The Political Behavior of the Mexican-American Elderly." *The Gerontologist,* 1977, 17(5), pp. 392-399.

Finds the elderly Mexican-American's political activity to be low and which is reflected in their low sense of efficacy. Their low level of political activity is attributed, in part, to low socioeconomic status, and language and cultural barriers.

Trela, James E. "Some Political Consequences of Senior Centers and Other Old Age Group Memberships." *The Gerontologist,* 1971, 2(2), pt. 1, pp. 118-123.

Senior citizen centers and other old age organizations, although largely recreational, provide a context for political exchange and heightened political consciousness.

Trela, James E. "Age Structure of Voluntary Associations and Political Self-Interest among the Aged." *The Sociological Quarterly,* 1972, 13(2), pp. 244-258.

Examines whether there is a relationship between the age structure of voluntary-association ties and sentiments of political self-interest among the elderly. Indicates that desire for political changes to benefit the elderly, and willingness to engage in behavior to secure change were greatest among members of age-graded associations, and lowest among the elderly with mixed-generational memberships.

Trela, James E. "Status Inconsistency and Political Action in Old Age." In Jaber F. Gubrium (Ed.), *Time, Roles, and Self in Old Age.* New York: Human Sciences Press, 1976, pp. 126-147.

Develops a framework in order to view the process of aging in terms of status consistency theory. This framework is then used to explore the effects of the aging experience on political attitudes and beliefs, and to analyze the potential of the aged for unified political action.

Trela, James E. "Social Class and Political Involvement in Age Graded and Non-Age Graded Associations." *International Journal of Aging and Human Development,* 1977-1978, 8(4), pp. 301-309.

Examines the relationship between social and political activity among retired persons with different age-related patterns of association membership. Findings reveal that for individuals who belong to non-age-graded associations, there are smaller class differences in political involvement. Also class differences disappear among members of age-graded associations exclusively.

Turk, Herman; Smith, Joel; Myers, Howard. "Understanding Local Political Behavior: The Role of the Older Citizen." In Ida H. Simpson and

John C. McKinney (Eds.), *Social Aspects of Aging.* Durham, N.C.: Duke University Press, 1966, pp. 254-276.

Suggests that older persons act and think differently from younger persons on the local political scene only insofar as they are less a part of the total community. When given equal membership, the findings indicate that the paradoxical political role of the elderly might disappear.

Turner, Barbara F. and Kahn, Robert L. "Age as a Political Issue." *Journal of Gerontology,* 1974, 29(5), pp. 572-580.

Examines the role of age as a political issue in an election between a 40-year-old challenger and an 84-year-old incumbent. Finds that the age of the two candidates did not significantly influence candidate preference.

B. Economy

Brotman, Herman B. "Income and Poverty in the Older Population in 1975." *The Gerontologist,* 1977, 17(1), pp. 23-26.

Tables show the median income and income distribution of older families and unrelated individuals, as well as the number and proportion of persons in households with incomes below the poverty level.

Clemente, Frank, and Summers, Gene F. "Industrial Development and the Elderly: A Longitudinal Analysis." *Journal of Gerontology,* 1973, 28(4), pp. 479-483.

Studies the effect of industrial development in a small community upon the elderly over a five-year period. Results show that such development is associated with a decline in the economic status of the older residents, especially the retirees.

Goldstein, Sidney. "Negro-White Differentials in Consumer Patterns of the Aged, 1960-1961." *The Gerontologist,* 1971, 2(3), pt. 1, pp. 242-249.

In comparing the income, expenditure, and savings patterns of aged white and black consumers, this study documents the disadvantaged position of the black aged. Important differences characterize the expenditure dimension of the consumer behavior of the two groups.

Cottrell, Fred. "The Technological and Societal Basis of Aging." In Clark Tibbitts (Ed.), *Handbook of Social Gerontology.* Chicago: The University of Chicago Press, 1960, pp. 92-119.

Examines how the development of high energy technologies, associated with the rise of industrialization, has led to a more complex social organization and a change in age-determined social roles.

Havighurst, Robert J. "The Future Aged: The Use of Time and Money." *The Gerontologist,* 1975, 15(1), pt. 2, pp. 10-15.

Gives projections about the use of free time and the economic status of the elderly.

Kreps, Juanita M. "Economic Status of the Rural Aged." In E. Grant Youmans (Ed.), *Older Rural Americans.* Lexington: University of Kentucky Press, 1967, pp. 144-168.

Notes that the rural aged are one of the lowest income groups in this country. The rural elderly's low-income level is due, in part, to their educational level which is less than that of the urban aged. Examines some recent economic trends and their impact on the rural elderly.

Liang, Jersey, and Fairchild, Thomas J. "Relative Deprivation and the Perception of Financial Adequacy among the Aged." *Journal of Gerontology,* 1979, 34(5), pp. 746-759.

Using a relative deprivation model to account for the perceived financial adequacy among the elderly, this analysis indicates that objective income only influences financial satisfaction in an indirect way. Feelings of relative deprivation in reference to others and to previous situations are factors which mediate between objective status and financial satisfaction.

Laing, Jersey; Kahana, Eva; and Doherty, Edmund. "Financial Well-Being among the Aged: A Further Elaboration." *Journal of Gerontology,* 1980, 35(3), pp. 409-420.

Reveals that the elderly's financial well-being is directly affected by relative deprivation and distributive justice and that it is indirectly influenced by social status and labor force participation. In addition, race and age are found to be significantly related to social comparison and financial satisfaction.

Peterson, David A. "Financial Adequacy in Retirement: Perceptions of Older Americans." *The Gerontologist,* 1972, 12(4), pp. 379-383.

In a survey of 462 older persons, over half perceived their current financial situation as inadequate, regardless of income level. The average older person felt his or her income would need to be increased by 33% to be adequate.

Zimmerman, Michael. "Old Age Poverty in Preindustrial New York City." In Bess B. Hess (Ed.), *Growing Old in America.* New Brunswick, N.J.: Transaction Books, 1976, pp. 81-104.

Using data from the past, the author's findings contradict some commonly held beliefs about the historical family in this country. His evidence reveals that a substantial proportion of the aged in New

York City in the early nineteenth century were not cared for by their families and were in need of assistance.

Chapter 13

WORK, RETIREMENT, AND LEISURE

A. Work

Bauder, Ward W., and Doerflinger, Jon A. "Work Roles among the Rural Aged." In E. Grant Youmans (Ed.), *Older Rural Americans.* Lexington: University of Kentucky Press, 1967, pp. 22-43.

Analyzes the work roles of the rural elderly. Focuses on the rural-urban differences in work, labor force participation, and retirement patterns.

Carp, Frances M. "Differences among Older Workers, Volunteers, and Persons Who Are Neither." *Journal of Gerontology,* 1968, 23(4), pp. 497-501.

Compares persons who continue to work past retirement age or are involved in some volunteer community service with those persons who do neither. Results reveal that paid work has a powerful influence on happiness, self-esteem, and relationships with other people. Persons who are involved in community service are not any happier, have no better self-concepts and social relationships than did those who neither worked nor did volunteer community service.

Clemente, Frank, and Summers, Gene F. "Age and the Journey to Work." *The Gerontologist,* 1974, 14(3), pp. 215-216.

The hypothesis that there is an inverse relationship between age and distance traveled to work is not supported by the data. However, the authors view their findings as tentative because of the limitations of their analysis.

Cohn, Richard M. "Age and the Satisfactions from Work." *Journal of Gerontology,* 1979, 34(2), pp. 264-272.

Indicates that there is a decline in the importance of intrinsic work satisfactions for the well-being of the older worker. These satisfactions do not seem to contribute to overall life satisfaction during the decades before normal retirement, and it is this change in the importance of intrinsic job satisfactions which allows for early retirement.

Cole, Stephen. "Age and Scientific Performance." *American Journal of Sociology,* 1979, 84(4), pp. 958-977.

Examines the association between age, scientific productivity, and creativity. Data from academic scientists in six different fields reveal that age has only a minor influence on scientific performance.

Goldstein, Sidney. "Socio-Economic and Migration Differentials between the Aged in the Labor Force and in the Labor Reserve." *The Gerontologist,* 1967, 7(1), pp. 31-40 and p. 79.

Indicates that older persons in high white-collar positions display the greatest tendency toward continued labor force participation. Also higher proportions of those with a college education continue working. But regardless of labor force status, the aged manifest a high degree of residential stability.

Doudy, Willis J.; Powers, Edward A.; and Keith, Patricia. "Work and Retirement: A Test of Attitudinal Relationships." *Journal of Gerontology,* 1975, 30(2), pp. 193-198.

Analyzes the relationship between work satisfaction and retirement attitudes. The results offer only marginal support for an inverse relationship between work satisfaction and retirement attitudes.

Holden, Karen C. "Comparability of the Measured Labor Force of Older Women in Japan and the United States." *Journal of Gerontology,* 1978, 33(3), pp. 422-426.

Older women in Japan are more likely to be employed than women in the U.S., but labor force data for the two countries are not entirely comparable. One reason for this problem of comparability is the difference in the definition of unpaid family workers in the two countries which contributes to the higher measured labor force participation in Japan, especially of the women and elderly. Another reason is that the Japanese census is taken during one of the peak agricultural seasons. Although older women are more likely to be only part-time and seasonal workers at this period, they report themselves as working because of instructions to do so.

Jaslow, Philip. "Employment, Retirement, and Morale among Older Women." *Journal of Gerontology,* 1976, 31(2), pp. 212-218.

Tests the hypothesis that older working women have better morale than those who do not work. With the exception of retired women with annual incomes of $5,000 or more, the study finds that employed women have higher morale than retirees. Those women who never worked have the lowest morale.

Keith, Patricia M.;Goudy, Willis J.; and Powers, Edward A. "Work-Nonwork Orientations among Older Men in Nonmetropolitan Communities." *Sociological Symposium,* 1979, no. 26, pp. 83-101.

Investigates work-nonwork orientations of males 50 years of age and older living in small towns. Research reveals that while work is of central importance in the lives of professionals and entrepreneurs, self-employment does not seem to be the crucial determinant. Even though type of occupation is associated with work orientation, occupation has an independent influence on nonwork activities.

Lopata, Helena Z., and Steinhart, Frank. "Work Histories of American Urban Women." *The Gerontologist,* 1971, 2(4), pt. 2, pp. 27-36.

Notes that the American social system has failed to prepare women for employment. Also much of the social science literature concerning occupations deals with male work histories and neglects those of females.

Murray, James R.; Powers, Edward A.; and Havighurst, Robert J. "Personal and Situational Factors Producing Flexible Careers." *The Gerontologist,* 1971, 2(4), pt. 2, pp. 4-12.

Provides a conceptual framework for the analysis of career changes between the ages of 40 and 65 as well as an instrument to study work and leisure at these ages.

Powers, Edward A., and Gourdy, Willis J. "Examination of the Meaning of Work to Older Workers." *Aging and Human Development,* 1971, 2(1), pp. 38-45.

Indicates that while work is a means for earning a living for a sizable number of older workers, there is still a minority for whom work serves more than an economic function. No major differences are found between age cohorts in the willingness of older workers to accept a hypothetical offer of an annuity up to the traditional age of retirement. After age 65, workers are much less willing to accept the hypothetical offer.

Rosenberg, George S. *The Worker Grows Old.* San Francisco: Jossey-Bass, 1970.

Based on a sample of white working-class persons between the ages of 45 to 79, this study examines the relationships betwen poverty, old age, and social isolation from friends and kin. Finds that age and poverty as well as widowhood and retirement were unrelated to kin contact. A larger proportion of younger than of older workers report that there is a closed-class system. Also older men who live in the poorest neighborhoods are more likely to have a conception of a closed-class system.

Schrank, Harris. "The Work Force." In Matilda W. Riley, Marilyn Johnson, and Anne Foner, *Aging and Society: A Sociology of Age Stratification,* vol. 3. New York: Russell Sage Foundation, 1972, pp. 160-197.

Applies the conceptual model of age stratification to the work force and focuses on the allocation process.

Seltzer, Mildred M., and Atchley, Robert C. "The Impact of Structural Integration into the Profession on Work Commitment, Potential for Disengagement, and Leisure Preferences among Social Workers." *Sociological Focus,* 1971, 5(1), pp. 9-17.

Examines work commitment, potential for disengagement, and leisure preferences among chapter presidents of the National Association of Social Workers and near-retired and retired social workers. Results reveal that although about 94% of the social workers have a high level of work commitment, there is a high potential for disengagement in about 60% of them. Findings also show that a high autonomous leisure preference is associated with age.

Sheppard, Harold L. (Ed.). *Towards an Industrial Gerontology,* Cambridge, Mass.: Schenkman Publishing Co., 1970.

Contains papers from a seminar on industrial gerontology employment problems of older workers.

Wedderburn, Dorothy. "Prospects for the Reorganization of Work." *The Gerontologist,* 1975, 15(3), pp. 236-241.

Stresses the need for positive intervention because the institutional factors influencing the elderly's situation are becoming more complex and increasingly beyond the individual's control.

Wright, James D., and Hamilton, Richard F. "Work Satisfaction and Age: Some Evidence for the 'Job Change' Hypothesis." *Social Forces,* 1978, 56(4), pp. 1140-1158.

Attempts to evaluate three competing answers to the question of why younger workers are relatively less satisfied than older workers. According to the evidence, the most plausible reason for older workers being more satisfied is that they have better jobs.

B. Retirement

Acuff, Gene, and Allen, Donald. "Hiatus in 'Meaning': Disengagement for Retired Professors." *Journal of Gerontology,* 1970, 25(2), pp. 126-128.

The Purpose in Life Scale was administered to emeritus professors in a southwestern state. Meaningful retirement for them includes continued professional involvement, contact with the extended family, good health, and a personal religious philosophy.

Albrecht, Ruth. "Pre-Retirement Training in the United States." *Sociological Symposium,* no. 1, Spring 1969, pp. 15-21.

Discusses some concepts, theories, and practies regarding pre-retirement training.

Atchley, Robert C. "Retirement and Work Orientation." *The Gerontologist,* 1971, 2(1), pt. 1, pp. 29-32.

Indicates that only a small minority of the respondents carry a high degree of work orientation over into retirement. Most of the retirees show a low degree of work orientation.

Atchley, Robert C. "The Meaning of Retirement." *Journal of Communication,* 1974, 24(4), pp. 97-100.

Investigates the various dimensions of meaning associated with the concept of retirement. Finds that persons view retirement as having a positive meaning on the dimensions of activity, emotional and moral evaluation, and physical potency.

Atchley, Robert C. "Adjustment to Loss of Job at Retirement." *International Journal of Aging and Human Development,* 1975, 6(1), pp. 17-27.

Presents a theory of how people adjust to the loss of a job at retirement. This theory seeks to integrate existing theories by means of the effect of retirement on the hierarchy of personal goals.

Atchley, Robert C. "Orientation toward the Job and Retirement Adjustment among Women." In Jaber F. Gubrium (Ed.), *Time, Roles, and Self in Old Age.* New York: Human Sciences Press, 1976, pp. 199-208.

Analyzes factors which might produce a high positive work orientation among women in retirement. Finds that the quality of the job is more important than other background variables in maintaining a high positive work orientation. Also once a woman develops a high positive work orientation, she tends to keep it.

Atchley, Robert C. *The Sociology of Retirement.* Cambridge, Mass.: Schenkman Publishing Co., Inc., 1976.

Attempts to provide a framework in which to view the retirement phenomenon and to identify the areas in which further research is needed.

Atchley, Robert C. "Issues in Retirement Research." *The Gerontologist,* 1979, 19(1), pp. 44-54.

Identifies some key issues and research questions concerning retirement. These issues and questions include consideration of how retirement is defined and the types of retirement factors affecting the decision and timing of retirements. Also included are the effects of retirement on couples, work organizations, communities, and society.

Back, Kurt W. "The Ambiguity of Retirement." In Ewald W. Busse and Eric Pfeiffer (Eds.), *Behavior and Adaptation in Late Life,* 2d ed. Boston: Little, Brown and Company, 1977, pp. 78-98.

Views retirement both from a societal and an individual perspective. Discusses topics such as the meaning of the status change in retirement, the retirement process, and the use of leisure time.

Back, Kurt W., and Guptill, Carleton S. "Retirement and Self-Ratings." In Ida H. Simpson and John C. McKinney (Eds.), *Social Aspects of Aging.* Durham,N.C.: Duke University Press, 1966, pp. 120-129.

Examines some of the dimensions of the self-concept of retired and pre-retired men. Finds that if the retiree is healthy, has a middle- or upper-stratum occupation, and is highly involved, he will feel less of a loss in the activity dimensions.

Ballweg, John A. "Resolution of Conjugal Role Adjustment after Retirement." *Journal of Marriage and the Family,* 1967, 29(2), pp. 277-281.

Reveals that retired husbands participate in more household tasks than do men in the same category still working.

Barfield, Richard, and Morgan, James N. *Early Retirement: The Decision and the Experience.* Ann Arbor: Institute of Social Research, The University of Michigan, 1969.

Based on data from older automobile workers and the general population, this study focuses on the decision to retire or to remain at work. The major finding is that financial factors (mainly expected retirement income) are of primary importance in the retirement decision. Another factor, which is found to be substantially correlated with planning early retirement, is subjective evaluation of health.

Barfield, Richard E. *The Automobile Worker and Retirement: A Second Look.* Ann Arbor: Institute for Social Research, The University of Michigan, 1970.

Deals with decision-making on early retirement among auto workers and is a sequel to the above report, *Early Retirement.* Findings reveal that poor health, the expectation of adequate retirement income, and dissatisfaction with the job are associated with planning retirement before age 65. Financial factors (mainly retirement income) are of primary importance in the decision to retire.

Barfield, Richard E., and Morgan, James N. "Trends in Planned Early Retirement." *The Gerontologist,* 1978, 18(1), pp. 13-18.

The comparison of plans for early retirement with respondents now and those of a decade ago reveals that recent historic events have been changing the position of different cohorts in a nonlinear way. Different age groups appear to be having different lifetime experiences which affect their retirement plans.

Barfield, Richard E., and Morgan, James N. "Trends in Satisfaction with Retirement." *The Gerontologist,* 1978, 18(1), pp. 19-23.

A survey which compares retirees interviewed eight to ten years earlier with those interviewed recently shows current retirees to be less satisfied with retirement. Health problems and somewhat low retirement income are major factors contributing to their dissatisfaction.

Bauder, Ward W. "Farmers' Definitions of Retirement." *The Gerontologist,* 1967, 7(3), pp. 207-212.

Farmers who accepted the retirement role had a higher net worth, were more likely to own land, and were more optimistic about their future income than those who rejected the role. Although the majority in this sample of farmers define retirement as something less than full cessation of work, more are counting on social security payments than on income from farm investments for retirement income.

Bell, Bill D. "Life Satisfaction and Occupational Retirement: Beyond the Impact Year." *International Journal of Aging and Human Development,* 1978-1979, 9(1), pp. 31-50.

Tests hypotheses derived from the crisis theory, the continuity theory, and the consistency theory relative to the prediction of life satisfaction following retirement. Of the four crisis hypotheses, only one hypothesis, that individuals underwent a decline in satisfaction with retirement, is confirmed. In the case of the continuity theory, the only hypothesis partially confirmed is that a positive association was obtained between satisfaction and orientational change in the voluntary association area. Lastly, of the three consistency theory hypotheses, only the hypothesis that expectational disconfirmations were not productive of lowered satisfaction is partially supported.

Bengtson, Vern L.; Chiriboga, David A.; and Keller, Alan B. "Occupational Differences in Retirement: Patterns of Role Activity and Life-Outlook among Chicago Teachers and Steelworkers." In Robert J. Havighurst, et al. (Eds.), *Adjustment to Retirement: A Cross-National Study.* New York: Humanities Press, 1969, pp. 53-70.

Compares Chicago steelworkers and teachers. Finds teachers to have higher activity levels in worker, friend, club member, and civic/political roles, while workers are higher in grandparent and parent roles. Teachers are community-centered and oriented toward community improvement, whereas workers are home-centered and hedonistic. Teachers also rate higher in measures of initiative and in autonomy.

Burgess, Ernest W. "A Comparison of Interdisciplinary Findings of the Study of Objective Criteria of Aging." In Clark Tibbitts and Wilma Donahue (Eds.), *Social and Psychological Aspects of Aging.* New York: Columbia University Press, 1962, pp. 671-677.

Compares tests results of older and younger workers to examine the criteria of aging and the determinants of retirement. Findings indicate that while there are no differences in productivity between younger and older workers as groups, there are great individual differences in both age groups. The overlap in the ratings of younger and older workers is significant, showing considerable individual differences in aging in the characteristics measured by the tests.

Busse, Ewald W., and Kreps, Juanita M. "Criteria for Retirement: A Re-examination." *The Gerontologist,* 1964, 4(3), pp. 115-119.

Points out that with the shortage of highly specialized manpower, the establishment of an objective criteria for retirement, other than age, is needed. Suggests that the criteria should be based on tests and established on a job-by-job basis.

Carp, Frances M. (Ed.), *The Retirement Process.* Washington, D.C.: United States Department of Health, Education, and Welfare, 1968.

Contains a collection of papers and discussions from a conference on retirement. Discusses new research findings and considers strategies and tactics for stimulating systematic research on the retirement process.

Carp, Frances M. (Ed.). *Retirement.* New York: Behavioral Publications, 1972.

A sequel to the *Retirement Process* (see above), this book focuses on "theories" of retirement which are presented by persons from diverse disciplines.

Chevan, Albert, and Fischer, Lucy R. "Retirement and Interstate Migration." *Social Forces,* 1979, 57(4), pp. 1365-1380.

Finds that the migration of the recently retired is related to retirement and climate. These two factors set the migration of the elderly apart from younger age groups. They lead to a third distinction between the migration of the old and the young which is the orientation of the older migrants to the Sunshine states.

Cox, Harold, and Bhak, Albert. "Symbolic Interaction and Retirement Adjustment: An Empirical Assessment." *International Journal of Aging and Human Development,* 1978-1979, 9(3), pp. 279-286.

Using a symbolic interaction perspective, the data reveal that the individual's significant others are crucial to the development of his or her preretirement attitudes and post-retirement adjustment.

Donahue, Wilma; Orbach, Harold L.; and Pollak, Otto. "Retirement: The Emerging Social Pattern." In Clark Tibbitts (Ed.), *Handbook of Social Gerontology.* Chicago: The University of Chicago Press, 1960, pp. 330-406.

Describes and reviews the growing body of knowledge concerning retirement.

Dressler, David M. "Life Adjustment of Retired Couples." *International Journal of Aging and Human Development,* 1973, 4(4), pp. 335-349.

Investigates the marital relationship and retirement experiences of couples living in an urban community. While there was some decrease in their level of social participation since retirement, overall, these couples appear to be satisfied with their marriages and life patterns. Results indicate that continuity of life patterns is an important determinant of successful adjustment to retirement.

Ekerdt, David J.; Bosse, Raymond; and Mogey, John M. "Concurrent Change in Planned and Preferred Age for Retirement." *Journal of Gerontology,* 1980, 35(2), pp. 232-240.

At two points, ten years apart, male workers were asked at what age they planned to retire and at what age they preferred to retire. Originally they preferred to retire earlier than the planned age for retirement. But by the second sampling preferences were changed toward older ages and tended to coincide with the planned age for retirement.

Elison, David L. "Work, Retirement, and the Sick Role." *The Gerontologist,* 1968, 8(3), pp. 189-192.

Contends that the social context of retirement, especially among blue-collar workers, is a precipitating factor in the illness of people after retirement.

Fengler, Alfred P. "Attitudinal Orientations of Wives toward Their Husband's Retirement." *International Journal of Aging and Human Development,* 1975, 6(2), pp. 139-152.

Investigates the extent to which wives believe they have been affected or will be affected by their husband's retirement. Findings reveal that more than 70% of the wives think that their husband's retirement had brought or would bring some changes or adjustments in their marital relationship.

Fillenbaum, Gerda G. "The Working Retired." *Journal of Gerontology,* 1971, 26(1), pp. 82-89.

Analyzes the ways in which the working retired differ from the nonworking retired. The working retired have more education, intend to work when retired, and are less likely to report a deterioration in health. Also the working retired, as compared to the nonworking retired, have less financial need to work, hold memberships in a larger number of associations, and enjoy success and recognition in work.

Fillenbaum, Gerda G. "On the Relation between Attitude to Work and Attitude to Retirement." *Journal of Gerontology,* 1971, 26(2), pp. 244-248.

Finds a very limited relationship between job attitude and retirement attitude among non-academic employees at a university and medical center. Suggests that only where work holds the central position in a person's life should job attitude affect retirement attitude.

Fox, Judith H. "Effects of Retirement and Former Work Life on Women's Adaptation in Old Age." *Journal of Gerontology,* 1977, 32(2), pp. 196-202.

Examines the effects of retirement on women that are still employed, retired, and who have been lifelong housewives. Findings reveal that women who have worked have just as many social resources, if not more, than those women who have been housewives most of their lives. When compared to women still employed, retirees have a lower perceived level of social contact, but are more involved in informal interaction with friends and neighbors.

Friedman, Eugene A., and Orbach, Harold L. "Adjustment to Retirement." In Silvano Arieti (Ed.), *The Foundations of Psychiatry, vol. 1, American Handbook of Psychiatry,* 2d ed. New York: Basic Books, 1974, pp. 609-647.

Discusses the emergence and institutionalization of retirement and provides a comprehensive review of the research on adjustment to retirement.

George, Linda K., and Maddox, George L. "Subjective Adaptation to Loss of the Work Role: A Longitudinal Study." *Journal of Gerontology,* 1977, 32(4), pp. 456-462.

Examines the relationship between retirement and adaptation in 58 male subjects. The findings indicate that there are high levels of adaptation in the subjects as reflected in the overwhelming stability of morale over time. In addition, marital status, occupational prestige, education, and self-perceived health are found to be significant predictors of adaptation.

Glamser, Francis D., and DeJong, Gordon F. "The Efficacy of Preretirement Preparation Programs for Industrial Workers." *Journal of Gerontology,* 1975, 30(5), pp. 595-600.

Evaluates individual briefing and group discussion types of preretirement programs to determine if they are effective in easing the transition to retirement. Although the workers' subjective reactions to both programs were positive, the group discussion proved to be the most effective for increasing knowledge of retirement issues, in preparing one for retirement, and alleviating uncertainty about the future.

Glamser, Francis D. "Determinants of a Positive Attitude toward Retirement." *Journal of Gerontology,* 1976, 31(1), pp. 104-107.

Results show that workers who expect a positive retirement experience in terms of finances, friends, social activity, and the level of preparedness are likely to have a positive attitude toward retirement. Finds no relationship between attitude toward retirement and commitment to work.

Goldstein, Sidney. "Socio-Economic and Migration Differentials between the Aged in the Labor Force and in the Labor Reserve." *The Gerontologist,* 1967, 7(1), pp. 31-40 and p. 79.

Indicates that older persons in high white-collar positions display the greatest tendency toward continued labor force participation. Also higher proportions of those with a college education continued working. But regardless of labor force status, the aged manifest a high degree of residential stability.

Goudy, Willis J., et al. "Changes in Attitudes toward Retirement: Evidence from a Panel Study of Older Males." *Journal of Gerontology,* 1980, 35(6), pp. 942-948.

Data from a panel study of older males for the periods 1964 and 1974 were obtained to study changes in retirement attitudes. Results indicate that changes in retirement attitudes over a decade are minor. Also there are differences in retirement attitudes between occupational groups, but the changes that occur within the groups are usually small.

Havighurst, Robert J., et al. (Eds.). *Adjustment to Retirement: A Cross-National Study.* New York: Humanities Press, 1969.

Deals with a study of retired steelworkers and teachers from various countries. Offers a description of the types of adjustment to retirement and makes comparisons between occupations within each country.

Havighurst, Robert J., et al. "Male Social Scientists: Lives After Sixty." *The Gerontologist,* 1979, 19(1), pp. 55-60.

Results show that there is a continuity of lifestyle over the period from ages 60 to 75, with little or no change caused by mandatory or voluntary retirement.

Hearn, Hershel L. "Aging and the Artistic Career." *The Gerontologist,* 1972, 12(4), pp. 357-362.

Focuses on a sample of retired musicians, actors, and painters. The career of the artist does not have the abrupt finality of compulsory retirement as many other careers do. An artist never retires and age is seen as only increasing one's experience and expertise.

Heyman, Dorothy K., and Jeffers, Frances C. "Wives and Retirement: A Pilot Study." *Journal of Gerontology,* 1968, 23(4), pp. 488-496.

Studies the wives of 33 retired men for differences between those who are happy and unhappy about their husband's retirement. Wives in the unhappy category tend to be older, engaged in manual occupations, in poorer health, and had lower ratings in activities and attitudes.

Keating, Norah C., and Cole, Priscilla. "What Do I Do With Him 24 Hours a Day? Changes in the Housewife Role After Retirement." *The Gerontologist,* 1980, 20(1), pp. 84-89.

A study of 400 retired teachers and wives reveals that there are no significant male-female differences with levels of communication in retirement and in satisfaction with division of household tasks. Women are significantly happier than men with the retirement stage of their life cycle in that it gives them a new sense of being needed.

Kerckhoff, Alan C. "Husband-Wife Expectations and Reactions to Retirement." *Journal of Gerontology,* 1964, 19(4), pp. 510-516.

Wives seem to be less deeply involved than husbands in expectations of and reactions to retirement. The husbands tend to have higher expectations of retirement and soon after retiring they have a greater sense of improvement and satisfaction than their wives. However, after about 5 years, husbands become less satisfied and they respond more negatively to retirement than their wives. In addition, upper-level couples respond the most favorably to retirement, followed by middle-level couples. Lower-level couples tend to be the least favorable in their reactions to the experience, and do not regard retirement as a particularly pleasant change in their lives.

Kerckhoff, Alan C. "Husband-Wife Expectations and Reactions to Retirement." In Ida H. Simpson and John C. McKinney (Eds.), *Social Aspects of Aging.* Durham, N.C.: Duke University Press, 1966, pp. 160-172.

Compares the responses of husbands and wives before, soon after, and well after retirement. Preretired husbands look forward to retirement, and retired husbands show a greater sense of satisfaction in retirement than do their wives. Men who are retired less than five years show the greatest satisfaction. Couples in which the husband was in a professional or managerial category did not welcome retirement but their reactions to the experience are generally positive, while those who were in the lower level occupations do not find the retirement experience pleasant and tend to respond more negatively.

Kerckhoff, Alan C. "Family Patterns and Morale in Retirement." In Ida H. Simpson and John C. McKinney (Eds.), *Social Aspects of Aging.* Durham, N.C.: Duke University Press, 1966, pp. 173-192.

Examines the relationship between family patterns and morale in retirement. The only variable which is consistently associated with morale for both husbands and wives is the level of the husbands' participation in household tasks. In households where husbands participate, both husbands' and wives' morale is higher than those of couples in households where husbands do not participate.

Kimmel, Douglas C.; Price, Karl F.; and Walker, James W. "Retirement Choice and Retirement Satisfaction." *Journal of Gerontology,* 1978, 33(4), pp. 575-585.

Compares persons who retired voluntarily with those whose retirement was nonvoluntary. The findings show that voluntary rather than nonvoluntary retirement is generally better for a person. Voluntary retirees tend to be better off than nonvoluntary retirees in income, health, occupational status, and feelings about retirement. Also voluntary retirees receive more family support for their decision to retire.

King, Charles E., and Howell, William. "Role Characteristics of Flexible and Inflexible Retired Persons." *Sociology and Social Research,* 1965, 49(2), pp. 153-165.

Examines the experiences of retired persons in the process of role change. Finds that occupational, marital, and organizational participation roles have an important influence on retirement.

Kreps, Juanita M. (Ed.). *Employment, Income, and Retirement Problems of the Aged.* Durham, North Carolina: Duke University Press, 1963.

Deals with various aspects of the problems arising from the changing age structure of our society. These problems include employment and income of older workers, retirement, and pensions.

Lipman, Aaron. "Role Conceptions of Couples in Retirement." In Clark Tibbitts and Wilma Donahue (Eds.), *Social and Psychological Aspects of Aging.* New York: Columbia Univesity Press, 1962, pp. 475-485.

Analyzes preretirement role orientations and new role conceptions emerging as a result of retirement. Lipman concludes that retirement brings a definite change in the traditional activities of the male which alter the preretirement division of males and females. It appears that role differentiation by sex is reduced with increased age and retirement. Because non-sex differentiated roles demand expressive rather than instrumental qualities, they tend to be well adapted for the personality system of both husband and wife in retirement.

McKinney, John C. "The Self and Social Structure: Some Theoretical Considerations Concerning Retirement." *Sociological Symposium,* no. 2, Spring 1969, pp. 123-136.

Discusses the relevance of the symbolic interactionist and structural functionalist perspectives for the study of retirement.

McPherson, Barry, and Guppy, Neil. "Pre-Retirement Life-Styles and the Degree of Planning for Retirement." *Journal of Gerontology,* 1979, 34(2), pp. 254-263.

Identifies some of the variables which influence the pre-retirement attitudes and decision-making of males presently in the labor force. The findings reveal that socioeconomic status, perceived health, organization affiliation, job satisfaction, and degree of leisure participation are positively associated with pre-retirement attitudes and decisions.

Maddox, George L. "Retirement as a Social Event in the United States." In John C. McKinney and Frank de Vyver (Eds.), *Aging and Social Policy.* New York: Appleton-Century-Crofts, 1966, pp. 117-135.

Asserts that the assumptions about the homogeneity of the elderly population and the meaning of retirement for the older male warrant critical review.

Maddox, George L. "Adaptation to Retirement." *The Gerontologist,* 1970, 10(1), pt. 2, pp. 14-18.

Notes some important conditions which affect adaptations to retirement. These conditions include the individual's work experience and the kinds of resources in the environment.

Medley, Morris L. "Marital Adjustment in the Post-Retirement Years." *The Family Coordinator,* 1977, 26(1), pp. 5-11.

Presents a comprehensive, theoretical framework in which to analyze marital adjustment in the post-retirement years.

Monk, Abraham. "Factors in the Preparation for Retirement by Middle-Aged Adults." *The Gerontologist,* 1971, 2(4), pt. 1, pp. 348-351.

A study of administrative and professional men between the ages of 50 and 59 indicates a denial of the idea of retirement and an absence of any preparations for retirement.

Orbach, Harold L. "Normative Aspects of Retirement." In Clark Tibbitts and Wilma Donahue (Eds.), *Social and Psychological Aspects of Aging.* New York: Columbia University Press, 1962, pp. 53-63.

Discusses the institutionalization of retirement, and the basic value orientations which underlie the conception of retirement as a form of social life.

Orbach, Harold L. "Social Values and the Institutionalization of Retirement." In Clark Tibbitts, and Wilma Donahue (Eds.), *Processes of Aging: Social and Psychological Perspectives, vol. 2.* New York: Atherton Press, 1963, pp. 389-402.

Considers the historical dynamics of retirement as a social phenomenon and analyzes the character of the basic value systems which have developed on the societal level to deal with retirement.

Palmore, Erdman B. "Differences in the Retirement Patterns of Men and Women." *The Gerontologist,* 1965, 5(1), pp. 4-8.

Finds that women retire for voluntary reasons more than men. The study also finds that retirement is steadily increasing among men but not among women. If this trend continues, according to Palmore, there should be little or no difference in male and female retirement rates in the next 15 or 20 years.

Palmore, Erdman B. "Why Do People Retire?" *Aging and Human Development,* 1971, 2(4), pp. 269-283.

Indicates that age is the most important factor for influencing retirement for both sexes. The second most important factor for men is poor health, whereas for women it is marital status. Two main types of reasons for retirement are inability to work and less of a need for earnings.

Palmore, Erdman B. "Compulsory Versus Flexible Retirement: Issues and Facts." *The Gerontologist,* 1972, 12(4), pp. 343-348.

Palmore summarizes the arguments, theories, and facts on compulsory and flexible retirement. He concludes with proposals for increasing flexible retirement policies.

Peretti, Peter O., and Wilson, Cedric. "Voluntary and Involuntary Retirement of Aged Males and Their Effect on Emotional Satisfaction, Usefulness, Self-Image, Emotional Stability, and Interpersonal Relationships." *International Journal of Aging and Human Development,* 1975, 6(2), pp. 131-138.

Voluntary retirement tends to have more positive effects on aged males than involuntary retirement in the areas of emotional satisfaction, usefulness, self-image, and emotional stability. In comparison with involuntary retirees, voluntary retirees belong to more social groups, have more frequent contact with others, and desire to sustain friendships.

Pollman, A. William. "Early Retirement: A Comparison of Poor Health to Other Retirement Factors." *Journal of Gerontology,* 1971, 26(1), pp. 41-45.

The primary reason for a group of industrial workers taking early retirement is an adequate retirement income. Poor health ranks second, followed by a desire for more free time.

Prasad, S. Benjamin. "The Retirement Postulate of the Disengagement Theory." *The Gerontologist,* 1964, 4(1), pp. 20-23.

Finds no empirical support for the postulate of the disengagement theory--that most men are ready to disengage or retire--when it is translated in terms of industrial workers.

Roman, Paul, and Taietz, Philip. "Organizational Structure and Disengagement: The Emeritus Professor." *The Gerontologist,* 1967, 7(3), pp. 147-152.

Indicates that a significant degree of continued engagement is found in a university setting in which opportunities for engagement are provided after retirement.

Rose, Charles L., and Mogey, John M. "Aging and Preference for Later Retirement." *Aging and Human Development,* 1972, 3(1), pp. 45-61.

Finds that the preference for later retirement is related to age and social class factors. However, age is found to be more than twice as important as social class factors in the preference for later retirement.

Rowe, Alan R. "The Retirement of Academic Scientists." *Journal of Gerontology,* 1972, 27(1), pp. 113-118.

Reveals that most academic scientists tend to accept retirement and do not find it particularly disruptive to their lives. They continue to engage in science after retirement to varying degrees.

Rowe, Alan R. "Scientists in Retirement." *Journal of Gerontology,* 1973, 28(3), pp. 345-350.

Studies scientists who retired from colleges, universities, and research and industrial organizations. Findings indicate that their retirement is a relatively contented one with a chance to continue to engage in science.

Rowe, Alan R. "Retired Academics and Research Activity." *Journal of Gerontology,* 1976, 31(4), pp. 456-461.

Data obtained from academic retirees from colleges and universities reveals that at retirement they continue to engage in research and/or writing. This is especially true of those academics who have high professional visibility.

Rowe, Alan R. "The Retired Scientist: The Myth of the Aging Individual." In Jaber F. Gubrium (Ed.), *Time, Roles, and Self in Old Age.* New York: Human Sciences Press, 1976, pp. 209-219.

Contends that as people grow old, they do not necessarily have to alter their lifestyle, especially as related to their vocation. Rowe's research on retired scientists supports this view.

Shanas, Ethel. "Adjustment to Retirement." In Frances M. Carp (Ed.), *Retirement*. New York: Behavioral Publications, 1972, pp. 219-243.

Considers two processes, substitution and accommodation, which operate in adjustment to retirement. Discusses the assumptions underlying each of these perspectives and the kinds of research associated with them.

Sheppard, Harold L. "Work and Retirement." In Robert H. Binstock and Ethel Shanas (Eds.), *Handbook of Aging and the Social Sciences*. New York: Van Nostrand Reinhold, 1976, pp. 286-309.

Deals with such topics as early retirement, unemployment and the older worker, the retirement decision, and adjustment to retirement.

Sheppard, Harold L. "The Issue of Mandatory Retirement." *Annals of the American Academy of Political and Social Science,* 1978, 438, pp. 40-49.

Discusses some research and policy issues concerning mandatory retirement and considers the relationship of mandatory retirement to the young in the labor force.

Sheppard, Harold L., and Rix, Sara E. *The Graying of Working America*. New York: The Free Press, 1977.

Deals with the future of retirement-age policy and the question of whether or not there is a limit to the process and policies underlying the current trend toward early retirement accompanied by increased years in retirement.

Simpson, Ida H.; Back, Kurt W.; and McKinney, John C. "Attributes of Work, Involvement in Society, and Self-Evaluation in Retirement." In Ida H. Simpson and John C. McKinney (Eds.), *Social Aspects of Aging*. Durham, N.C.: Duke University Press, 1966, pp. 55-74.

Deals with variations in social involvement among retired workers. The findings indicate that the influence of work is not completely lost with retirement, but that many patterns of social involvement supported by work continue. Also if social involvements have not been built up before retirement, they are unlikely to be started in retirement.

Simpson, Ida H.; Back, Kurt W.; and McKinney, John C. "Orientation toward Work and Retirement, and Self-Evaluation in Retirement." In Ida H. Simpson and John C. McKinney (Eds.) *Social Aspects of Aging*. Durham, N.C.: Duke University Press, 1966, pp. 75-89.

Results reveal that attitudes toward work are the primary influence on preretirement orientations to retirement among upper-white-collar workers, and that income deprivation in retirement is the main influence on semi-skilled workers. None of the explanations account for the great variability within the middle stratum.

Simpson, Ida H. "Problems of the Aging in Work and Retirement." In Rosamonde R. Boyd, and Charles G. Oakes, Eds.), *Foundations of Practical Gerontology,* 2d ed. Columbia, South Carolina: University of South Carolina Press, 1975, pp. 157-172.

Discusses the problems of the older worker and gives some suggestions for successful planning for retirement.

Stokes, Randall G., and Maddox, George L. "Some Social Factors on Retirement Adaptation." *Journal of Gerontology,* 1967, 22(3), pp. 329-333.

Finds that satisfaction in retirement tends to be a function of time in that blue-collar workers adapt to retirement more successfully than white-collar workers in the beginning. However, in the long run, it is the white-collar workers who make the most successful adaptation.

Streib, Gordon F. "New Roles and Activities for Retirement." In George L. Maddox (Ed.), *The Future of Aging and the Aged.* Durham, N.C.: Duke University Press, 1971, pp. 18-53.

Discusses the need for flexibility in the lifestyles of the elderly which takes advantage of the abundant time in the later years, and permits them to engage in new roles which they were not able to pursue in earlier years.

Streib, Gordon F., and Schneider, Clement J. *Retirement in American Society: Impact and Process.* Ithaca, N.Y.: Cornell University Press, 1971.

Investigates some of the factors which affect the decision to retire and determines the impact of retirement upon health, income, and the social and psychological adjustment of retirees.

Strauss, Harold; Aldrich, Bruce W.; and Lipman, Aaron. "Retirement and Perceived Status Loss: An Inquiry into Some Objective and Subjective Problems Produced by Aging." In Jaber F. Gubrium (Ed.), *Time, Roles, and Self in Old Age.* New York: Human Sciences Press, 1976, pp. 220-234.

Studies factors associated with the maintenance of feelings of self-respect and social worth among retirees. Findings suggest that highly educated persons experienced the least perceived status loss after retirement. Although the association between high educational attainment and the absence of feelings of status loss are more apparent among males, it is statistically significant for both sexes.

Sussman, Marvin B. "An Analytic Model for the Sociological Study of Retirement." In Frances M. Carp (Ed.), *Retirement.* New York: Behavioral Publications, 1972, pp. 29-73.

Examines the important components of retirement which when linked to an analytic model seem to offer the best explanation for the retirement process.

Thompson, Gayle B. "Work Versus Leisure Roles: An Investigation of Morale among Employed and Retired Men." *Journal of Gerontology,* 1973, 28(3), pp. 339-344.

Investigates the variation in the morale of retired men and men still working. The findings reveal that the retirees have lower morale than employed men. The lower morale of retirees cannot be attributed just to the fact that they are retired. Their morale is lower because they have more negative evaluations of their health, are more functionally disabled, and are older and poorer.

Thompson, Wayne E.; Streib, Gordon F.; and Kosa, John. "The Effect of Retirement on Personal Adjustment: A Panel Analysis." *Journal of Gerontology,* 1960, 15(2), pp. 165-169.

The findings suggest that the negative effects of retirement have been overestimated. Retirement has a negative effect on adjustment only when there are feelings of income inadequacy and there is difficulty in keeping occupied. But even under these circumstances, there is no evidence of extreme maladjustment.

Wolfbein, Seymour L., and Burgess, Ernest W. "Employment and Retirement." In Ernest W. Burgess (Ed.), *Aging in Western Societies.* Chicago: The University of Chicago Press, 1960, pp. 54-75.

Discusses the factors that influence the decision to retire or to continue working in a cross-national context.

C. Leisure

Atchley, Robert C. "Retirement and Leisure Participation: Continuity or Crisis?" *The Gerontologist,* 1971, 2(1), pt. 1, pp. 13-17.

Examines Miller's crisis identity theory to explain the relationship between retirement and leisure participation. Proposes the identity continuity theory as an alternative.

Carp, Frances M. "Retirement Travel." *The Gerontologist,* 1972, 12(1), pp. 73-78.

The findings suggest that for most retirees travel is infrequent. Major obstacles are money, poor health, lack of an automobile, and the inconvenience and physical stress of public transportation.

Cottrell, Fred. "The Sources of Free Time." In Robert W. Kleemeier, (Ed.), *Aging and Leisure.* New York: Oxford University Press, 1961, pp. 55-81.

Examines the changing relationships between the productive process and other aspects of society.

Christ, Edwin A. "The 'Retired' Stamp Collector: Economic and Other Functions of a Systematized Leisure Activity." In Arnold M. Rose and Warren A. Peterson (Eds.), *Older People and Their Social World.* Philadelphia: F.A. Davis, 1965, pp. 93-112.

Suggests that leisure activities such as stamp collecting with its associations, communications system, and economic structure may become powerful sources of satisfaction after retirement.

Cowgill, Donald O., and Baulch, Norma. "The Use of Leisure Time by Older People." *The Gerontologist,* 1962, 2(1), pp. 47-50.

Reveals that the average elderly person has about five hours of leisure available each day and much of this time is spent at home. The most frequent use of time is watching television, followed by home hobbies and reading.

Friedsam, Hiram J., and Martin, Cora A. "Travel by Older People as a Use of Leisure." *The Gerontologist,* 1973, 13(2), pp. 204-207.

Compared to non-travelers, travelers tend to have higher incomes, more education, and report their health as good. Travel functions to help maintain kin networks and is an important use of leisure for older persons.

Gordon, Chad; Gaitz, Charles M.; and Scott, Judith. "Leisure and Lives: Personal Expressivity across the Life Span." In Robert H. Binstock and Ethel Shanas (Eds.), *Handbook of Aging and the Social Sciences.* New York: Van Nostrand Reinhold, 1976, pp. 310-341.

Specifies the major objectives of leisure activities and places them on a continuum of expressive involvement intensity. Uses a life-cycle stage model to relate leisure activities to the value themes of urban middle-class America.

Havighurst, Robert J. "The Nature and Values of Meaningful Free-Time Activity." In Robert W. Kleemeier (Ed.), *Aging and Leisure.* New York: Oxford University Press, 1961, pp. 309-344.

Based on data from the Kansas City Study of Adult Life, this chapter describes the values of leisure activities and their relationship to age, sex, social class, and personal adjustment. Discusses use of time in regard to lifestyle, retirement, and fulfillment.

Havighurst, Robert J. "The Nature and Values of Meaningful Free-Time Activity." In Clark Tibbitts and Wilma Donahue (Eds.), *Social and Psychological Aspects of Aging.* New York: Columbia University Press, 1962, pp. 899-904.

Discusses groups of people who are regarded as successful and unsuccessful users of leisure time along with new concepts of leisure. According to Havighurst, the use of time remains on a plateau with respect to age from 40 to 65 or 75, and is part of one's personality.

Havighurst, Robert J. "Leisure and Aging." In Adeline M. Hoffman (Ed.), *The Daily Needs and Interests of Older People.* Springfield, Ill.: Charles C. Thomas, 1970, pp. 165-174.

Defines leisure and a set of free-time patterns and discusses factors determining leisure activity.

Hoar, Jere. "A Study of Free-Time Activities of 200 Aged Persons." *Sociology and Social Research,* 1961, 45(2), pp. 157-162.

The results reveal that free-time activities decline in number and change with age. Membership in organizations and attendance at meetings tend to decrease as age increases. Most of the respondents said that they had voted at the most recent national election. Women reported that they read in their spare time, whereas men said that they did gardening.

Kaplan, Max. *Leisure: Lifestyle and Lifespan: Perspectives for Gerontology.* Philadelphia: W.B. Saunders, 1979.

Deals with the social roles of retirement and leisure and how these roles are interrelated. Discusses several environments for leisure roles and some types of activity experiences.

Kleemeier, Robert W. (Ed.), *Aging and Leisure.* New York: Oxford University Press, 1961.

This collection of articles on the meaningful use of time among the elderly represents a variety of perspectives from persons in the fields of social science.

Kleemeier, Robert W. "Leisure and Disengagement in Retirement." *The Gerontologist,* 1964, 4(4), pp. 180-184.

Discusses leisure and work substitute activities versus inactivity. Concludes that the choice one must make is not between activity and inactivity, but between the kinds and levels of activities.

Lawton, M. Powell. "Leisure Activities for the Aged." *The Annals of the American Academy of Political and Social Science,* 1978, 438, pp. 71-80.

Reviews research on activity patterns and their meaning to the elderly. Discusses the major determinants of activity choice and the meaning of activities.

Miller, Stephen J. "The Social Dilemma of the Aging Leisure Participant." In Arnold M. Rose and Warren A. Peterson (Eds.), *Older People and Their Social World.* Philadelphia: F.A. Davis, 1965, pp. 77-92.

According to the author, the dilemma of persons participating in leisure activities is that they must justify an identity in terms of their leisure activities which by definition are nonessential in character. He discusses the nature of leisure in contemporary culture, the ways in which the elderly may justify their career of recreation, and the effects of age on participation in the systemized leisure group.

Oliver, David B. "Career and Leisure Patterns of Middle-Aged Metropolitan Out-Migrants." *The Gerontologist,* 1971, 2(4), pt. 2, pp. 13-20.

Studies the adjustment to retirement before the usual retirement age in a sample of middle-aged persons who moved from a metropolitan city to a resort area. Contributing to the successful adjustment of this group, is the fact that they are self-directed toward leisure instead of work, and they value family relationships and friendships above all.

Palmore, Erdman B. "The Effects of Aging on Activities and Attitudes." *The Gerontologist,* 1968, 8(4), pp. 259-263.

Contrary to the assumption that most people become less active as they age, in this longitudinal study there is no significant overall decrease in activities among men and only small decreases among women.

Peppers, Larry G. "Patterns of Leisure and Adjustment to Retirement." *The Gerontologist,* 1976, 16(5), pp. 441-446.

Reveals that there are no specific "acceptable" retirement activities. The subjects in this research were engaged in a wide range of pursuits. While there was little change at retirement in the kinds of leisure activities they enjoyed prior to retirement, there was a significant increase in the number of activities in which many retirees engaged in.

Pfeiffer, Eric, and Davis, Glenn C. "The Use of Leisure Time in Middle Life." *The Gerontologist,* 1971, 2(3), pt. 1, pp. 187-195.

Indicates that we still live in a work-oriented society. The majority of the subjects said they would work even if it were not necessary, and that they derived greater satisfaction from their work than from leisure activities.

Sherman, Susan R. "Leisure Activities in Retirement Housing." *Journal of Gerontology,* 1974, 29(3), pp. 325-335.

Residents living in retirement settings had more leisure activities than those residing in conventional housing. There is a moderately positive relationship between activity scores and several measures of outlook on life.

Thompson, Wayne E., and Streib, Gordon F. "Meaningful Activity in a Family Context." In Robert W. Kleemeier (Ed.), *Aging and Leisure.* New York: Oxford University Press, 1961, pp. 177-211.

Describes the family of the later years and its relevance to the question of how people use their leisure time.

Vogel, Bruce S., and Schell, Robert E. "Vocational Interest Patterns in Late Maturity and Retirement." *Journal of Gerontology,* 1968, 23(1), pp. 66-70.

Compares the pattern of interests of older retired men to that of younger more recently retired men. The younger retirees express a stronger interest in solitary activities involving greater independence, prestige, and material gain. The older retirees show a stronger interest in social interactional activities and activities involving supervisory responsibilities of a somewhat lower status level.

Zborowski, Mark. "Aging and Recreation." *Journal of Gerontology,* 1962, 17(3), pp. 302-309.

The subjects were given a list of activities and asked to check the ones in which they engaged in at age 40 and those in which they were presently engaged . The findings reveal that aging has an insignificant effect on recreational patterns and preferences. The general tendency is to retain the patterns which have been developed in the past.

PART 5

ENVIRONMENT AND AGING

Chapter 14

DEMOGRAPHY

Beard, Belle B. "Longevity and the Never-Married." In Clark Tibbitts and Wilma Donahue (Eds.), *Social and Psychological Aspects of Aging.* New York: Columbia University Press, 1962, pp. 36-50.

Investigates singleness in relation to longevity. Finds that single persons in their later years outlive those who have married.

Beard, Belle B. "Longevity and Fertility: A Study of Centenarians." *Sociological Symposium,* no. 2, Spring 1969, pp. 23-35.

Investigates whether or not people who live to extreme old age have larger than average families. Results reveal that if a genetic relationship exists between longevity and fertility, it has not been determined.

Biggar, Jeanne C. "Who Moved among the Elderly, 1965 to 1970: A Comparison of Types of Older Movers." *Research on Aging,* 1980, 2(1), pp. 73-91.

Patterns of selectivity for the elderly parallel those for general migration, but the factors leading to the elderly's migration may be quite different. Migration, especially interstate migration, differentially selects the elderly in higher income and educational levels, while local mobility selects the more dependent elderly.

Biggar, Jeanne C.; Longino, Charles F.; Flynn, Cynthia B. "Elderly Interstate Migration: Impact on Sending and Receiving States, 1965 to 1970. *Research on Aging,* 1980, 2(2), pp. 217-232.

Examines the characteristics of persons age 60 and over who were interstate migrants between 1965 and 1970. The findings reveal that elderly interstate migrants are less dependent in terms of demographic and socioeconomic characteristics than those that stay behind as well as those that they joined in their new state of residence.

Biggar, Jeanne C. "Reassessing Elderly Sunbelt Migration." *Research on Aging,* 1980, 2(2), pp. 177-190.

The Sunbelt states were primary destinations for migrants over age 60 between 1965 and 1970. The 15 Sunbelt states attracted more than half of the older migrants who crossed state lines during this period.

Bock, E. Wilbur, and Webber, Irving L. "Suicide among the Elderly: Isolating Widowhood and Mitigating Alternatives." *Journal of Marriage and the Family,* 1972, 34(1), pp. 24-31.

Indicates that the elderly widowed have a higher suicide rate than the elderly married. This difference is explained, in part, by the greater social isolation of the widowed, especially the widowers. Widowers have more difficulty than widows in making substitutions for the loss of a spouse. Having relatives near by and belonging to organizations aids in the reduction of the suicidal potential of the widowed.

Brotman, Herman B. "Population Projections: pt. 1, Tomorrow's Older Population (to 2000)." *The Gerontologist,* 1977, 17(3), pp. 203-209.

Notes that the older population is growing faster than the younger population. Also the older segment of the elderly population is growing faster than the younger segment. Predicts that the existing disparity between the numbers of older men and women will continue to increase in the future.

Brotman, Herman B. "Life Expectancy: Comparison of National Levels in 1900 and 1974 and Variations in State Levels, 1969-1971." *The Gerontologist,* 1977, 17(1), pp. 12-22.

Uses data on life expectancy to show the differences between cohorts as well as the disparities of sex and color within the cohort. Also gives differences among the residents of various states and among the residents of the same state.

Brotman, Herman B. "Income and Poverty in the Older Population in 1975." *The Gerontologist,* 1977, 17(1), pp. 23-26.

Tables show the median income and income distribution of older families and unrelated individuals along with the number and proportion of persons in households with incomes is below the poverty levels.

Bultena, Gordon L., and Marshall, Douglas G. "Family Patterns of Migrant and Nonmigrant Retirees." *Journal of Marriage and the Family,* 1970, 32(1), pp. 89-92.

Compares older persons who have retired in their home communities and those who moved to Florida or Arizona upon retirement. Results indicate that the migrants tend to be more isolated from their children than nonmigrants. This isolation is more of a function of the residential mobility of children than the migration of their parents after retirement.

Cain, Leonard D. "Age Status and Generational Phenomena: The New Old People in Contemporary America." *The Gerontologist,* 1967, 7(2), pt. 1, pp. 83-92.

Those persons who are already past 65 matured in a dramatically different world than those who are just entering this age group. Because of this, special significance should be given to gerontological planning for the new generation of old people.

Chevan, Albert, and Korson, J. Henry. "The Widowed Who Live Alone: An Examination of Social and Demographic Factors." *Social Forces,* 1972, 51(1), pp. 45-53.

Examines various demographic and social factors to determine their influence on the living arrangements of the widowed. Findings reveal that the percentage of the widowed living alone peaks at ages 65 to 69 and then declines at ages 80 and over. The groups least disposed to living alone include American Indians, Asians, and whites with Spanish surnames. The widowed with six years of education or less are found living alone less often than those with more education.

Chevan, Albert, and O'Rourke, John F. "Aging Regions in the United States." *Journal of Gerontology,* 1972, 27(1), pp. 119-126.

Finds that older people are not distributed across the nation in a homogeneous fashion, and that there are different styles of aging which may be geographically associated with the groups established in this study.

Chevan, Albert, and Fischer, Lucy R. "Retirement and Interstate Migration." *Social Forces,* 1979, 57(4), pp. 1365-1380.

Finds that migration of the recently retired is related to retirement and climate. These two factors set the migration of the elderly apart from younger age groups. Also these factors lead to a third distinction between the migration of the old and the young which is the orientation of the older migrants to the Sunshine states.

Cleland, Courtney B. "Mobility of Older People." In Arnold M. Rose and Warren A. Peterson (Eds.), *Older People and Their Social World.* Philadelphia: F.A. Davis, 1965, pp. 323-339.

Suggests that a typology of communities can contribute to analyzing the migration of the elderly. Gives an in-depth look to a North Dakota community.

Conrad, Frederick A. "Sex Roles as Factors in Longevity." *Sociology and Social Research,* 1962, 46(2), pp. 195-202.

Discusses sex differences in longevity and concludes that inadequate attention has been given to sex roles in studies of sex mortality differentials. Makes some suggestions for further research.

Cowgill, Donald O. "The Demography of Aging in the Midwest." In Arnold M. Rose and Warren A. Peterson (Eds.), *Older People and Their Social World.* Philadelphia: F.A. Davis, 1965, pp. 275-310.

Examines the distribution and composition of the elderly in the nine states which constitute the Corn Belt and Wheat Belt regions.

Cowgill, Donald O. "The Demography of Aging." In Adeline M. Hoffman (Ed.), *The Daily Needs and Interests of Older People.* Springfield, Ill.: Charles C. Thomas, 1970, pp. 27-69.

Discusses a number of topics dealing with demography. These topics include historical perspectives on human longevity and population structure, age and the demographic transition; and the aging, growth, life expectancy, and social characteristics of the American population.

Cowgill, Donald O. "The Aging of Populations and Societies." *The Annals of the American Academy of Political and Social Science,* 1974, 415, pp. 1-18.

Notes that modern societies have been slow in adapting their institutions to the new demographic phenomenon of aged populations. As a result, the elderly have suffered a decline in status. However, there are some signs that this trend is being reversed in the most modernized societies.

Cutler, Neal E., and Harootyan, Robert A. "Demography of the Aged." In Diana S. Woodruff and James E. Birren (Eds.), *Aging: Scientific Perspectives and Social Issues.* New York: D. Van Nostrand Co., 1975, pp. 31-69.

Provides descriptive demographic data regarding older persons along with some basic demographic concepts.

Flynn, Cynthia B. "General Versus Aged Interstate Migration, 1965-1970." *Research on Aging,* 1980, 2(2), pp. 165-176.

Compares the migration patterns of the elderly and the general population. Makes state-by-state comparisons of the volumes and rates of in- and out-migration for both groups.

Fuguitt, Glenn V., and Tordella, Stephen J. "Elderly Net Migration: The New Trend of Nonmetropolitan Population Change." *Research on Aging,* 1980, 2(2), pp. 191-204.

Deals with the changes which have taken place in elderly migration patterns and contrasts them with the rest of the population. The results indicate decreasing levels of net migration in metropolitan areas and increasing levels in nonmetropolitan areas for the 1950-1975 period for all age groups.

Fujii, Sharon. "Minority Group Elderly: Demographic Characteristics and Implications for Public Policy." In C. Eisendorfer (Ed.), *Annual Review of Gerontology and Geriatrics.* New York: Springer, vol. 1, 1980, pp. 261-284.

Provides a description in terms of demographic characteristics and policy issues for the aged in the following minority groups: the blacks, Hispanic/Latinos, American Indians, and Pacific/Asians.

Glick, Paul C. "The Future Marital Status and Living Arrangements of the Elderly." *The Gerontologist,* 1979, 19(3), pp. 301-309.

Forecasts that the greater longevity of women than men is likely to result in 250 women for every 100 men above age 85 by the year 2000 if the present trend continues. Also at that time the proportion of women from ages 65 to 79 who eventually become divorced is expected to double, and well over one-half of all elderly women might be living alone before the year 2000.

Goldscheider, Calvin. "Differential Residential Mobility of the Older Population." *Journal of Gerontology,* 1966, 21(1), pp. 103-108.

Focusing on the residential mobility of persons 50 years of age and older, the data reveal that persons in this age group are less mobile, less likely to desire to move, and are less successful in anticipating their mobility behavior than those in younger age groups. Most people gave dissatisfaction with current housing and neighborhood as reasons for moving or desiring to move.

Goldstein, Sidney. "Socio-Economic and Migration Differentials between the Aged in the Labor Force and in the Labor Reserve." *The Gerontologist,* 1967, 7(1), pp. 31-40 and p. 79.

Indicates that older persons in high white-collar positions display the greatest tendency toward continued labor force participation. Also higher proportions of those with a college education continue to work. But regardless of labor force status, the aged manifest a high degree of residential stability.

Hauser, Phillip M., and Vargas, Raul. "Population Structure and Trends." In Ernest W. Burgess (Ed.), *Aging in Western Societies.* Chicago: The University of Chicago Press, 1960, pp. 29-53.

Focuses on the age structure of the United States and some selected European countries. Discusses the factors associated with changes in the age structure.

Hauser, Phillip M. "Aging and World-Wide Population Change." In Robert H. Binstock and Ethel Shanas (Eds.), *Handbook of Aging and the Social Sciences.* New York: Van Nostrand Reinhold, 1976, pp. 59-86.

Discusses worldwide aging and the extension of life within the framework of population developments and trends.

Heaton, Tim B.; Clifford, Willam B.; and Fuguitt, Glenn V. "Changing Patterns of Retirement Migration: Movement between Metropolitan and Nonmetropolitan Areas." *Research on Aging,* 1980, 2(1), pp. 93-104.

Compares migration rates between metropolitan and nonmetropolitan areas for males both in and out of the work force. The findings show that retired males are more likely to move between metropolitan and nonmetropolitan areas. The rate of metropolitan to nonmetropolitan migrations for retired males is higher than the rate for the counter-stream, especially among those in the 45-64 age group.

Kennedy, John M., and DeJong, Gordon F. "Aged in Cities: Residential Segregation in 10 USA Central Cities." *Journal of Gerontology,* 1977, 32(1), pp. 97-102.

Uses census data to determine the degree of segregation of the elderly in cities and how this pattern varied from 1960 to 1970. The analysis shows a disproportionate share of the elderly residing within the central city. While there is considerable age segregation within certain parts of the city, the degree of segregation did not increase between 1960-1970.

Lee, Everett S. "Migration of the Aged." *Research on Aging,* 1980, 2(2), pp. 131-135.

Discusses why the migration of older persons has increased over time and will continue to increase in the future.

Lesnoff-Caravaglia, Gari. "The Five Per Cent Fallacy." *International Journal of Aging and Human Development,* 1978-1979, 9(2), pp. 187-192.

The findings of this investigation support the study by Kastenbaum and Candy and demonstrate that the percentage of persons dying in nursing homes and extended care facilities far exceeds the widely accepted five per cent.

Longino, Charles F., Jr. "Going Home: Aged Return Migration in the United States, 1965-1970." *Journal of Gerontology,* 1979, 34(5), pp. 736-745.

Shows that the states that attract both return and nonreturn migrants, except for Arizona and Nevada, are coastal states and not necessarily in the southern half of the U.S. States in the southeastern part of the nation strongly attract only return migrants. Return migrants tend to be negatively selected on socioeconomic characteristics relative to other interstate migrants.

Longino, Charles F. "Residential Relocation of Older People: Metropolitan and Nonmetropolitan." *Research on Aging,* 1980, 2(2), pp. 205-216.

Indicates that between 1965 and 1970 over half of intrastate and interstate migrants aged 60 and over moved between or within metropolitan areas. Those who changed residential environments, tended to move from metropolitan to nonmetropolitan areas.

Manton, Kenneth G.; Sandomirsky, Sharon Poss; and Wing, Steven. "Black/White Mortality Crossover: Investigation from the Perspective of the Components of Aging." *The Gerontologist,* 1979, 19(3), pp. 291-300.

Focuses on the factors associated with the aging of specific vital functions in blacks and whites as a possible explanation for the lower mortality rates of blacks in comparison with whites at advanced ages.

Marshall, James R. "Changes in Aged White Male Suicide: 1948-1972." *Journal of Gerontology,* 1978, 33(5), pp. 763-768.

Examines the recent drop in the suicide rate of 65-to 74-year-old white males. Results indicate that the drop is related to the improved economic status of the elderly.

Miller, Marv. "Geriatric Suicide: The Arizona Study." *The Gerontologist,* 1978, 18(5), pt. 1, pp. 488-495.

White males aged 60 and over in Maricopa County, Arizona, who committed suicide were matched with men who died of natural causes. The findings reveal that the latter group were more likely to have had a confidant at the time of their death than those who committed suicide. Also suicide rates were considerably higher for unmarried men. A major factor in the suicides of older men in this country appears to be poor planning for, and poor adjustment to, retirement.

Myers, George C. "Cross-National Trends in Mortality Rates among the Elderly." *The Gerontologist,* 1978, 18(5), pt. 1, pp. 441-448.

Sees reduction in the U.S. mortality rates for the elderly during 1970-1975 as a continuation of a long-term trend. A cross-national analysis shows that the death rates for the elderly in the U.S. in 1975 were lower than for the other developed countries that were studied. However, declines in mortality in the U.S. over the 1970-1975 and 1950-1975 periods were exceeded by reductions in other countries at certain ages. In many countries, the male rates increased during these periods.

Neugarten, Bernice L. "The Future of the Young-Old." *The Gerontologist,* 1975, 15(1), pt. 2, pp. 4-9.

Discusses the population size, the health status, and family structure of the elderly in the year 2000. Neugarten suggests that a distinction be made between older persons, the "young-old" (55-75), and the "old-old" (75+).

O'Rourke, John F., and Chevan, Albert. "A Factorial Ecology of Age Groups in the United States, 1960." In Jaber Gubrium (Ed.), *Late Life: Communities and Environmental Policy.* Springfield, Ill.: Charles C. Thomas, 1974, pp. 32-58.

Based on the 1960 census data, the authors analyzed the factorial distribution of three age groups in our society and attempted to establish relationships between people as members of age groups and the kinds of places in which they live. A major finding is that there is greater variation between age groups than between ecological areas.

Palmore, Erdman B. "The Relative Importance of Social Factors in Predicting Longevity." In Erdman B. Palmore and Frances C. Jeffers (Eds.), *Prediction of Life Span.* Lexington, Mass.: Heath Lexington Books, 1971, pp. 237-247.

Based on a longitudinal study of persons aged 60 to 94, the results show that work satisfaction, happiness rating, physical functioning, and tobacco use are the four strongest predictors of longevity.

Palmore, Erdman B. "Potential Demographic Contributions to Gerontology." *The Gerontologist,* 1973, 13(2), pp. 236-242.

Asserts that demography could make an important contribution to gerontology. Suggests some types of demographic analysis that could lead to significant advances in gerontology.

Palmore, Erdman B., and Stone, Virginia. "Predictors of Longevity: A Follow-up of the Aged in Chapel Hill." *The Gerontologist,* 1973, 13(1), pp. 88-90.

Reveals that socioeconomic factors tend to increase longevity. Physical mobility is the strongest predictor of longevity while education and occupation account for nearly half of the explained variance in longevity.

Pieper, Hanns G. "Aged Americans: A Profile of A Growing Minority." In John R. Barry and C. Ray Wingrove (Eds.), *Let's Learn About Aging: A Book of Readings.* Cambridge, Mass.: Schenkman, 1977, pp. 7-21.

Based mainly upon 1970 U.S. census data and using five-year age groups as units of analysis, this paper describes the demographic characteristics of the elderly population.

Siegel, Jacob S. "On the Demography of Aging." *Demography,* 1980, 17(4), pp. 345-364.

Discusses some of the issues and problems in the study of aging and the contributions that demographers can make.

Serow, William. "Return Migration of the Elderly in the USA: 1955-1960 and 1965-1970." *Journal of Gerontology,* 1978, 33(2), pp. 288-295.

Examines trends in total and return migration of persons aged 65 and over. Although recent census data does not show a significant increase in the rate of return migration among the elderly, as the older population increases in the next decades, the share of total migration represented by return migration will be greater.

Shanas, Ethel, and Hauser, Philip M. "Zero Population Growth and the Family Life of Old People." *Journal of Social Issues,* 1974, 30(4), pp. 79-92.

Deals with the place of the elderly in a technologically advanced society. Discusses the current older population and their families, as well as what the situation of the elderly and their families would be like under conditions of zero population growth.

Sheldon, Henry D. "The Changing Demographic Profile." In Clark Tibbitts (Ed.), *Handbook of Social Gerontology.* Chicago: University of Chicago Press, 1960, pp. 27-61.

Examines the changes in the age structure of the population of the United States between 1900 and 1950. Emphasizes the growth in the number and proportion of middle-aged and older persons as well as their geographic distribution.

Sheldon, Henry D. "Distribution of the Rural Aged Population." In E. Grant Youmans (Ed.), *Older Rural Americans.* Lexington: University of Kentucky Press, 1967, pp. 117-142.

Compares the proportion of older persons living in rural and urban areas and discusses changes in the age structure of the rural population.

Stahura, John M., and Stahl, Sidney M. "Suburban Characteristics and Aged Net Migration." *Research on Aging,* 1980, 2(1), pp. 3-22.

Deals with the extent to which the elderly are attracted to or leave the suburbs and tries to determine whether the push-pull and gravity theories can be used to explain this phenomenon. The results reveal that most suburbs are experiencing net aged outmigration. A combination of the two theories explained 43 percent of the variance in the net migration of older persons.

Uhlenberg, Peter. "Changing Structure of the Older Population of the USA during the Twentieth Century." *The Gerontologist,* 1977, 17(3), pp. 197-202.

Focuses upon the characteristics of successive cohorts in the 60-64 age bracket at the beginning of each decade from 1900 to 2000. Uhlenberg notes that the period of rapid change in the demographic structure of the older population is over and that for the rest of this century change will occur at a slower pace.

Uhlenberg, Peter. "Demographic Change and Problems of the Aged." In Matilda W. Riley, *Aging from Birth to Death: Interdisciplinary Perspectives.* Boulder, Colo.: Westview Press, 1979, pp. 153-166.

Discusses how demographic and social change has produced widely varied life course experiences for cohorts born a generation apart, and has altered the nature of old age by changing the characteristics of the persons occupying this stage of life.

Van Es, J.C., and Bowling, Michael. "A Model for Analyzing the Aging of Local Populations: Illinois Counties betwen 1950 and 1970." *International Journal of Aging and Human Development,* 1978-1979, 9(4), pp. 377-387.

Develops and applies a model relating migration and its effect on age structure to those community characteristics which are most likely to influence decisions on migration.

Wenz, Friedrich V. "Aging and Suicide: Maturation or Cohort Effect?" *International Journal of Aging and Human Development,* 1980, 11(4), pp. 297-305.

Examines the mean suicide potential of various age groups. The findings support the cohort explanation relating suicide and aging. Old age and widowhood may aggravate but they do not motivate any tendency for self-destruction.

Wiggins, James W., and Schoeck Helmut. "A Profile of the Aging: U.S.A." *Geriatrics,* 1961, 16(7), pp. 336-342.

Attempts to describe the noninstitutionalized, "normal" aging population in this country. Data reveal that the aging are not characteristically dependent, inadequate, ill, or senile and that current stereotypes of the elderly are inaccurate.

Chapter 15

HEALTH AND TRANSPORTATION

A. Physical Health

Carp, Frances M., and Kataoka, Eunice. "Health Care Problems of the Elderly of San Francisco's Chinatown." *The Gerontologist,* 1976, 16(1), pt. 1, pp. 30-38.

The elderly residents of Chinatown have a great need for health care services and inadequate personal resources for obtaining them. Solutions to their problems involve an effort on the part of the broader society.

Coe, Rodney M., and Barnhill, Elizabeth. "Social Participation and Health of the Aged." In Arnold M. Rose and Warren A. Peterson (Eds.), *Older People and Their Social World.* Philadelphia: F.A. Davis, 1965, pp. 211-223.

Finds a moderately positive association between the degree of social participation and perceived level of health.

Coe, Rodney M. "Professional Perspectives on the Aged." *The Gerontologist,* 1967, 7(2), pt. 1, pp. 114-119.

Examines attitudes of members of the health profession toward aging as a process, the elderly as patients, and perceptions of appropriate therapy. Stereotypes continue to influence professionals' treatment of the aged and to hamper effective coordination of services required by the elderly patient.

Ellenbogen, Bert L. "Health Status of the Rural Aged." In E. Grant Youmans (Ed.), *Older Rural Americans.* Lexington: University of Kentucky Press, 1967, pp. 195-220.

Discusses the physical and mental health of the rural elderly and the provision of health services for them. Gives some ways for improving health care for the rural aged.

Gray, Robert M., and Kasteler, Josephine M. "An Investigation of the Effects of Involuntary Relocation on the Health of Older Persons." *Sociological Symposium,* no. 2, Spring, 1969, pp. 49-58.

Compares the health activities and attitudes of elderly persons who were involuntarily relocated with those who had not been moved. Results show that relocation is stressful. Persons who were relocated had lower health scores than those who did not change residence.

Haug, Marie. "Doctor Patient Relationships and the Older Patient." *Journal of Gerontology,* 1979, 34(6), pp. 852-860.

Finds that persons in the study aged 60 and over are more likely to accept the authority of physicians in their attitude and behavior than those younger. Older respondents scored lower than the younger respondents on health knowledge and are more accepting of authority in society.

Heyman, Dorothy K., and Jeffers, Frances C. "Effect of Time Lapse on Consistency of Self-Health and Medical Evaluations of Elderly Persons." *Journal of Gerontology,* 1963, 18(2), pp. 160-164.

Studies self-health ratings of elderly people on a longitudinal basis. On the first examination, the physical function rating was related to self-health rating, but not to health attitude score. On the next round, all three variables were significantly related to one another. These findings substantiate an earlier study by Maddox (1962) which found self-health appraisals to be realistic in older persons.

Jeffers, Frances C., and Nichols, Claude R. "The Relationship of Activities and Attitudes to Physical Well-Being in Older People." *Journal of Gerontology,* 1961, 16(1), pp. 67-70.

Examines the relationship of older people's physical functioning to their attitudes and activities. Finds that older people with no disability have higher total attitude and activity scores than those with mild to severe disabilities. All categories of the activity scale are positively and significantly associated with physical functioning rating except for religious activity. The disabled older person appears to be more highly motivated to take part in religious activity than the well person. Also finds an inverse relationship between attitude toward religion and physical functioning.

Kent, Donald P., and Matson, Margaret B. "The Impact of Health on the Aged Family." *The Family Coordinator,* 1972, 21(1), pp. 29-36.

Tensions arising from the cost of illness, psychological stress, and role disruptions are frequent reactions to health problems and have important implications for family relations. Suggests that policymakers should concentrate on the family as the central unit around which to build health services for the elderly.

Lipman, Aaron, and Sterne, Richard S. "Aging in the United States: Ascription of a Terminal Sick Role." *Sociology and Social Research,* 1969, 53(2), pp. 194-203.

Discusses the "sick role" as a socially legitimate excuse from the performance demand of the value of personal self-reliance and independence. Suggests some possible consequences of the enforced ascription of the sick role to the elderly.

Maddox, George L. "Some Correlates of Differences in Self-Assessment of Health Status among the Elderly." *Journal of Gerontology,* 1962, 17(2), pp. 180-185.

Indicates that the objective state of an older person's health is the most important determinant of his or her self-assessment of health status. Persons who are preoccupied with their health, or who are poorly adjusted to their environment are more likely to assess their health as poor. Older subjects and those with higher status are more likely to be optimistic about their health.

Marden, Parker G., and Burnight, Robert C. "Social Consequences of Physical Impairment in an Aging Population." *The Gerontologist,* 1969, 9(1), pp. 39-46.

Demonstrates that physical impairments have important social effects. These effects may be manifested in such areas as psychological well-being, attitudes toward family relationships, and the perception of enjoyment of church, friends, and organizations.

Marden, Parker G., and Burnight, Robert C. "Social Consequences of Physical Impairment in an Aging Population." In Donald P. Kent, Robert Kastenbaum, and Sylvia Sherwood (Eds.), *Research Planning and Action for the Elderly: The Power and Potential of Social Science.* New York: Behavioral Publications, 1972, pp. 445-464.

Reveals that physical impairments have an important impact on social factors. This is true whether males and females are viewed separately or whether comparisons are made between the two sexes.

Markides, Kyriakos S., and Martin, Harry W. "Predicting Self-Related Health among the Aged." *Research on Aging,* 1979, 1(1), pp. 97-112.

Analyzes self ratings of health of persons age 60 and over. Finds that older persons are fairly realistic in perceptions of their health and that the strongest determinant of self-rated health is the health index. The elderly of lower socioeconomic levels tend to evaluate their health as poorer than those of higher socioeconomic levels.

Myles, John F. "Institutionalization and Sick Role Identification among the Elderly." *American Sociological Review,* 1978, 43(4), pp. 508-521.

Investigates the extent to which institutionalization alters the relationship between objective and perceived health status. The results reveal that given comparable levels of illness and disability, the institutionalized respondents are less likely than the noninstitutionalized respondents to view themselves as ill.

Nuttbrock, Larry, and Kosberg, Jordan I. "Images of the Physician and Help-Seeking Behavior of the Elderly: A Multivariate Assessment." *Journal of Gerontology,* 1980, 35(2), pp. 241-248.

Investigates the relationship between the elderly's attitudes toward physicians and help-seeking behavior. Indicates that a high level of perceived physician affectivity is associated with the predisposition and actual behavior of seeking medical help, whereas a perception of physicians as lacking affectivity is associated with not seeking help.

Osborn, Richard W. "Social and Economic Factors in Reported Chronic Morbidity." *Journal of Gerontology,* 1971, 26(2), pp. 217-223.

Explores the relationship between social rank and chronic disease. Reveals that those who are out of the work force have low incomes and high levels of reported chronic disease. The respondents report that chronic disease forced them out of the work force. Suggests that reported chronic disease is not the result of income differences, but that for older urban males income depends on chronic disease.

Rose, Arnold M. "Physical Health and Mental Outlook Among the Aging." In Arnold M. Rose and Warren A. Peterson (Eds.), *Older People and Their Social World.* Philadelphia: F.A. Davis, 1965, pp. 201-209.

Those persons who report themselves as healthy are more likely to be men, better educated, middle class rather than lower class, and partly employed rather than fully retired. In addition, the healthy aged give more evidence of "aging-group consciousness" as they are more inclined to resent their decline in status because of their age.

Rosecranz, Howard A., and Pihlblad, C. Terence. "Measuring the Health of the Elderly." *Journal of Gerontology,* 1970, 25(2), pp. 129-133.

Attempts to construct a health index based on self-reported statements. Makes a validation of the index by relating it to the degree of physical mobility or physical impairment and to the individual's self perception of his or her health.

Rosow, Irving, and Breslau, Naomi. "A Guttman Health Scale for the Aged." *Journal of Gerontology,* 1966, 21(4), pp. 556-559.

Presents a Guttman scale for measuring the functional health of older people which is based on respondents' judgments, and relies on objective referents of people's activities and specific functional capacities.

Shanas, Ethel. "Family Responsibility and the Health of Older People." *Journal of Gerontology,* 1960, 15(4), pp. 408-411.

Indicates that most older people live close to at least one child and see him or her often. Also the poorer the health of the older person, the more likely he or she is to be living in the same household with an adult child. When faced with parental health problems, children tend to assume their obligations and responsibilities.

Shanas, Ethel. *The Health of Older People: A Social Survey.* Cambridge: Harvard University Press, 1962.

Reports the findings from a survey of the health needs of older people. Some of the major findings are: (1) only a minority of older people believe they are sick; (2) the reasons older people do not use medical care are primarily psychological, not financial; (3) older people, in general, are not isolated from their families; and (4) the American public believes that old age and ill health are synonymous.

Shanas, Ethel. "Health Care and Health Services for the Aged." *The Gerontologist,* 1965, 5(4), p. 240 and p. 276.

Contains a brief survey of the health status of older people which points up the huge span of health services that is required by them.

Shanas, Ethel. "Health and Incapacity in Later Life." In Ethel Shanas, et al., *Old People in Three Industrial Societies.* New York: Atherton Press, 1968, pp. 18-48.

Some of the findings regarding the health of older people in Denmark, Britain, and the United States reveal that only a small proportion of persons 65 and over are in institutions. In each of the three countries, more old people are found to be bedfast at home than are residents in institutions. Also the majority of the elderly living at home in all three countries are able to perform minimal tasks needed for personal care without assistance from others. Finally, incapacity in the elderly increases with age and the most severely incapacitated old people are those aged 80 and over.

Shanas, Ethel. "Health and Adjustment in Retirement." *The Gerontologist,* 1970, 10(1), pt. 2, pp. 19-21.

Indicates that poor health is a major cause of retirement, but retirement does not cause poor health.

Shanas, Ethel. "Measuring the Home Health Needs of the Aged in Five Countries." *Journal of Gerontology,* 1971, 26(1), pp. 37-40.

Using the measures of functional incapacity, this study points out the need by the elderly in five countries for community health services.

Sherwood, Sylvia. "Gerontology and the Sociology of Food and Eating." *Aging and Human Development,* 1970, 1(1), pp. 61-85.

Relates food and eating patterns to social contacts and societal conditions along with aging and the problems of aging.

Sussman, Marvin B. "Use of the Longitudinal Design in Studies of Long-Term Illness: Some Advantages and Limitations." *The Gerontologist,* 1964, pt. 2, 4(2), pp. 25-29.

Discusses several reasons for selecting a longitudinal design and some of the methological problems encountered in this type of study.

Tissue, Thomas. "Another Look at Self-Rated Health among the Elderly." *Journal of Gerontology,* 1972, 27(1), pp. 91-94.

Indicates that self-rated health in old age is associated most closely with other indicators of health, and not with morale or self-image.

Wessen, Albert F. "Some Sociological Characteristics of Long-Term Care." *The Gerontologist,* 1964, 4(2), pt. 2, pp. 7-14.

The following propositions describe the present picture of long-term care: (1) long-term care will increase both quantitatively and qualitatively in the future; (2) long-term care involves major role dislocations for patients and their families; and (3) long-term care is caught in our society's negative cultural attitudes toward the elderly.

Youmans, Grant E. "Age Group, Health, and Attitudes." *The Gerontologist,* 1974, 14(3), pp. 249-254.

Examines the attitudes of four age groups in both urban and rural areas to perceived health status. The findings reveal that in the urban area negative attitudes toward health show only a modest increase with the onset of old age, whereas in the rural area in each of the age groups there are more ailments and more negative attitudes.

Zola, Irving K. "Oh Where, Oh Where Has Ethnicity Gone?" In Donald Gelfand and Alfred Kutzik (Eds.), *Ethnicity and Aging.* New York: Springer Publishing Co., 1979, pp. 66-80.

Reviews and interprets the development of ethnic and cultural research in the field of health care.

B. Mental Health

Baizerman, Michael, and Ellison, David L. "A Social Role Analysis of Senility." *The Gerontologist,* 1971, 2(2), pt. 1, pp. 163-170.

Views senility as a social role. Discusses the social consequences of labeling someone as senile and suggests some foci for research on senility and mental disorders.

Clark, Margaret, and Anderson, Barbara G. *Culture and Aging: An Anthropological Study of Older Americans.* Springfield, Ill.: Charles C. Thomas, 1967.

Based on a sample of 435 elderly persons in San Francisco in which some of them are considered mentally healthy, while others have undergone treatment for mental disorders. The major focus is on the personal and social factors relevant to a good or poor adaptation in old age.

Gelfand, Donald E. "Ethnicity, Aging and Mental Health." *International Journal of Aging and Human Development,* 1979-1980, 10(3), pp. 289-298.

Discusses the relationship of ethnicity to the mental health problems of the elderly in our society and offers recommendations for research and training in this area.

Lowenthal, Marjorie F. "Some Social Dimensions of Psychiatric Disorders in Old Age." In Richard H. Williams, Clark Tibbitts, and Wilma Donahue (Eds.), *Processes of Aging: Social and Psychological Perspectives,* vol. 2. New York: Atherton Press, 1963, pp. 224-246.

Presents the preliminary findings of a research program on geriatric mental illness which compares hospitalized and nonhospitalized older persons.

Lowenthal, Marjorie F. *Lives in Distress: The Paths of the Elderly to the Psychiatric Ward.* New York: Basic Books, 1964.

Analyzes the precipitating factors which led to elderly persons being admitted to a psychiatric ward in a San Francisco hospital.

Lowenthal, Marjorie F. "Social Isolation and Mental Illness in Old Age." *American Sociological Review,* 1964, 29(1), pp. 54-70.

Examines the relationship between isolation and mental disorders in old age. The findings indicate that lifelong extreme isolation is not necessarily conducive to the development of the types of mental disorders that require hospitalization in old age. However, lifelong marginal social adjustment may be conducive to the development of mental illness. In addition, physicial illness may be the critical antecedent to both isolation and mental disorders.

Lowenthal, Marjorie F., and Berkman, Paul L. and Associates. *Aging and Mental Disorder in San Francisco: A Social Psychiatric Study.* San Francisco: Jossey-Bass, 1967.

Concerns the detection and correlates of mental illness among elderly persons and the conditions under which they are able to maintain themselves or be maintained in the community. The findings of this study indicate that the great majority of the elderly are living independent and productive lives. Also low morale is not an inevitable accompanient or prediction of mental illness. In addition, except in extreme cases, isolation is more a result rather than a course of mental illness.

Lowenthal, Marjorie F., and Robinson, Betsy. "Social Networks and Isolation." In Robert H. Binstock and Ethel Shanas (Eds.), *Handbook of Aging and the Social Sciences.* New York: Van Nostrand Reinhold, 1976, pp. 432-456.

Deals with the sociopsychological characteristics of older persons that are relatively isolated from social networks and the extent to which this isolation reflects a change from previous patterns.

Rose, Arnold M. "Mental Health of Normal Older Persons." In Arnold M. Rose and Warren A. Peterson (Eds.), *Older People and Their Social World.* Philadelphia: F.A. Davis, 1965, pp. 193-199.

Points out that for most persons, old age brings disturbances to one's roles and self-conceptions that tend to result in minor forms of ill health. Mild depressions or neuroses are also more likely to occur.

Simon, Alexander; Lowenthal, Marjorie F.; and Epstein, Leon J. *Crisis and Intervention.* San Francisco: Jossey-Bass, 1970.

Describes the mental, physical, and socioeconomic conditions of elderly residents of San Francisco who are hospitalized with psychiatric disorders.

C. Transportation

Carp, Frances M. "Retired People as Automobile Passengers." *The Gerontologist,* 1972, 12(1), pp. 66-72.

Reveals that for two-thirds of retired persons who do not drive, riding as a passenger in a private automobile is an important means of transportation for them. Their greatest problem is the lack of opportunity for rides.

Cottrell, Fred. "Transportation of Older People in a Rural Community." *Sociological Focus,* 1971, 5(1), pp. 29-40.

Focuses on transportation for the aging in a rural community. The study shows that free transportation, delivered door-to-door on call, is used by those who are unable to provide their own transportation. The heaviest users are women beyond age 70 and living alone.

Cutler, Stephen J. "The Availability of Personal Transportation, Residential Location, and Life Satisfaction among the Aged." *Journal of Gerontology,* 1972, 27(3), pp. 383-389.

Finds low life-satisfaction scores among those elderly who do not have personal transportation available to them, and who live at greater distances from the facilities and services of the community.

Cutler, Stephen J. "The Effects of Transportation and Distance on Voluntary Association Participation among the Aged." *International Journal of Aging and Human Development,* 1974, 5(1), pp. 81-93.

Reveals that in a community in which public and commercial modes of transportation are not available, the absence of personal transportation is related to lower levels of voluntary association participation among the elderly. Also the role of transportation in facilitating voluntary association participation of the elderly increases both as distance of residence from the sites of associations increases, and as the analytical focus shifts from the number of memberships to frequency of attendance at meetings.

Cutler, Stephen J. "Transportation and Changes in Life Satisfaction." *The Gerontologist,* 1975, 15(2), pp. 155-159.

Indicates that the quality of an older person's life is partly dependent upon the availability of personal transportation.

Chapter 16

LIVING ENVIRONMENTS

Bauder, Ward W., and Doerflinger, Jon A. "Work Roles among the Rural Aged." In E. Grant Youmans (Ed.), *Older Rural Americans.* Lexington: University of Kentucky Press, 1967, pp. 22-43.

Analyzes the work roles of the rural elderly and focuses on the rural-urban differences in work, labor force participation, and retirement patterns.

Bell, Bill D. "The Impact of Housing Relocation on the Elderly: An Alternative Methodological Approach." *International Journal of Aging and Human Development,* 1976, 7(1), pp. 27-38.

Compares the effect of housing relocation on the patterns of interaction and life satisfaction on older persons living in congregate housing and those living independently. Results reveal no significant differences in frequencies of interaction between the two groups, but life satisfaction is higher for those living in independent housing units.

Bennett, Ruth, and Nahemow, Lucille. "Socialization and Social Adjustment in Five Residential Settings for the Aged." In Donald P. Kent, Robert Kastenbaum, and Sylvia Sherwood (Eds.), *Research Planning and Action for the Elderly: The Power and Potential of Social Science.* New York: Behavioral Publications, 1972, pp. 514-524.

Investigates socialization, social adjustment, and mental status to determine if they vary according to institutional totality. Finds socialization to be better in residential settings which are low in totality. Socialization is only slightly related to mental status.

Brand, Frederick N., and Smith, Richard T. "Life Adjustment and Relocation of the Elderly." *Journal of Gerontology,* 1974, 29(3), pp. 336-340.

To determine the relationship between involuntary relocation and the life adjustment and health of older people, interview data were obtained from elderly persons who had experienced enforced relocation and those who had not relocated. Results reveal that the relocated residents show greater life dissatisfaction than the control group who did not move. Elderly blacks seem to adjust better after relocation than whites. Life satisfaction is lower among those persons who were in poor health and forced to relocate.

Britton, John H., and Britton, Jean O. "The Middle-Aged and Older Rural Person and His Family." In E. Grant Youmans (Ed.), *Older Rural Americans.* Lexington, Ky.: University of Kentucky Press, 1967, pp. 44-74.

Reviews the research literature on living arrangements of older persons, relationships of the elderly with their families, and family norms for aging in rural communities.

Britton, Joseph H.; Mather, William G.; and Lansing, Alice K. "Expectations for Older Persons in a Rural Community: Living Arrangements and Family Relationships." *Journal of Gerontology,* 1961, 16(2), pp. 156-162.

Most of the residents of the rural community investigated believed that older persons should live alone in their own homes unless they were not able to care for themselves, had financial difficulties, or were lonely. Under these conditions they believed it was appropriate for older persons to live with their family or in a home for the aged. Some of the other expectations for the elderly were that they should maintain responsibility for themselves, enjoy their children and grandchildren, and do as they wish for their own enjoyment.

Bultena, Gordon L. "Structural Effects on the Morale of the Aged: A Comparison of Age-Segregated and Age-Integrated Communities." In Jaber F. Gubrium (Ed.), *Late Life: Communities and Environmental Policy.* Springfield, Ill.: Charles C. Thomas, 1974, pp. 18-31.

Based on interview data from three age-integrated communities, this study reveals that residents of planned retirement communities have higher morale than those living in regular communities. Retirement communities also facilitate the adaptations of older migrants to the retirement role.

Bultena, Gordon L., and Wood, Vivian. "The American Retirement Community: Bane or Blessing?" *Journal of Gerontology,* 1969, 24(2), pp. 209-217.

Examines differences in the personal adjustment of retired persons who moved to retirement communities and those who moved to age-integrated communities. Finds migrants to retirement communities have higher morale. However, this may be due partly to the fact that those in retirement communities are in a higher socioeconomic bracket and more often perceive their health as good or very good. Compared to the aged-integrated community, the retirement community offers greater opportunities for interaction and more support for leisure-oriented lifestyles which are conducive to adjusting to the retirement role.

Bultena, Gordon, and Wood, Vivian. "Normative Attitudes toward the Aged Role among Migrant and Nonmigrant Retirees." *The Gerontologist,* 1969, 9(3), pt. 1, pp. 204-208.

Indicates that the elderly who move to retirement areas are more liberal in their assessment as to what constitutes proper behavior among the aged than those persons retiring in their home communities.

Burgess, Ernest W. (Ed.). *Retirement Villages.* Ann Arbor: Division of Gerontology, The University of Michigan, 1961.

Contains a compilation of papers from a conference on retirement villages. Discusses the design and functioning of retirement villages along with suggestions for research.

Cantor, Marjorie H. "Life Space and Social Support System of the Inner City Elderly of New York." *The Gerontologist,* 1975, 15(1), pt. 1, pp. 23-27.

A survey of persons 60 years of age and over living in the inner city of New York reveals that most of the services they need, with the exception of medical care, are readily accessible to them. Also the locale provides them with a viable social support system. In spite of problems, especially about personal safety, the majority of respondents believe the city satisfies their needs.

Carp, Frances M. *A Future for the Aged: Victoria Plaza and Its Residents.* Austin: The University of Texas Press, 1966.

Identifies characteristics associated with adjustment to living in Victoria Plaza, a public housing project for the elderly, and investigates the processes of interpersonal contact and group formation.

Carp, Frances, M. "The Impact of Environment on Old People." *The Gerontologist,* 1967, 7(2), pt. 1, pp. 106-108 and p. 135.

Reveals that the change to Victoria Plaza, a new public housing facility for older persons, increases satisfaction among the residents as well as producing more favorable attitudes about themselves and toward others.

Carp, Frances M. "Person-Situation Congruence in Engagement." *The Gerontologist,* 1968, 8(3), pp. 184-188.

Suggests that older persons who were involved in social activities before they moved to Victoria Plaza, a public housing project, tend to be more satisfied, better adjusted, and more popular with other residents in their new setting.

Carp, Frances M. "Housing and Minority-Group Elderly." *The Gerontologist,* 1969, 9(1), pp. 20-24.

Reports that despite poor housing, the Mexican-American elderly are satisfied with their living conditions and do not want to move to a new public housing facility. Reasons given for not moving are pride in home ownership and interpersonal bonds with relatives and friends.

Carp, Frances M. "The Mobility of Older Slum-Dwellers." *The Gerontologist,* 1972, 12(1), pp. 57-65.

Suggests that most elderly slum dwellers remain in their own neighborhood because of the lack of transportation and not because of the neighboring pattern of lower-class persons.

Carp, Frances M. "Mobility among Members of an Established Retirement Community." *The Gerontologist,* 1972, 12(1), pp. 48-56.

Compares residents in a retirement community with other retirees in San Antonio. The retirement community residents tend to go more places, do more things, and be better satisfied with their situation.

Carp, Frances M. "Short-Term and Long-Term Prediction of Adjustment to a New Environment." *Journal of Gerontology,* 1974, 29(4), pp. 444-453.

Supports the role of person-situation congruence in determining the adjustment of the elderly to a new living situation. Indicates the feasibility of identifying characteristics of community-resident elderly which can be used to predict their adjustment in another setting.

Carp, Frances M. "Long-Range Satisfaction with Housing." *The Gerontologist,* 1975, 15(1), pt. 1, pp. 68-72.

Data collected at the end of eight years from tenants of Victoria Plaza, a public housing project, and a comparison group reveal that the satisfaction of the elderly with their housing and living arrangements continues to have a lasting effect.

Carp, Frances M. "Life-Style and Location within the City." *The Gerontologist,* 1975, 15(1), pt. 1, pp. 27-34.

Indicates that although living in the center city for the elderly has many disadvantages, they are outweighed by the advantages. The city appears to have good potential as an environment for the aged.

Carp, Frances M. "Impact of Improved Housing on Morale and Life Satisfaction." *The Gerontologist,* 1975, 15(6), pp. 511-515.

Reveals the importance of the living environment upon the morale and life satisfaction of older persons. Tenants of Victoria Plaza, a public housing project, are happier than those elderly with generally unsatisfactory housing arrangements living elsewhere in the community.

Carp, Frances M. "Housing and Living Environments of Older People." In Robert H. Binstock and Ethel Shanas (Eds.), *Handbook of Aging and the Social Sciences.* New York: Van Nostrand Reinhold, 1976, pp. 244-271.

Discusses the effects of housing and living environments on older people, the need to create a wider variety and larger supply of living environments, and implications of studies in housing for the elderly.

Carp, Frances M. "Impact of Improved Living Environment on Health and Life Expectancy." *The Gerontologist,* 1977, 17(3), pp. 242-249.

Focuses on long-range differences between elderly residents of Victoria Plaza, a public housing project, and a comparison group. Carp tentatively concludes that a good living environment for the elderly may not only improve their psychological and social well-being, but it may extend their life and improve their health as well.

Carp, Frances M. "Effects of the Living Environment on Activity and Use of Time." *International Journal of Aging and Human Development,* 1978-1979, 8(1), pp. 75-91.

Shows that in Victoria Plaza, a public housing facility for the elderly, where there is increased opportunities for activity, the activity rates of older persons are raised. Also the data reveal the existence of a "latent demand" for activity within the community-resident elderly.

Carp, Frances M., and Abraham Carp. "Person-Environment Congruence and Sociability." *Research on Aging,* 1980, 2(4), pp. 395-415.

Examines the long-term effects on older persons who moved from an isolating living environment to one rich in social opportunities. Results indicate that compared to those elderly who did not move, the majority of elderly who moved enjoy increased sociability and improved life satisfaction.

Clark, Margaret. "Patterns of Aging among the Elderly Poor of the Inner City." *The Gerontologist,* 1971, 2(1), pt. 2, pp. 58-66.

Suggests one approach to social planning for the inner-city aged to examine the ways in which the aged poor develop informal structures for the solution of basic problems of survival. Planned programs could then be constructed to develop these arrangements among people.

Cohen, Carl I., and Sokolvsky, Jay. "Social Engagement Versus Isolation: The Case of the Aged in SRO Hotels." *The Gerontologist,* 1980, 20(1), pp. 36-44.

Disputes the current belief that most aged SRO (single-room occupancy) residents are complete isolates. The findings show that high percentages of SRO persons have never married or have had short-lived marriages. Also SROs have had long periods of living alone and relative isolation as compared to other urban samples.

Cottrell, Fred. "Transportation of Older People in a Rural Community." *Sociological Focus,* 1971, 5(1), pp. 29-40.

Focuses on transportation for the aging in a rural community. Shows that free transportation (delivered door-to-door on call) is used by those who are unable to provide their own transportation. The heaviest users are women beyond age 70 and living alone.

Cowgill, Donald O. "Residential Segregation by Age in American Metropolitan Areas." *Journal of Gerontology,* 1978, 33(3), pp. 446-453.

Computes the dissimilarity of the residential distribution for the population over and under age 65 for 241 Standard Metropolitan Statistical Areas. The major factor associated with the level and rate of increase in segregation is the rate of growth of the population of the SMSAs. Larger communities tend to be more differentiated and those with fewer aged and more nonwhites are more age segregated.

Dick, Harry R.; Friedsam, Hiram J.; and Martin, Cora Ann. "Residential Patterns of Aged Persons Prior to Institutionalization." *Journal of Marriage and the Family,* 1964, 26(1), pp. 96-98.

Indicates that changes in the number and types of housing and living arrangements appear to be mostly a function of changes in family structure and health. The sex of the older person is also a significant factor.

Donahue, Wilma. "Housing and Community Services." In Ernest W. Burgess (Ed.), *Aging in Western Societies,* Chicago: The University of Chicago Press, 1960, pp. 106-155.

Reviews ways of meeting the housing needs of the elderly in several European countries. Identifies concepts and principles in housing the elderly, and describes community services to help utilize existing living arrangements and newer housing developments.

Eckert, J. Kevin. *The Unseen Elderly.* San Diego State University: The Campanile Press, 1980.

Provides a description of the lifestyle of persons aged 50 years and over living in SRO (single-room occupancy) hotels in downtown San Diego, California. Stresses the adjustments that they make to their needs and problems, as well as the support systems available to them in such a setting.

Ellenbogen, Bert L. "Health Status of the Rural Aged." In E. Grant Youmans (Ed.), *Older Rural Americans.* Lexington: University of Kentucky Press, 1967, pp. 195-220.

Discusses the physical and mental health of the rural elderly and the provision of health services for them. Gives some ways for improving health care for the rural aged.

Erickson, Rosemary, and Eckert, Kevin. "The Elderly Poor in Downtown San Diego Hotels." *The Gerontologist,* 1977, 17(5), pp. 440-446.

Compares residents of skid-row, working-class, and middle-class hotels in downtown San Diego. The middle-class subjects are very different from those in the skid-row and working-class hotels in that they exhibit a more intact primary support system. All residents are found to be independent, self-reliant, and not dependent on social services.

Gersuny, Carl. "The Rhetoric of the Retirement Home Industry." *The Gerontologist,* 1970, 10(4), pt. 1, pp. 282-286.

By analyzing the brochures published by managements of retirement homes, this paper examines the rhetoric of persuasion used in the recruitment and socialization of clients.

Golant, Stephen M. "Spatial Context of Residential Moves by Elderly Persons." *International Journal of Aging and Human Development,* 1977-1978, 8(3), pp. 279-289.

Focuses on older residential movers as a distinctive population group. Results reveal that most moves by the elderly are within the same county or state, and the majority of elderly live in the state in which they were born.

Golant, Stephen M. "Residential Concentrations of the Future Elderly." *The Gerontologist,* 1975, 15(1), pt. 2, pp. 16-23.

Discusses some future locational patterns of the elderly in states, in metropolitan areas, central cities, neighborhoods, and retirement communities.

Goldscheider, Calvin. "Differential Residential Mobility of the Older Population." *Journal of Gerontology,* 1966, 21(1), pp. 103-108.

Focusing on the residential mobility of persons 50 years of age and older, the data reveal that persons in this age group are less mobile, less likely to desire to move, and are less successful in anticipating their mobility behavior than those in younger age groups. Most people gave dissatisfaction with current housing and neighborhood as reasons for moving or desiring to move.

Gray, Robert M., and Kasteler, Josephine M. "An Investigation of the Effects of Involuntary Relocation on the Health of Older Persons." *Sociological Symposium,* no. 2, Spring 1969, pp. 49-58.

Compares the health activities and attitudes of elderly persons who were involuntarily relocated with those who had not been moved. Results show that relocation is stressful. Persons who were relocated had lower health scores than those who did not change residence.

Gubrium, Jaber F. "Environmental Effects on Morale in Old Age and the Resources of Health and Solvency." *The Gerontologist,* 1970, 10(4), pt. 1, pp. 294-297.

The data indicate that for those elderly with poor behavior resources (health and solvency) an age-concentrated environment is positively associated with morale. Finds no relationship between age-concentration and morale for those elderly with high resources.

Gubrium, Jaber F. (Ed.). *Late Life: Communities and Environmental Policy.* Springfield, Ill.: Charles C. Thomas, 1974.

Focuses on the physical, formal, and cross-cultural environments of the elderly and concludes with some issues on environmental policy.

Gutowski, Michael, and Field, Tracey. *The Graying of Suburbia.* Washington, D.C.: The Urban Institute, 1979.

Compares the characteristics of elderly suburban households and elderly central city households. Contends that the number of elderly persons living in the suburbs will continue to grow because of the large middle-aged population now living in the suburbs who are expected to age in place. Discusses the current and future needs of the elderly suburban population.

Hamovitch, Maurice B., and Peterson, James E. "Housing Needs and Satisfactions of the Elderly." *The Gerontologist,* 1969, 9(1), pp. 30-32.

Indicates that those elderly interviewed are generally well-pleased with their housing. Factors they consider important are being with people of their own kind and of the same age. Also important are climate, location, shopping facilities, and acess to medical personnel.

Hampe, Gary D., and Blevins, Audie L. "Primary Group Interaction of Residents in a Retirement Hotel." *International Journal of Aging and Human Development,* 1975, 6(4), pp. 309-320.

Data from residents living in a retirement hotel reveal that they have a high level of satisfaction with their housing arrangements. Suggests that this satisfaction is due to better living conditions and the involvement of the individual in primary groups.

Heintz, Katherine M. *Retirement Communities: For Adults Only.* New Brunswick, N.J.: Center for Urban Policy Research, 1976.

Investigates the social characteristics of the residents of metropolitan area retirement communities and the impact of these retirement communities upon the larger social environment. The residents of the retirement communities are younger, wealthier, better educated, and of higher occupational status than the elderly in the general population. They express a high degree of satisfaction with their housing accommodations and, despite their physical segregation, the retirement community residents participate in the social and political activities of the larger community.

Hochschild, Arlie R. *The Unexpected Community.* Berkeley: The University of California Press, 1973.

Deals with 43 people, mostly widows, who live in Merrill Court, a small apartment house for the elderly. The residents form their own community and subculture. Describes in detail the customs, friendships, and neighboring that take place among them.

Hochschild, Arlie R. "Communal Life-Styles for the Old." *Society,* 1973, 10(5), pp. 50-57.

Deals with a study of the residents of Merrill Court, a small apartment house for the elderly. Emphasizes how disengagement may be prevented when older persons are supported by a community of appropriate peers.

Jackson, Jacquelyne J. "Social Impacts of Housing Relocation upon Urban Low-Income Black Aged." *The Gerontologist,* 1972, 12(1), pp. 32-37.

Compares black aged applicants who were accepted for a public housing project with those who were not accepted. Results indicate that those who were accepted tended to be males, married, and more sociable. Also those who described themselves as being dependent and pessimistic were admitted more often than those who were not.

Jacobs, Jerry. *Fun City: An Ethnographic Study of a Retirement Community.* New York: Holt, Rinehart and Winston, 1974.

This case study of Fun City, a retirement community, focuses on the ways in which the residents have attempted to adapt to their new mode of life. The concluding chapter deals with some theories of aging and how they fit the lifestyles of Fun City residents.

Jacobs, Jerry. "An Ethnographic Study of a Retirement Setting." *The Gerontologist,* 1974, 14(6), pp. 483-487.

This study of the lifestyles of residents of Fun City, a retirement community, found that the process of disengagement is not inevitable or universal as the theory suggests. Also the findings reveal that life in Fun City had some undesirable features and was contrary to many of the needs and expectations of the residents.

Jacobs, Jerry. *Older Persons and Retirement Communities: Case Studies in Social Gerontology.* Springfield, Ill.: Charles C. Thomas, 1975.

Compares three case studies: High Heaven, a campus based retirement complex, Fun City, a retirement community, and Merrill Court, an apartment building for retired persons. Stresses that ethnographic case studies are not necessarily parochial and that the data can be applied to larger theoretical issues. Also such studies constitute an important perspective from which to study the effects of social settings upon individuals and vice versa.

Jacobs, Ruth H. "The Friendship Club: A Case Study of the Segregated Aged." *The Gerontologist,* 1969, 9(4), pt. 1, pp. 276-280.

Reports that there is a sense of community among the residents of a senior citizens housing project, but at the same time the residents feel rejected and alienated by the larger society.

Johnson, Sheila K. *Idle Haven: Community Building among the Working-Class Retired.* Berkeley: University of California Press, 1971.

This study of Idle Haven, a mobile-home park explores the social relationships of the residents, their leisure pursuits, and some of the formal aspects of the social structure of the park. The study reveals Idle Haven is a tightly knit, homogeneous community which is inhabited by the working-class elderly and provides security and companionship for them.

Kennedy, John M., and DeJong, Gordon F. "Aged in Cities: Residential Segregation in 10 USA Central Cities." *Journal of Gerontology,* 1977, 32(1), pp. 97-102.

Census data were used to determine the degree of segregation of the elderly in cities and how this pattern varied from 1960 to 1970. The analysis shows that a disproportionate share of the elderly reside within the central city. While there is considerable age segregation within certain parts of the city, the degree of segregation did not increase between 1960 and 1970.

Kivett, Vira R., and Learner, R. Max. "Perspectives on the Childless Rural Elderly: A Comparative Analysis." *The Gerontologist,* 1980, 20(6), pp. 708-715.

There are few significant differences between the childless rural elderly and the general population of rural elderly in terms of needs and resources. However, the childless rural elderly in this study are at high risk for certain kinds of dependency.

Kleemeier, Robert W. "The Use and Meaning of Time in Special Settings." In Clark Tibbitts and Wilma Donahue (Eds.), *Social and Psychological Aspects of Aging.* New York: Columbia University Press, 1962, pp. 913-918.

Discusses the influence of certain kinds of environments or special settings upon human activities and use of time. Offers several hypotheses in regard to special settings for the elderly.

Kleemeier, Robert W. "Attitudes toward Special Settings for the Aged." In Richard H. Williams, Clark Tibbitts, and Wilma Donahue (Eds.), *Processes of Aging: Social and Psychological Perspectives,* vol. 2. New York: Atherton Press, 1963, pp. 101-121.

Discusses special settings for the elderly, the place of special settings, and the attitudes toward them.

Kreps, Juanita M. "Economic Status of the Rural Aged." In E. Grant Youmans (Ed.), *Older Rural Americans.* Lexington: University of Kentucky Press, 1967, pp. 144-168.

Notes that the rural aged are one of the lowest income groups in this country. The rural elderly's low income level is due, in part, to their educational level which is less than that of the urban aged. Examines some recent economic trends and their impact on the rural elderly.

Larson, Calvin J. "Alienation and Public Housing for the Elderly." *International Journal of Aging and Human Development,* 1974, 5(3), pp. 217-229.

Findings from the study of two public housing projects for the elderly show that the alienating effects of the move into the project vary inversely with the tenants' ability to maintain established social relationships and to acquire new ones.

Lawton, M. Powell, and Cohen, Joseph. "The Generality of Housing Impact on the Well-Being of Older People." *Journal of Gerontology,* 1974, 29(2), pp. 194-204.

To determine the impact of rehousing on the well-being of older persons, this study compares a group of elderly persons that were rehoused with a group of elderly persons that remained in their own homes. Results show that the rehoused were higher in morale, more satisfied with their housing, more involved in external activities, and significantly poorer in health.

Lawton, M. Powell; Kleban, Morton H.; and Carlson, Diane A. "The Inner-City Resident: To Move or Not to Move." *The Gerontologist,* 1973, 13(4), pp. 443-448.

The results show that those residents who were the most competent were motivated to leave, and those who were the least competent did not wish to leave. However, when residents actually did leave, their leaving was determined by circumstances relatively unrelated to their characteristics.

Lawton, M. Powell; Nahemow, Lucille; and Teaff, Joseph. "Housing Characteristics and the Well-Being of the Elderly Tenants in Federally Assisted Housing." *The Journal of Gerontology,* 1975, 30(5), pp. 601-607.

Indicates that private, nonprofit sponsorship of housing and small community size are associated with higher friendship scores and greater activity participation. Small community size is also associated with greater housing satisfaction.

Lee, Gary R., and Lassey, Marie L. "Rural-Urban Differences among the Elderly: Economic, Social, and Subjective Factors." *Journal of Social Issues,* 1980, 36(2), pp. 62-74.

Deals with the issue of rural versus urban settings in the subjective well-being of the elderly. Considers some possible compensations of rural residence.

Lopata, Helena Z. "Living Arrangements of American Urban Widows." *Sociological Focus,* 1971, 5(1), pp. 41-61.

Examines the attitudes expressed by older widows in the metropolitan Chicago area toward living with their married children. Finds that older widows enjoy the ease and independence of living alone and believe that there would be problems in living with their married children.

Lopata, Helena Z. "Social Relations of Widows in Urbanizing Societies." *The Sociological Quarterly,* 1972, 13(2), pp. 259-271.

Urbanization and increasing societal complexity are modifying the lifestyles of widows in various communities of the world. Many widows are living in situations which do not permit them to utilize the emerging social resources.

Lopata, Helena Z. "Support Systems of Elderly Urbanites: Chicago in the 1970s." *The Gerontologist,* 1975, 15(1), pt. 1, pp. 35-41.

Notes that the urban elderly are generally not involved in a complex support system. Maintains that their social engagement in multi-dimensional support systems is dependent mostly on personal resources.

Lovald, Keith A. "Social Life of the Aged Homeless Man in Skid Row." *The Gerontologist,* 1961, 1(1), pp. 30-33.

Describes the economic situation, living arrangements, and recreational activities of unattached elderly men living in the Gateway district of Minneapolis.

McKain, Walter C., Jr. "Community Roles and Activities of Older Rural Persons." In E. Grant Youmans (Ed.), *Older Rural Americans.* Lexington: University of Kentucky Press, 1967, pp. 75-96.

Discusses some of the formal and informal social participation of older people and examines some factors associated with their participation.

Marshall, Victor W. "Game-Analysable Dilemmas in a Retirement Village: A Case Study." *International Journal of Aging and Human Development*, 1973, 4(4), pp. 285-291.

Views retirement communities which provide lifetime residency for a substantial entrance payment and monthly fees as a conflict of interest between the administration and the residents. Draws on game theory to explain a particular case and suggests that this theory has wide applicability for gerontological issues.

Marshall, Victor W. "Socialization for Impending Death in a Retirement Village." *American Journal of Sociology*, 1975, 80(5), pp. 1124-1144.

Analyzes how the legitimation of death is successfully accomplished at Glen Brae, a retirement village. Contends that congregate living facilities can provide optimal settings for this type of socialization.

Martin, William C. "Activity and Disengagement: Life Satisfaction of In-Movers into a Retirement Community." *The Gerontologist*, 1973, 13(2), pp. 224-227.

Based on a study of in-movers into a retirement community, the author examines the activity and disengagement theories in relation to life satisfaction. He concludes that both theories can correctly describe the socio-psychological processes of aging and that a combination of structural disengagement and age-segregated interpersonal activity may result in high life satisfaction.

Messer, Mark. "The Possibility of an Age-Concentrated Environment Becoming a Normative System." *The Gerontologist*, 1967, 7(4), pp. 247-251.

Offers some evidence that disengagement is facilitated by a segregated environment such as a public housing project for the elderly. This type of environment serves as a buffer to the conflicting role expectations of a younger population and makes adjustment to old age easier.

Montgomery, James E. "Housing of the Rural Aged." In E. Grant Youmans (Ed.), *Older Rural Americans*. Lexington: University of Kentucky Press, 1967, pp. 169-174.

Discusses factors affecting the housing needs of the rural elderly, their current housing conditions, and efforts to improve housing for the aged in rural areas.

Montgomery, James E. "The Housing Patterns of Older Families." *The Family Coordinator*, 1972, 21(1), pp. 37-46.

Gives an overview of housing for the elderly and examines their housing needs and alternatives.

Niebanck, Paul L. *The Elderly in Older Urban Areas.* Philadelphia: Institute for Environmental Studies, University of Pennsylvania, 1965.

Provides a comprehensive description of the elderly residents who are subject to relocation and the impact of relocation upon them. Discusses programs to improve the relocation process.

Pampel, Fred C., and Choldin, Harvey M. "Urban Location and Segregation of the Aged: A Block-Level Analysis." *Social Forces,* 1978, 56(4), pp. 1121-1139.

Analyzes residential patterns of the aged in two cities to determine the extent to which they are disproportionately living near city centers in low-income neighborhoods and segregated from other age groups. While a moderate degree of segregation is found between the aged and the non-aged, the conception of the aged as being segregated into undesirable urban areas is overstated.

Poorkaj, Houshang. "Social-Psychological Factors and Successful Aging." *Sociology and Social Research,* 1971, 56(3), pp. 289-300.

Examines the relationship between living arrangements and successful aging, as well as the utility of the activity and disengagement theories for interpreting successful aging. The major finding of the study is that those living in an age-integrated community have a higher level of morale than those living in an age-segregated retirement community.

Rabushka, Alvin, and Jacobs, Bruce. *Old Folks at Home.* New York: The Free Press, 1980.

Reports the results of a survey of elderly homeowners. Finds that the majority of elderly do not consider their homes to need significant repairs or maintenance work. Such factors as education, financial status, and health tends to correlate with poor housing conditions. On the average, the homes of the blacks have at least one more critical defect than do those of whites.

Rose, Arnold M. "Perspectives on the Rural Aged." In E. Grant Youmans (Ed.), *Older Rural Americans.* Lexington: University of Kentucky Press, 1967, pp. 6-21.

Analyzes the rural aged in terms of three factors: the aging process, characteristics of rural life today, and characteristics of rural life some 60 years ago when the present generation of older people were in their formative years.

Rosow, Irving. "Retirement Housing and Social Integration." *The Gerontologist,* 1961, 1(1), pp. 85-91.

Hypothesizes that old people who have become socially alienated will be integrated more effectively in a segregated neighborhood than in an integrated neighborhood. Suggests some possible functions that residential segregation may serve.

Rosow, Irving. "Retirement Housing and Social Integration." In Clark Tibbitts and Wilma Donahue (Eds.), *Social and Psychological Aspects of Aging.* New York: Columbia University Press, 1962, pp. 327-340.

Discusses the social effects of different types of living arrangements on older persons and examines them in the light of existing knowledge and research.

Schooler, Kermit K. "The Relationship between Social Interaction and Morale of the Elderly as a Function of Environmental Characteristics." *The Gerontologist,* 1969, 9(1), pp. 25-29.

Argues that the proper interpretation of a relationship between the maintenance of social relationships and emotional well-being depends upon some understanding of the residential environment in which they occur.

Seguin, Mary M. "Opportunity for Peer Socialization in a Retirement Community." *The Gerontologist,* 1973, 13(2), pp. 208-214.

Reveals that there is ample opportunity for peer socialization among the residents of a retirement community. The residents generate both an informal social network and a formal social structure through which they enact expressive and instrumental roles.

Shanas, Ethel. "Living Arrangements of Older People." *The Gerontologist,* 1961, 1(1), pp. 27-29.

The findings from a survey of the health needs of older people reveal that most older persons are not isolated from their children. The majority of elderly persons live in close proximity to at least one child and see him or her often.

Shanas, Ethel. "Living Arrangements of Older People in the United States." In Clark Tibbitts and Wilma Donahue (Eds.), *Social and Psychological Aspects of Aging.* New York: Columbia University Press, 1962, pp. 459-463.

A major finding from a study of the health needs of older people is that older people are not physically isolated from their children. A great majority of the aged with children have at least one child in the same household, within walking distance, or only a short ride away.

Shanas, Ethel. "Living Arrangements and Housing of Old People." In Ewald W. Busse and Eric Pfeiffer (Eds.), *Behavior and Adaptation in*

Late Life, 2d ed. Boston: Little, Brown and Company, 1977, pp. 111-129.

The first part of this article focuses on the household composition of the elderly and the supportive role of children, relatives, and neighbors in integrating the aged into the larger community. The second part deals with the housing of the elderly and the types of housing available to them.

Sheldon, Henry D. "Distribution of the Rural Aged Population." In E. Grant Youmans (Ed.), *Older Rural Americans*. Lexington: University of Kentucky Press, 1967, pp. 117-142.

Compares the proportion of older persons living in rural and urban areas and discusses changes in the age structure of the rural population.

Sheley, Joseph F. "Mutuality and Retirement Community Success: An Interactionist Perspective in Gerontological Research." *International Journal of Aging and Human Development*, 1974, 5(1), pp. 71-79.

Interviews from male residents in a retirement community reveal that they are satisfied with retirement as well as life in their community. The residents' satisfaction with community life is linked to their having similar backgrounds and interests which give them a sense of belonging.

Sherman, Susan R. "The Choice of Retirement Housing among the Well-Elderly." *Aging and Human Development*, 1971, 2(2), pp. 118-138.

Examines some of the reasons the elderly chose retirement housing. The best liked aspect of retirement housing was the presence of friends. Other reasons included provision of meals, improved and attractive living quarters in an urban environment, close proximity to age peers, recreational facilities, and security. Some of the reasons given by the elderly in conventional housing for not moving into retirement housing were a distaste for age segregation, a fear of regimentation, and boredom.

Sherman, Susan R. "Satisfaction with Retirement Housing: Attitudes, Recommendations and Moves." *Aging and Human Development*, 1972, 3(4), pp. 339-366.

Compares the satisfaction of older persons who live in various types of retirement housing with those elderly living in conventional housing. The factors that are related to satisfaction with housing include: proximity, security, balance of independence-dependence, and provision of creature comforts.

Sherman, Susan R. "Methodology in a Study of Residents of Retirement Housing." *Journal of Gerontology*, 1973, 28(3), pp. 351-358.

Describes the methodology used in a longitudinal study of residents of six retirement housing sites. Gives the criteria for selection of the sites, interview construction, as well as matching procedures and methods used to minimize attrition.

Sherman, Susan R. "Leisure Activities in Retirement Housing." *Journal of Gerontology,* 1974, 29(3), pp. 325-335.

Interview data from residents of six retirement sites and from residents living in conventional housing reveal the following results about leisure activities. Residence in two retirement settings, and in some instances four, is associated with more leisure activities than was residence in conventional housing. There is a moderately positive relationship between activity scores and several measures of outlook on life.

Sherman, Susan R. "Patterns of Contacts for Residents of Age-Segregated and Age-Integrated Housing." *Journal of Gerontology,* 1975, 30(1), pp. 103-107.

Finds different types of social integration and patterns of contact for residents of retirement housing and residents of conventional housing. The author concludes that either type of living arrangement can be satisfactory provided persons make the choice according to their own preferences.

Sherman, Susan R. "Mutual Assistance and Support in Retirement Housing." *Journal of Gerontology,* 1975, 30(4), pp. 479-483.

Compares networks of mutual assistance for the elderly living in retirement housing with those elderly living in conventional housing. Retirement housing residents do not suffer from a lack of assistance from children, but neither do they benefit overall from greater assistance from neighbors.

Smith, Bruce W., and Hiltner, John. "Intraurban Location of the Elderly." *Journal of Gerontology,* 1975, 30(4), pp. 469-472.

Reveals that the location patterns of the elderly differ significantly from that of younger persons. However, only weak associations are found between the elderly's location and their living in older neighborhoods, multiple-family dwelling units, and tracts closer to the central business district.

Starr, Bernice C. "The Community." In Matilda W. Riley, Marilyn Johnson, and Anne Foner, *Aging and Society: A Sociology of Age Stratification,* vol. 3. New York: Russell Sage Foundation, 1972, pp. 198-235.

Introduces age as a central element of community analysis. Discusses the age structure of the community, the changing community needs of persons as they age, and the impact of migration.

Stephens, Joyce. "Romance in the SRO: Relationships of Elderly Men and Women in a Slum Hotel." *The Gerontologist,* 1974, 14(4), pp. 279-282.

Mutual suspicion and avoidance tend to characterize the relationships between elderly men and women living in a SRO (single-room occupancy) slum hotel. For the men, the seeking out of female company usually means the services of a prostitute. The women do not relate well to each other because of the competition, hostility, and jealousy that exists between them.

Stephens, Joyce. "Society of the Alone: Freedom, Privacy, and Utilitarianism as Dominant Norms in the SRO." *Journal of Gerontology,* 1975, 30(2), pp. 230-235.

Finds that the majority of elderly tenants in a SRO (single-room occupancy) hotel are lifelong social isolates. The impersonal world of the SRO allows them to live a lifestyle of their own choosing and encourages freedom, privacy, and utilitarianism to extreme degrees.

Stephens, Joyce. *Loners, Losers, and Lovers: Elderly Tenants in a Slum Hotel.* Seattle: University of Washington Press, 1976.

Using the technique of participant observation, the author gives a descriptive analysis of the social world of the elderly tenant living in a SRO (single-room occupancy) slum hotel. She describes the roles and role patterns found within the SRO society, the norms and values that serve to maintain relationships, and the nature of the relationships between the tenants and the outside world.

Streib, Gordon F., and Streib, Ruth B. "Communes and the Aging: Utopian Dream and Gerontological Reality." *American Behavioral Scientist,* 1975, 19(2), pp. 176-189.

Notes that it is unlikely that true communal organizations for the elderly can develop on any scale in this country at the present time. Discusses an example of a new type of experiment which has some of the elements of an urban commune.

Struyk, Raymond J. "The Housing Situation of Elderly Americans." *The Gerontologist,* 1977, 17(2), pp. 130-139.

Contrasts data on households headed by persons 65 years of age or older with figures for all households. Concludes that among elderly-headed households, 17% of those residing in urban areas and 30% of those in rural areas are living in dwellings which are physically deficient, plagued by problems such as heating and plumbing, or are located in an unpleasant neighborhood environment.

Sundeen, Richard A., and Mathieu, James T. "The Urban Elderly: Environments of Fear." In Jack Goldsmith and Sharon S. Goldsmith (Eds.), *Crime and the Elderly.* Lexington, Mass.: Lexington Books, 1976, pp. 51-66.

Explores some of the factors that increase or lessen the fear of victimization among the elderly in three communities: a central city, an urban municipality, and a retirement community. Findings show that within the central city social support is the most important factor in diffusing the fear of crime. In the urban municipality, a feeling of belonging to the community and perceived safety of the neighborhood at night helped to decrease the fear of robbery and burglary. Finally, the number of persons in one's residence did not appear to be as important as other factors in reducing the fear of crime.

Sundeen, Richard A. "The Fear of Crime and Urban Elderly." In Marlene A.Y. Rifai (Ed.), *Justice and Older Americans.* Lexington, Mass.: Lexington Books, 1977, pp. 13-24.

Discusses the relationship between the fear of crime victimization and some factors which represent life circumstances among urban elderly. High levels of fear of burglary are related to a low sense of participation in one's community, while high levels of fear of robbery are related to a low level of self-perceived health. Also perception of less security in one's neighborhood during the day is related to being female.

Taietz, Phillip. "Community Complexity and Knowledge of Facilities." *Journal of Gerontology,* 1975, 30(3), pp. 357-362.

Examines the relationship between the type of community in which the elderly live and their knowledge of the community. Results reveal that there is a negative relationship between community complexity and knowledge of facilities for rural communities, but for large cities the relationship is positive.

Teaff, Joseph D., et al. "Impact of Age Integration on the Well-Being of the Elderly Tenants in Public Housing." *Journal of Gerontology,* 1978, 33(1), pp. 126-133.

Analyzes the relationship between age-integrated and age-segregated housing and the well-being of elderly tenants. Results show that elderly persons living in age-segregated housing participate more in organized activities and have higher morale and housing satisfaction than those in age-integrated settings.

Tissue, Thomas. "Old Age, Poverty, and the Central City." *Aging and Human Development,* 1971, 2(4), pp. 235-247.

Compares the lifestyles of older men living in poverty in the central city to their counterparts in outlying areas. Although the men living in the central city have led more mobile and solitary lives in the past and their present lifestyles differ greatly from those men in the outlying areas, the two lifestyles produce the same levels of satisfaction and morale.

Toseland, Ron, and Rasch, John. "Factors Contributing to Older Persons' Satisfaction with Their Communities." *The Gerontologist,* 1978, 18(4), pp. 395-402.

Indicates that community variables are the most important predictors of community satisfaction. These variables are physical safety, recreation and health care facilities, and satisfaction with the individual dwelling unit.

Twente, Esther E. *Never Too Old: The Aged in Community Life.* San Francisco: Jossey-Bass, 1970.

Concerns elderly persons in small communities, their families, and other groups with whom they affiliate. Addressed primarily to social workers.

Ward, Russell A. "The Implication of Neighborhood Age Structure for Older People." *Sociological Symposium,* 1979, no. 26, pp. 42-63.

Discusses the importance as well as the consequences of residential age structure on the well-being of the elderly.

Winiecke, Linda. "The Appeal of Age-Segregated Housing for the Elderly Poor." *International Journal of Aging and Human Development,* 1973, 4(4), pp. 293-305.

The majority of the respondents who are interested in age-segregated housing as compared to those who express no interest tend to be young, are renters, do not see their children often, and complain more of being lonely and bored.

Yee, William, and Van Arsdol, Maurice D. "Residential Mobility, Age, and the Life Cycle." *Journal of Gerontology,* 1977, 32(2), pp. 211-221.

Reveals that age has an inverse relationship to mobility and underlies a life-cycle step explanation of mobility for a homogeneous population aggregate. Also transition points in the family life cycle appear to define normative events that are followed by later residential changes.

Youmans, Grant E. "Family Disengagement among Older Urban and Rural Women." *Journal of Gerontology,* 1967, 22(2), pp. 209-211.

Compares older and younger urban women and older and younger rural women to determine the extent of disengagement in their family life. The findings reveal slight but statistically significant evidence of disengagement only in the rural area.

Youmans, E. Grant (Ed.). *Older Rural Americans.* Lexington: University of Kentucky Press, 1967.

Provides a sociological perspective on older persons living in rural environments. Discusses the social, economic, and health conditions of older rural persons, as well as the condition and place of older rural persons in three major subcultures--the American Indians, the Spanish-speaking people of the Southwest, and blacks.

Youmans, E. Grant. "Disengagement among Older Rural and Urban Men." In E. Grant Youmans (Ed.), *Older Rural Americans.* Lexington: University of Kentucky Press, 1967, pp. 97-116.

Compares rural and urban men aged 60 to 64 and those aged 75 and over in three areas of life: economic, family relationships, and leisure-time activities. The findings show that economic disengagement increases substantially with age among the men. In both residential areas, the older men had only slightly more disengagement in family life and leisure-time activities than the younger men.

Youmans, E. Grant. "Orientations to Old Age." *The Gerontologist,* 1968, 8(3), pp. 153-158.

In his study of middle-aged persons living in a rural community, Youmans finds that they have no expectations to disengage in old age from their present hobbies and community activities. Most of the respondents expect to be as happy in old age as they are at present.

Youmans, E. Grant. "Generation and Perceptions of Old Age: An Urban-Rural Comparison." *The Gerontologist,* 1971, 2(4), pt. 1, pp. 284-288.

Compares generational differences in perceptions of old age of those living in a metropolitan center and those in a rural county. The older generation show more concern about worries and work problems, and a stronger conviction about the positive aspects of age than do younger persons.

Youmans, E. Grant. "Perspectives on the Older American in a Rural Setting." In John C. Cull and Richard E. Hardy, *The Neglected Older American.* Springfield, Ill.: Charles C. Thomas, 1973, pp. 65-85.

Compares older and younger persons in a rural area and in an urban area for differences in values and beliefs. Finds that older persons in the rural area scored higher than urban older persons on most measures of authoritarianism. Both younger and older persons in the rural area are more fundamentalistic in their religious outlook than their urban counterparts. Also older urban persons give significantly stronger support to the value of achievement, and less support for dependency than do older rural persons.

Youmans, E. Grant. "The Rural Aged." *The Annals of the American Academy of Political and Social Science,* 1977, 429, pp. 81-90.

Reviews some studies on the objective and subjective conditions of life for the rural elderly. Indicates that older rural Americans have small incomes, inadequate transportation, a restricted social life, and poor physical and mental health.

Youmans, E. Grant. "Attitudes: Young-Old and Old-Old." *The Gerontologist,* 1977, 17(2), pp. 175-178.

Compares the attitudes of young-old and old-old persons living in rural and urban communities. In the urban community more favorable attitudes as well as substantial differences in attitude scores are found between the old-old and the young-old. In the rural community there are only slight differences between the attitude scores of the young-old and old-old.

Chapter 17

INSTITUTIONALIZATION

Anderson, Nancy N. "Institutionalization, Interaction, and Self-Conception in Aging." In Arnold M. Rose and Warren A. Peterson (Eds.), *Older People and Their Social World.* Philadelphia: F.A. Davis, 1965, pp. 245-257.

Suggests that interaction explains self-conception more adequately than does institutionalization.

Bennett, Ruth, and Nahemow, Lucille. "Institutional Totality and Criteria of Social Adjustment in Residences for the Aged." *Journal of Social Issues,* 1965, 21(4), pp. 44-78.

Examines the relationship between institutional totality and the clarity and complexity of social adjustment criteria. Shows that in homes for the aged, participation in formal and informal activities emerge as a major adjustment criterion. In retirement housing, participation in informal social relationships is an important adjustment criterion. Adjustment criteria are the clearest and most complex in settings which are established as permanent and which approximate self-contained communities.

Borup, Jerry H.; Gallego, Daniel T.; and Heffernan, Pamela G. "Relocation and Its Effect on Mortality." *The Gerontologist,* 1979, 19(2), pp. 135-139.

Finds that the stress of relocation on nursing home patients does not increase the probability of mortality. No significant differences are found between the mortality rates of handicapped and nonhandicapped patients, and male and female patients.

Coe, Rodney M. "Self-Conception and Institutionalization." In Arnold M. Rose and Warren A. Peterson (Eds.), *Older People and Their Social World.* Philadelphia: F.A. Davis, 1965, pp. 225-243.

Reveals that institutionalization has a tremendous impact on the self-conception of chronically ill, aged patients. A fairly large number of patients appear to be depersonalized to an extreme degree.

Curry, Timothy J., and Ratliff, Bascom W. "The Effects of Nursing Home Size on Resident Isolation and Life Satisfaction." *The Gerontologist,* 1973, 13(3), pt. 1, pp. 295-298.

Finds that small nursing homes facilitate the development of a greater number of friendships. However, nursing home size does not influence life satisfaction to any great degree.

Dick, Harry R., and Friedsam, Hiram J. "Adjustment of Residents of Two Homes for the Aged." *Social Problems,* 1964, 11(3), pp. 282-290.

Examines the adjustment of residents in two homes for the aged. Morale appears to decline during institutionalization even though some favorable adjustments were made to the home. Although good health is significant for high morale, it is not necessary for a favorable attitude toward the home.

Dudley, Charles J., and Hillery, George A., Jr. "Freedom and Alienation in Homes for the Aged." *The Gerontologist,* 1977, 17(2), pp. 140-145.

Compared to those living in other types of residential organizations, the residents of homes for the aged have higher scores on alienation and deprivation of freedom.

Eribes, Richard A., and Bradley-Rawls, Martha. "The Underutilization of Nursing Home Facilities by Mexican-American Elderly in the Southwest." *The Gerontologist,* 1978, 18(4), pp. 363-371.

To Mexican-Americans the nursing home is not seen as a culturally viable alternative, but only as a last resort. Mexican-American families try to keep their elderly out of institutionalized facilities, and prefer to handle the medical care of their elderly in other ways.

Friedman, Edward P. "Spatial Proximity and Social Interaction in a Home for the Aged." *Journal of Gerontology,* 1966, 21(4), pp. 566-570.

Shows that spatial proximity proves to be the most important single variable in explaining friendship formation among elderly women in a home for the aged. Friendship choice and the relationship between proximity does not decline as the length of residence of the person making the choice increases. Also proximity is shown to be a more important factor in those choices in which reciprocity is present than in those in which it is absent.

Friedman, Edward P. "Age, Length of Institutionalization, and Social Status in a Home for the Aged." *Journal of Gerontology,* 1967, 22(4), pt. 1, pp. 474-477.

Reveals that for residents in a home for elderly women, age and length of institutionalization are related to friendship formation. A significant correlation is found between extreme old age, long length of institutionalization, and high social status within the institution.

Gelfand, Donald E. "Visiting Patterns and Social Adjustment in an Old Age Home." *The Gerontologist,* 1968, 8(4), pp. 272-275 and p. 304.

The two most important determinants of social adjustment in the old age home studied are outside visiting and sociability.

Gubrium, Jaber F. "On Multiple Realities in a Nursing Home." In Jaber F. Gubrium (Ed.), *Late Life: Communities and Environmental Policy.* Springfield, Ill.: Charles C. Thomas, 1974, pp. 61-98.

Examines the following three dimensions of the social organization of multiple realities in a nursing home: (1) the constraints of situations as they influence patient care; (2) definitions of the reality of patient care; and (3) the accommodations that actors with different definitions make to one another.

Gubrium, Jaber F. *Living and Dying at Murray Manor.* New York: St. Martin's Press, 1975.

Using the participant-observation method, this book documents the way in which daily care in a nursing home is accomplished. It analyzes how the participants carry out their roles and invoke their rights and duties.

Ingram, Donald K., and Barry, John R. "National Statistics on Deaths in Nursing Homes: Interpretations and Implications." *The Gerontologist,* 1977, 17(4), pp. 303-308.

An increasingly large number of elderly persons are dying while residents of nursing homes. As a result, the authors feel that some orientation about death, and the problems of the dying patient must become part of the formal training of all nursing home personnel.

Jacobs, Ruth H. "One-Way Street: An Intimate View of Adjustment to a Home for the Aged." *The Gerontologist,* 1969, 9(4), pt. 1, pp. 268-275.

Suggests that conflict may serve positive functions in institutions for the elderly.

Jones, Dean C. "Social Isolation, Interaction, and Conflict in Two Nursing Homes." *The Gerontologist,* 1972, 12(3), pt. 1, pp. 230-234.

Reveals that considerable social isolation, hostility, mistrust, and overt conflict exist between nursing home patients.

Kahana, Eva. "The Humane Treatment of Old People in Institutions." *The Gerontologist,* 1973, 13(3), pt. 1, pp. 282-289.

Discusses issues in practices relating to a humane environment in institutions. Proposes a conceptual model for environment-individual interaction as a way of humanizing institutional settings.

Kahana, Eva. "Matching Environments to Needs of the Aged: A Conceptual Scheme." In Jaber F. Gubrium (Ed.), *Late Life: Communities and Environmental Policy.* Springfield, Ill.: Charles C. Thomas, 1974, pp. 201-214.

Presents a conceptual model for matching environments to the needs of the aged and demonstrates how this model has been used in a study of three nursing homes.

Kart, Cary S., and Manard, Barbara. "Quality of Care in Old Age Institutions." *The Gerontologist,* 1976, 16(3), pp. 250-256.

Singles out the following five characteristics for identifying a good nursing home or rest home: ownership, size, socioeconomic status of facility, social integration, and professionalism of staff.

Kastenbaum, Robert, and Candy, Sandra E. "The 4% Fallacy: A Methodological and Empirical Critique of Extended Care Facility Population Statistics." *International Journal of Aging and Human Development,* 1973, 4(1), pp. 15-21.

Finds that a minimum of 20% of all elderly persons who died in 1971 in metropolitan Detroit were living in a nursing home and 24% were residents of some type of extended care facility. The population statistics which indicate that only 4% of those over age 65 are in nursing homes and other extended care facilities are misleading.

Keith, Patricia M. "An Exploratory Study of Sources of Stereotypes of Old Age among Administrators." *Journal of Gerontology,* 1977, 32(4), pp. 463-469.

Explores the effects of client, personal, and organizational characteristics on the stereotypes of the elderly held by nursing home administers. Suggests that the sex of clients and other status characteristics may affect attitudes toward the aged, and possibly the quality of care which is provided.

Makarushka, Julia L., and McDonald, Robert D. "Informed Consent, Research, and Geriatric Patients: The Responsibility of Institutional Review Committees." *The Gerontologist,* 1979, 19(1), pp. 61-66.

Examines the responsibilities of the Institutional Review Committee to the older patient as a potential research subject. Discusses the functions of the informed consent process and the effects of inappropriate informed consent procedures.

Manard, Barbara B.; Kart, Cary S.; and Van Gils, Dirk W.L. *Old-Age Institutions.* Lexington, Mass.: Lexington Books, 1975.

The beginning chapters provide an overview of the elderly population and old-age institutions. The later chapters focus on the diversity of living arrangements both within and outside of institutions in the states of Massachusetts, Virginia, and Utah.

Markson, Elizabeth. "A Hiding Place to Die." *Trans-Action,* 1971, 9(1-2), pp. 48-54.

The following factors contribute to the abandonment of the elderly to a state mental hospital to die: old age itself, the high probability of dying, and low social status along with lack of power.

Markson, Elizabeth W. "Ethnicity as a Factor in the Institutionalization of the Ethnic Elderly." In Donald Gelfand and Alfred Kutzik (Eds.), *Ethnicity and Aging.* New York: Springer Publishing Co., 1979, pp. 341-356.

Finds that placing the aged of different ethnic groups into the same mental institution produces discontent and often open confrontation.

Myles, John F. "Institutionalization and Sick Role Identification among the Elderly." *American Sociological Review,* 1978, 43(4), pp. 508-521.

Investigates the extent to which institutionalization alters the relationship between objective and perceived health status. The results reveal that given comparable levels of illness and disability, the institutionalized respondents are less likely than the noninstitutionalized respondents to view themselves as ill.

Noelker, Linda, and Harel, Zev. "Predictors of Well-Being and Survival among Institutionalized Aged." *The Gerontologist,* 1978, 18(6), pp. 562-567.

Finds that the primary predictors of personal well-being for residents in long-term care facilities are a positive preception of the facility, the staff, and the other residents as well as a desire to live in the facility.

Palmore, Erdman. "Total Chance of Institutionalization among the Aged." *The Gerontologist,* 1976, 16(6), pp. 504-507.

Factors related to total chance of institutionalization are living arrangements, marital status, number of children living, and sex. The factors increasing one's access to institutions include finances, education, and race.

Reingold, Jacob, and Dobrof, Rose. "Organization Theory and Home for the Aged." *The Gerontologist,* 1965, 5(2), pp. 88-95 and p. 112.

Maintains that a productive approach to studying institutions for the aged is through organizational theory. Shows how the specialization that exists among staff members in homes for the aged illustrates how organizational analysis can be utilized.

Rosenblatt, Daniel, and Taviss, Irene. "The Home for the Aged--Theory and Practice." *The Gerontologist,* 1966, 6(3), pp. 165-168.

Discusses the major points of the theories of Goffman, and Cumming and Henry dealing with aging and total institutions, and examines them in the light of a study in a home for the aged.

Siegel, Barry, and Lasher, Judith. "Deinstitutionalizing Elderly Patients: A Program of Resocialization." *The Gerontologist,* 1978, 18(3), pp. 293-300.

Three components of a deinstitutionalization program are a proper diagnosis, a change in social structure, and familiarity with the proposed new setting. The results show that efforts to deinstitutionalize patients must be based on changes in expectations of staff and changes in the patients' definition of their own situations.

Smith, Kristen F., and Bengtson, Vern L. "Positive Consequences of Institutionalization: Solidarity between Elderly Parents and Their Middle-Aged Children." *The Gerontologist,* 1979, 19(5), pp. 438-447.

Indicates that in only about 10 percent of parent-child combinations does institutionalization have a negative effect on their relationship. The majority of the families find that the elderly parents' institutionalization strengthens ties and renews closeness between parent and child.

Stannard, Charles I. "Old Folks and Dirty Work: The Social Conditions for Patient Abuse in a Nursing Home." *Social Problems,* 1973, 20(3), pp. 329-342.

Shows how patient abuse by aides and orderlies can occur in a nursing home without the nurses being aware of it.

Vincente, Leticia; Wiley, James; and Carrington, Allen. "The Risk of Institutionalization before Death." *The Gerontologist,* 1979, 19(4), pp. 361-367.

Nearly 39 percent of the sample in this study were admitted to a nursing home at least once before death. Chances of being institutionalized are higher for the unmarried, the old, and those who live alone.

Wax, Murray. "The Changing Role of the Home for the Aged." *The Gerontologist,* 1962, 2(3), pp. 128-133.

Predicts that during the next decade homes for the aged will be in competition with housing arrangements that provide a wide range of services to the independent elderly and with associations seeking to rehabilitate the chronically ill elderly.

Weinstock, Comilda, and Bennett, Ruth. "Problems in Communication to Nurses among Residents of a Racially Heterogeneous Nursing Home." *The Gerontologist,* 1968, 8(2), pp. 72-75.

Strained interaction is reflected mainly in the negative attitudes of the white patients toward the black staff, and not from the staff members having negative attitudes toward the elderly.

Wessen, Albert F. "Some Sociological Characteristics of Long-Term Care." In Arnold M. Rose and Warren A. Peterson (Eds.), *Older People and Their Social World.* Philadelphia: F.A. Davis, 1965, pp. 259-271.

Suggests that long-term care must be seen as a distinctive problem of medical care with its own unique characteristics and needs. Presents some propositions describing the present picture of long-term care.

Chapter 18

DEATH AND DYING

Back, Kurt W., and Baade, Hans W. "The Social Meaning of Death and the Law." In John C. McKinney and Frank de Vyver (Eds.). *Aging and Social Policy.* New York: Appleton-Century-Crofts, 1966, pp. 302-329.

Examines the social meaning of death and its relation to the older person. The authors rely primarily on the formal structures of society, especially as it is expressed and applied in law.

Back, Kurt W. "Metaphors as Test of Personal Philosophy of Aging." *Sociological Focus,* 1971, 5(1), pp. 1-8.

Investigates the utility of a technique whereby metaphors are used for the words "time" and "death". The major finding in this study is that women are more accepting of death, and are more aware of the passage of time, especially in the later years. This is also true of older people in general as compared to those in the middle years.

Bengtson, Vern L.; Cuellar, Jose B.; and Ragan, Pauline K. "Stratum Contrasts and Similarities in Attitudes toward Death." *Journal of Gerontology,* 1977, 32(1), pp. 76-88.

Examines differences between blacks, Mexican-Americans, and whites in their attitudes toward death. Analysis by age and race reveals that middle-aged persons express the greatest fears of death and the elderly express the least. Blacks expect to live the longest and Mexican-Americans expect to die at earlier ages.

Blauner, Robert. "Death and Social Structure." *Psychiatry, Journal for the Study of Interpersonal Processes,* 1966, 29, pp. 378-394.

Discusses how modern societies control death through bureaucratization and some of the consequences of this control.

Glaser, Barney G. "The Social Loss of Aged Dying Patients." *The Gerontologist,* 1966, 6(2), pp. 77-80.

The aged dying patient is often looked upon by the nursing personnel as a low social loss. However, there are some conditions which balance out this evaluation and its consequences.

Glaser, Barney G., and Strauss, Anselm L. "Temporal Aspects of Dying as a Non-Scheduled Status Passage." *The American Journal of Sociology,* 1965, 71(1), pp. 48-59.

Based on a study of how hospital personnel handle dying which is seen as passing between the status of the living and the dead with no imposed schedule.

Glaser, Barney G., and Strauss, Anselm L. *Awareness of Dying.* Chicago: Aldine Publishing Co., 1965.

Describes the conspiracy engaged in by medical personnel and family members to prevent patients from becoming aware of their terminal illnesses. In contrast to this deception, is the system of open awareness which encourages more effective interaction with dying patients.

Glaser, Barney G., and Strauss, Anselm L. *Time for Dying.* Chicago: Aldine, 1968.

Focuses on the temporal features of dying in hospitals in relation to the work of the hospital personnel and to dying itself as a social process.

Gubrium, Jaber F. "Death Worlds in a Nursing Home." *Urban Life,* 1975, 4(3), pp. 317-338.

Examines dying and death as main events in Murray Manor, a nursing home.

Haberstein, Robert W. "The Social Organization of Death." In *International Encyclopedia of the Social Sciences.* New York: Macmillan, 1968, pp. 26-28.

Deals with death as a passage, the channeling of death responses, and the ritualization of funerals.

Haug, Marie. "Aging and the Right to Terminate Medical Treatment." *Journal of Gerontology,* 1978, 33(4), pp. 586-591.

The findings reveal similar views among all age groups on the desirability of maintaining control of final decisions by the patient or family in permitting a person to die. Although older persons are the most likely to disagree with the patient's or family's right to discontinue treatment, this disagreement is the opinion of only a minority of the elderly.

Kalish, Richard A. "The Aged and the Dying Process: The Inevitable Decisions." *Journal of Social Issues,* 1965, 21(4), pp. 87-96.

Considers the major problems in the "management of dying".

Kalish, Richard A. "Death and Dying in a Social Context." In Robert H. Binstock and Ethel Shanas (Eds.), *Handbook of Aging and the Social Sciences.* New York: Van Nostrand Reinhold, 1976, pp. 483-507.

Discusses the meanings of death, reactions to death, the dying process, caring for the dying, and encountering the death of others.

Keith, Pat M. "Life Changes and Perceptions of Life and Death among Older Men and Women." *Journal of Gerontology,* 1979, 34(6), pp. 870-878.

Analyzes changes in marital status, health, church involvement, and informal family and friendship contacts in relation to perceptions of life and death among older persons. Respondents were classified as negativists, activists, and passivists. Results indicate that those persons who experienced discontinuity are more frequently negativists or passivists, whereas those who experienced continuity are activists and positivists. In addition, men and women differ in their perceptions of life and death in that women are more likely to be positivists and passivists, and men tend to be negativists and activists.

Lipman, Aaron, and Marden, Philip W. "Preparation for Death in Old Age." *Journal of Gerontology,* 1966, 21(3), pp. 426-431.

Examines the extent to which retired persons living in public housing had made provisions for death. While the majority of respondents had made some preparations, the only factors significantly related to having made provisions for death are source of income, race, and education. A significantly higher proportion of persons who had made preparations for death receive none of their income from welfare as compared with those whose income is provided in part or in whole by welfare. Whites and those with higher educational attainment have made more provisions for death than non-whites and those with lower educational attainment.

Marshall, Victor W. "Organizational Features of Terminal Status Passage in Residential Facilities for the Aged." *Urban Life,* 1975, 4(3), pp. 349-368.

Compares the way in which residents organize their dying careers in a home for the aged and in a retirement village.

Marshall, Victor W. "Socialization for Impending Death in a Retirement Village." *American Journal of Sociology,* 1975, 80(5), pp. 1124-1144.

Analyzes how the legitimation of death is successfully accomplished at Glen Brae, a retirement village. Contends that congregate living facilities can provide optimal settings for this type of socialization.

Marshall, Victor W. *Last Chapters: A Sociology of Aging and Dying.* Monterey, Calif.: Brooks/Cole, 1980.

Examines the relationship between aging and dying both at the individual and social level. Also provides an assessment of several important strands of theory in social gerontology.

Matthews, Sarah. "Old Women and Identity Maintenance: Outwitting the Grim Reaper." *Urban Life,* 1975, 4(3), pp. 339-348.

Discusses the strategies among old women to maintain a desired self-identity in dying and death.

Pine, Vanderlyn R., and Phillips, Derek L. "The Cost of Dying: A Sociological Analysis of Funeral Expenditures." *Social Problems,* 1970, 17(3), pp. 405-417.

Shows a positive relationship between one's position in the status hierarchy and expenditures for funerals. At each status level, expenditures for funerals are higher among older persons than for younger persons.

Riley, J.W., Jr. "Death and Bereavement." In *International Encyclopedia of the Social Sciences.* New York: Macmillan, 1968, pp. 19-26

Discusses death and its relation to culture, society, and the individual.

Rosenfeld, Jeffrey P. "Old Age, New Beneficiaries: Kinship, Friendship and (Dis) Inheritance." *Sociology and Social Research,* 1979, 64(1), pp. 86-98.

Examines the inheritances that the elderly will to family and friends. Disinheritances of kin occur most frequently among the hospitalized elderly and residents of retirement communities.

Rosenfield, Jeffrey P. *The Legacy of Aging: Inheritance and Disinheritance in Social Perspective.* Norwood, N.J.: Ablex, 1979.

Deals with the social characteristics of will-writers and relates the lifestyles of the elderly to the wills that they write.

Sudnow, David. Passing On: *The Social Organization of Dying.* Englewood Cliffs, N.J.: Prentice-Hall, 1967.

Describes how care is given dying patients, how family members are informed of the deaths of their relatives, and how the social organization of the hospital is affected by and affects the occurrence of death within its confines.

Ward, Russell A. "Age and Acceptance of Euthanasia." *Journal of Gerontology,* 1980, 35(3), pp. 421-431.

The fact that older persons tend to accept euthanasia less than younger persons is attributed to the elderly's lower educational attainment and greater religiosity. Also lower life satisfaction and anomia are related to more favorable attitudes toward euthanasia among the elderly.

PART 6

PERIODICALS

Chapter 19

SELECTED AGING JOURNALS

Activities, Adaptation and Aging, 1980. The Haworth Press, 149 Fifth Ave., New York, NY 10010. (Quarterly).

Emphasizes activities for the elderly using an interdisciplinary approach.

Ageing International, 1974. International Federation on Ageing, 1909 K St., N.W., Washington, DC 20049. (Quarterly).

Published in several languages, this bulletin gives cross-cultural information on research results in social gerontology as well as program innovations and developments in aging policies within international organizations.

Aging and Work. 1969. (Formerly Industrial Gerontology). National Council on the Aging, Inc., 600 Maryland Ave., S.W., Washington, DC 20024. (Quarterly).

Focuses on the older worker and job satisfaction, job performance, discrimination, retirement, and other related topics.

Educational Gerontology. 1976. Hemisphere Publishing Corp., 1025 Vermont Ave., N.W., Washington, DC 20005. (Quarterly).

Contains articles relevant to adult education. Book reviews, periodicals, book lists, and government documents are included in a section on learning resources.

Generations. 1976. Western Gerontological Society, 833 Market St., San Francisco, CA. 94103. (Quarterly).

Generations is the newsletter of the Western Gerontological Society. Each issue is devoted to a topic concerning aging.

Geriatrics, 1946. Harcourt Brace Jovanovich, Inc., 757 Third Ave., New York, NY 10017. (Monthly).

Although this journal focuses primarily on the medical aspects of aging, from time to time it contains articles of interest to social gerontologists.

The Gerontologist. 1961. Gerontological Society of America, 1411 K St., N.W., Washington, DC 20005. (Bi-monthly).

Designed for practioners, educators, and researchers in the aging field, this journal contains articles on research, theory, demographic analysis, social policy, and program evaluation.

International Journal of Aging and Human Development. 1973. (Formerly Aging and Human Development), Baywood Publishing Co., 120 Marine St., P.O. Box D, Farmingdale, NY 11735. (Quarterly).

Focuses on the social and psychological studies of later life.

Journal of Applied Gerontology. 1982. Southern Gerontological Society, P.O. Box 3183, University of South Florida, Tampa, FL 33620. (Quarterly).

Provides a forum for applied gerontological research and practice.

Journal of Gerontology, 1946. Gerontological Society of America, 1411 K St., N.W., Washington, DC 20005. (Bi-monthly).

Publishes articles dealing with or related to the problems of aging from the areas of biology, medicine, psychology, and the social sciences.

Journal of The American Geriatrics Society. 1953. American Geriatrics Society, 10 Columbus Circle, New York, NY 10019. (Monthly).

Focuses on the medical aspects of aging, but often contains articles of interest to those in the social sciences.

Omega. 1970. Baywood Publishing Co., 120 Marine St., Farmingdale, NY 11735. (Quarterly).

Emphasizes the social and psychological studies of death, dying, and bereavement.

Research on Aging. 1979. Sage Publications, Inc., 275 S. Beverly Dr., Beverly Hills, CA 90212. (Quarterly).

Focusing on the role of research in social gerontology and knowledge about the aging process and the aged, this journal covers a wide range of disciplines including sociology, history, psychology, anthropology, economics, and political science.

Chapter 20

SELECTED SOCIOLOGICAL JOURNALS AND RELATED FIELDS

American Behavioral Scientist. 1957. Sage Publications, 275 S. Beverly Dr., Beverly Hills, CA 90212. (Bi-monthly).

Focuses on research and theoretical articles. Each issue is devoted to a special topic. The September/October 1970 issue was devoted to aging and was published as a separate volume in the Sage Contemporary Social Science Issues Series.

American Journal of Sociology. 1895. University of Chicago Press, 5801 Ellis Ave., Chicago, IL 60637. (Bi-monthly).

The oldest American journal in the field of sociology, this publication emphasizes general theoretical and methodological issues in a broad range of areas. Articles relevant to aging and the aged appear from time to time.

American Sociological Review. 1936. American Sociological Association, 1722 N. St., N.W., Washington, DC 20036. (Bi-monthly).

The official journal of the American Sociological Association, this publication's major focus is on work that contributes to the knowledge of society. It includes articles that contain new theoretical developments, results of research, and methodological innovations. Articles relating to the elderly appear occasionally.

The Annuals of the American Academy of Political and Social Science. 3937 Chestnut St., Philadelphia, PA 19104. (Bi-monthly).

Each issue contains articles on some important social or political problem. The July issue of 1978 and the September issue of 1974 were devoted to the elderly.

Family Relations. 1952. (Formerly Family Coordinator), National Council on Family Relations, 1219 University Ave., S.E., Minneapolis, MN 55414. (Quarterly).

Aimed toward practitioners in the family field, this journal contains articles dealing with theory, research, marriage and the family, adolescence, and aging and the aged.

Journal of Marriage and Family Living. 1938. (Formerly Marriage and Family Living), National Council on Family Relations, 1219 University Ave., Minneapolis, MN 55414. (Quarterly).

Contains articles on theory and research in marriage and family relations.

Journal of Social Issues. 1944. Society for the Psychological Study of Social Issues, P.O. Box 1248, Ann Arbor, MI 48106. (Quarterly).

Focuses on research on the psychological aspects of important issues. Its aim is the communication of scientific findings in a nontechnical way. The October 1965 issue had as its theme: "Old Age As a Social Issue."

Pacific Sociological Review. 1958. 275 S. Beverly Dr., Beverly Hills, CA 90212. (Quarterly).

The official journal of The Pacific Sociological Association, this publication includes articles on sociological theory, research, and methods.

Public Opinion Quarterly. 1937. Columbia University Press, 136 S. Broadway, Irvington-on-Hudson, NY 10533. (Quarterly).

Consists of research and theoretical articles. Its major purpose is to "illuminate problems of communication and public opinion."

Rural Sociology. 1936. Rural Sociology Society, 325 Morgan Hall, The University of Tennessee, Knoxville, TN 37916. (Quarterly).

Deals with all aspects of rural life and covers such areas as demography, criminology, and politics.

Social Forces. 1922. University of North Carolina Press, P.O. Box 2288, Chapel Hill, N.C. 27514. (Quarterly).

Associated with the Southern Sociological Society, this journal focuses primarily on articles pertaining to sociological research and theory.

Social Policy. 1970. Suite 500, 184 Fifth Ave., New York, NY 10010. (Five times a year).

Oriented toward major social issues and the encouraging of change in the structure of American society. Major content areas include aging and the aged, mass communications, ecology, health and illness, and urban sociology.

Social Problems. 1953. 208 Rockwell Hall, State University College, 1300 Elmwood Ave., Buffalo, NY 14222. (Five times a year).

Emphasizes the analysis of social problems and the political economy.

Society. 1963. (Formerly Trans-Action), P.O. Box A, Rutgers - The State University, New Brunswick, N.J. 08903. (Bi-monthly).

Written for a general audience, its articles cover a wide variety of topics in the social sciences.

Sociological Focus. 1967. Department of Sociology, University of Cincinnati, Cincinnati, OH 45221. (Quarterly).

The official journal of the North Central Sociological Association. Covers a wide variety of sociological topics with an emphasis on research and analysis with implications for public policy.

Sociological Inquiry. 1930. University of Texas Press, Box 7819, Austin, TX 87812. (Quarterly).

Serves the needs of social scientists with varied theoretical and methodological perspectives. It is designed to implement the scientific aims of Alpha Kappa Delta, a national sociology honor society, by communicating and reviewing developments of sociological interest.

Sociological Quarterly. 1960. Southern Illinois University, Carbondale, IL 62901. (Quarterly).

Primarily theory and research oriented, this journal covers a broad scope of topics. It is the official publication of the Midwest Sociological Society.

Sociological Symposium. 1968. Department of Sociology, Virginia Polytechnic Institute, Blacksburg, VA 24061. (Quarterly).

Each issue focuses on a special topic. The spring issue of 1969 was devoted to the "Sociology of the Elderly" and the spring issue of 1979 to "Social Gerontology."

Sociology and Social Research. 1916. University of Southern California, Los Angeles, CA 90007. (Quarterly).

Stresses research articles and projects on methodology. Content areas include administrative behavior, marriage and divorce, and health and illness.

Urban Life. 1972. (Formerly: Urban Life and Culture), Sage Publications, 275 S. Beverly Dr., Beverly Hills, CA 90212. (Quarterly).

Emphasizes urban ethnographic articles which employ the techniques of participant observation and qualitative interviewing. A special issue (October 1975) was devoted to the topic of: "Toward A Sociology of Death and Dying."

PART 7

RESOURCE MATERIALS ON AGING

Chapter 21

BIBLIOGRAPHIES, ABSTRACTS, AND REFERENCE WORKS

Atchley, Robert C. *The Social Forces in Later Life,* 3d ed. Belmont, Calif: Wadsworth, 1980.

Contains a 68-page bibliography covering a wide variety of literature in the field.

Balkema, John B. *A General Bibliography on Aging.* Washington, D.C.: National Council on the Aging, 1972.

Containing only monographic or non-journal literature, this annotated bibliography covers the years from 1967 to 1972.

Balkema, John B. *The Aged in Minority Groups: A Bibliography.* Washington, D.C.: National Council on the Aging, 1973.

Gives primary consideration to Asians, Indians, Jews, blacks and persons of Spanish origin.

Barnes, Nell D. *Black Aging: An Annotated Bibliography.* Monticello, Ill.: Vance Bibliographies, 1979.

Includes mainly monographs, articles, and government documents published after 1970.

Begus, Sarah; Goodman, Allen C.; and Hankin, Janet R. *An Annotated Bibliography of Recent Research on the Elderly.* Monticello, Ill.: Vance Bibliographies, 1982.

Annotated in detail, this bibliography contains research published after 1975 in the field of gerontology. Emphasizes studies of metropolitan elderly Jewish populations. The bibliography is arranged alphabetically by author and lists the topic of each article or book discussed.

Binstock, Robert H., and Shanas, Ethel (Eds.). *Handbook of Aging and the Social Sciences.* New York: Van Nostrand Reinhold, 1976.

Provides comprehensive knowledge, major reference sources, and suggestions for further research on the social aspects of aging. The social aspects are approached and developed within the framework of the subject matter of various social science disciplines.

Boston, Guy D. *Crime Against the Elderly: A Selected Bibliography.* Washington: Department of Justice, Law Enforcement Assistance Administration, National Institute of Law Enforcement and Criminal Justice, 1977.

Covering the years 1975 to 1977, this work contains annotations primarily from books and periodicals on fear of crime, reducing victimization, and other topics related to crime and crime prevention.

Current Literature on Aging. 1963. Washington, DC: National Council on the Aging Library. (Quarterly).

Lists and annotates selected recent books and articles which are arranged under subject headings.

Davis, Lenwood G. *the Black Aged in the United States: An Annotated Bibliography.* Westport, Conn.: Greenwood Press, 1980.

Contains annotations of books, articles, dissertations, and theses that deal with various aspects of the black elderly.

De Luca, Lucy; McIlvaine, B.; and Mundkur, Mohini. *Aging: An Annotated Guide to Government Documents.* Storrs: University of Connecticut Library, 1975.

Covering the period from 1960 to 1974, this guide to government publications contains annotated references which are arranged by subject areas. Out of print, but the University of Connecticut Library will reproduce copies for a fee.

Dissertation Abstracts International. Ann Arbor, Michigan: University Microfilms International, 1938. (Formerly Dissertation Abstracts.)

Abstracts of dissertations mainly from American universities are arranged by author within subject areas. Since 1966 there has been a separate section for humanities and social sciences. Dissertations are available for purchase on microfilm or paper. Also computer searches may be made through the Datrix (Direct Access to Reference Information) System.

Edwards, Willie M., and Flynn, Frances. *Gerontology: A Core List of Significant Works.* Ann Arbor, Michigan: Institute of Gerontology, 1978.

Focusing on social gerontology, this volume contains a listing of publications that the authors believe to be of special importance for a basic collection in gerontological materials.

Edwards, Willie M., and Flynn, Frances. *Gerontology: A Cross-National Core List of Significant Works.* Ann Arbor, Michigan: Institute of Gerontology, 1982.

Mainly composed of books, monographs, and selected issues of gerontological journals from Canada, the United Kingdom, and the United States. Includes some material from eight additional countries.

Eisdorfer, Carl (Ed.). *Annual Review of Gerontology and Geriatrics.* New York: Springer Publishing Co., 1980.

Designed to cover the field of aging, section headings include the "Biological Sciences," "Behavorial and Social Sciences," "Policy and Planning," and "Social Services."

Hepler, Harold R. "A Coordinated and Supplementary Bibliography on the Sociology of the Elderly." *Sociological Symposium,* no. 2, supplement, Spring 1969, pp. 179-221.

Contains paper, articles, books, and dissertations from the 1950s and the 1960s.

Hulicka, Irene M. *Empirical Studies in the Psychology and Sociology of Aging.* New York: Thomas Y. Crowell, 1977.

Contains abstracts of many of the most relevant articles in the psychology and sociology of aging.

Kaplan, Max. *Leisure, Recreation, Culture and Aging: An Annotated Bibliography.* Washington, D.C.: National Council on the Aging, 1983.

Includes over 100 books and articles which are cross-referenced by topics.

Krout, John A. *The Rural Elderly: An Annotated Bibliography of Social Science Research.* Westport, Conn.: Greenwood Press, 1983.

Lists 590 citations from both pure and applied research in the area of the rural elderly.

McIlvaine, B., and Mundkur, Mohini. *Aging: A Guide to Reference Sources, Journals and Government Publications.* Storrs: University of Connecticut Library, 1978.

Contains reference sources on aging from the social sciences and medical sciences published in the United States after 1970. A section on United States, state, foreign, and international government publications on aging published from 1975 to 1977 is also included. Out of print, but available at some libraries. The University of Connecticut Library will reproduce copies for a fee.

Mangen, David J., and Peterson, Warren A. (Eds.). *Research Instruments in Social Gerontology,* vol. 1: *Clinical and Social Psychology.* Minneapolis: University of Minnesota Press, 1982.

The first book of this three-volume series focuses on instruments to measure the reactions of older persons to aging and the assessment of aging made by younger persons.

Mangen, David J., and Peterson, Warren A. (Eds.). *Research Instruments in Social Gerontology,* vol. 2: *Social Roles and Social Participation.* Minneapolis: University of Minnesota Press, 1982.

Deals with the range of instruments for measuring social roles filled by older persons. Topics include the family, friendship, work and retirement, and religion.

Mangen, David J., and Peterson, Warren A. (Eds.). *Research Instruments in Social Gerontology*, vol. 3: *Health, Program Evaluation, and Demography.* Minneapolis: University of Minnesota Press, 1983.

The last book in this series reviews measurement in the areas of health, demography, and program evaluation. Discusses topics such as the effectiveness of long-term care, the elderly's utilization of health services, and geographic mobility.

Martin, Carol Ann. *The Elderly and Crime-- A Disheartening Dilemma: A Selected Bibliography.* Monticello, Ill.: Vance Bibliographies, 1980.

A 27-page bibliography on crime and the elderly which lists books from a wide variety of sources.

Missinne, Leo, and Seem, Bonnie. *Comparative Gerontology: A Selected Annotated Bibliography.* Washington, D.C.: International Federation on Ageing, 1979.

An annotated bibliography on comparative gerontology listing books and articles published since 1960.

Moore, Julie L.; Tuchin, Mort S.; and Birren, James E. "A Bibliography of Doctoral Dissertations on Aging from American Institutions of Higher Learning, 1934-1969." *Journal of Gerontology*, 1971, 26(3), pp. 391-422.

Dissertations are arranged under five major headings. Of particular interest to sociologists is the heading "Social Aspects" which includes such subheadings as "Status and Role Changes," "Social Interactions and Isolation," "Family Relationships" (later changed to "Intergenerational Relationships"), and "Demography."

Moore, Julie L., and Birren, James E. "A Bibliography of Doctoral Dissertations on Aging from American Institutions of Higher Learning, 1969-1971." *Journal of Gerontology*, 1972, 27(3), pp. 399-402.

This is the first supplement to the original work which was published in the *Journal of Gerontology*, 1971, 26(3), pp. 391-422. (See the above entry.) Additional supplements by years covered, and authors appear below.

2nd Supplement, 1973, 28(3), pp. 380-386; 1970-1972, Moore, J.L., Birren, J.E.

3rd Supplement, 1974, 29(4), pp. 459-467; 1971-1973, Mueller, J.E., Moore, J.L., and Birren, J.E.

4th Supplement, 1975, 30(4), pp. 484-489; 1972-1974, Mueller, J.E., Moore, J.L., and Birren, J.E.

5th Supplement, 1976, 31(4), pp. 471-483; 1973-1975, Mueller, J.E.; Moore, J.L., and Birren, J.E.

6th Supplement, 1977, 32(4), pp. 480-490; 1974-1976, Mueller, J.E.

7th Supplement, 1978, 33(4), pp. 605-615; 1975-1977, Mueller, J.E. and Kronauer, M.L.

8th Supplement, 1979, 34(4), pp. 591-603; 1976-1978, Mueller, J.E. and Kronauer, M.L.

9th Supplement, 1980, 35(4), pp. 603-617; 1977-1979, Mueller, J.E. and Kronauer, M.L.

10th Supplement, 1981, 36(4), pp. 496-512; 1978-1980, Mueller, J.E.

11th Supplement, 1982, 37(4), pp. 496-512; 1979-1981, Mueller, J.E. and Longo, M.K.

12th Supplement, 1983, 38(4), pp. 498-511; 1980-1982, Mueller, J.E. and Moore, J.L.

13th Supplement, 1984, 39(5), pp. 631-640; 1981-1983, Mueller, J.E. and Moore, J.L.

Oldakowski, Raymond K. *A Bibliography of Elderly Migration Literature.* Monticello, Ill.: Vance Bibliographies, 1983.

An 11-page bibliography on studies of elderly migration.

Place, Linna F.; Parker, Linda; and Berghorn, Forrest J. *Aging and the Aged: An Annotated Bibliography and Library Research Guide.* Boulder, Colo.: Westview Press, 1981.

Includes anthologies and journal articles as well as books and monographs. The bibliography is organized along three broad subject areas: physiological and psychological aspects of aging, social aspects of aging, and environment and the elderly.

Riley, Matilda W., et al. *Aging and Society: An Inventory of Research Findings,* vol. 1. New York: Russell Sage Foundation, 1968.

Organizes and summarizes the findings of social scientific research on middle-aged and older persons. Interprets these findings in the light of sociological theory and professional practice.

Roone, M. Leigh, and Wingrove, C. Ray. *Gerontology: An Annotated Bibliography.* Washington, D.C.: University Press of America, 1977.

Contains articles, books, and government documents published between 1966 to 1977. Out of print but available at some libraries.

Sharma, Prakash C. *Sociology of Retirement: A Selected Bibliographic Research Guide (1950-1973).* Monticello, Ill.: Vance Bibliographies, 1978.

Contains over 150 books and articles relating to the sociology of retirement.

Sharma, Prakash C. *A Selected Bibliographic Research Guide to Attitude toward Aging.* Monticello, Ill.: Vance Bibliographies, 1979.

Lists about 65 books and articles which were published primarily during 1950 to 1975 regarding attitudes toward aging.

Shock, Nathan W. *A Classified Bibliography of Gerontology and Geriatrics.* Stanford, Calif: Stanford University Press, 1971.

The major emphasis in this bibliography is on biology and medicine. However, under the major heading of "Social and Economic Aspects" are the subheadings of "Crime," "Demography," "Social Groups," and other areas of sociological interest. International in scope, this bibliography contains listings from journal articles, books, and government documents.

Shock, Nathan W. *A Classified Bibliography of Gerontology and Geriatrics: Supplement One, 1949 to 1955.* Stanford, Calif: Stanford University Press, 1957.

Shock, Nathan W. *A Classified Bibliography of Gerontology and Geriatrics: Supplement Two, 1956-1961.* Stanford, Calif: Stanford University Press, 1963.

Shock, Nathan W. "Current Publications in Gerontology and Geriatrics." *Journal of Gerontology,* 1950-1980.

A continuation of *A Classified Bibliography of Gerontology and Geriatrics* since 1962. (See above). "Current Publications in Gerontology and Geriatrics" appeared in each issue of the *Journal of Gerontology* from 1950 to 1980. The headings are the same as those in the author's original bibliography.

Sinnott, Jan D., et al. *Applied Research in Aging: A Guide to Methods and Resources.* Boston: Little, Brown and Co., 1983.

A guide to techniques and resources for persons doing applied research in aging. The Appendix includes bibliographic references and a list of organizations and clearing houses dealing with the elderly.

Sociological Abstracts. 1952. Sociological Abstracts, Inc., P.O. Box 22206, San Diego, CA 92122.

Abstracts contain articles from most American sociological journals and many foreign ones. Also includes papers presented at annual meetings of the various regional sociological societies. An entire section is devoted to social gerontology with subject headings such as "Ageism," "Aging," and the "Aged."

Sourcebook on Aging, 2d ed. Chicago: Marquis Academic Media, 1979.

Contains information on the current status of the elderly derived from a variety of government and private sources. Areas covered include health, retirement, legislation, and statistical data. Also contains a section on state and area agencies and associations concerned with the elderly.

Tibbitts, Clark (Ed.). *Handbook of Social Gerontology: Societal Aspects of Aging.* Chicago: University of Chicago Press, 1960.

Seeks to identify and structure the field of aging as well as providing a comprehensive view of it.

U.S. Department of Health, Education and Welfare. *Aging in the Modern World: An Annotated Bibliography.* Washington, D.C.: Government Printing Office, 1963.

Includes journal articles from 1958 to 1963 and monographs from 1900 to 1963.

U.S. Administration on Aging. *Words on Aging: A Bibliography of Selected Annotated References.* Washington, D.C.: Government Printing Office, 1970.

Written for persons working in the field of aging, this annotated bibliography contains relevant journal articles (1963-1967) and selected books (1900-1967) on the various facets of aging including social relationships and social adjustment.

U.S. Administration on Aging. *More Words on Aging: Supplement 1971.* Washington, D.C.: Government Printing Office, 1971.

A supplement to *Words on Aging* which contains references from 1968 to 1970.

University of Southern California. *Catalogs of the Library of Ethel Percy Andrus Gerontology Center.* Boston: G.K. Hall, 1976 (2 vols.)

Contains a list of the library's collection of books, reports, conference proceedings, government documents, and dissertations in gerontology. At present it is out of print and is available only on microfilm.

Chapter 22

STATISTICAL SOURCES

Administration on Aging. *Statistical Reports on Older Americans.* Washington, D.C.: Government Printing Office.

This publication replaced two previous series of reports: *Facts and Figures on Older Americans* and *Statistical Memos.* Titles in this series are:

No. 1. American Indian Population 55 Years of Age and Older: Geographical Distribution, 1970 (Part 1 of 2 (1977)

No. 2. Income and Poverty Among the Elderly: 1975 (1977)

No. 3. Some Prospects for the Future Elderly Population (1978)

No. 4. Social, Economic, and Health Characteristics of Older American Indians (Part 2 of 2) (1978)

No. 5. Characteristics of the Black Elderly - 1980 (1980)

No. 6. The Older Worker (1980)

This series has been discontinued. Copies of the above titles are available in most libraries. Some reproductions still may be obtained. Contact Donald G. Fowles, Administration on Aging, Department of Health and Human Services, 330 Independence Ave., S.W., Washington, D.C. 20201.

National Council on the Aging. *The Myth and Reality of Aging in America.* Washington, D.C.: National Council on the Aging, 1975.

Done by Louis Harris and Associates for the National Council on the Aging. This study represents "the first major national poll of the public's attitude toward aging and the aged." Includes the attitudes of older persons about themselves, their conditions, and experiences.

National Council on the Aging. *Aging in the Eighties: America in Transition.* Washington, D.C.: National Council on the Aging, 1981.

This second study done by Louis Harris and Associates for the National Council on the Aging, updates some of the issues and attitudes about aging that have taken place since the previous study was made. (See entry above).

National Council on the Aging. *Fact Book on Aging: A Profile of America's Older Population.* Washington, D.C.: The National Council on the Aging, 1978.

Using tables, charts, and narrative, this book summarizes data in eight areas of aging: demography, income, employment, physical and mental health, housing, transportation and criminal victimization.

U.S. Bureau of the Census. *Current Population Reports.* Washington, D.C.: Government Printing Office. Periodic reports of the older population are included in Special Studies, Series P-23. Titles are:

No. 43	1973	Some Demographic Aspects of Aging in the United States
No. 57	1975	Social and Economic Characteristics of the Older Population
No. 59	1976	Demographic Aspects of Aging and the Older Population in the United States
No. 78	1979	The Future of the American Family- Prospective Trends in the Size and Structure of the Elderly Population, Impact of Mortality Trends, and Some Implications
No. 85	1979	Social and Economic Characteristics of the Older Population: 1978
No. 128	1983	America in Transition: An Aging Society
	1984	Demographic and Socioeconomic Aspects of Aging (Forthcoming)

Note: Series P-20 Population Characteristics and Series P-60 Consumer Income also contain some excellent data on the elderly population. See Series P-25, No. 922, *Projections of the Population of the United States,* 1982-2050, October 1982.

U.S. Bureau of the Census. *Social Indicators.* Washington, D.C.: Government Printing Office, 1973-

Published every three years, this comprehensive report contains statistical information that describes trends and developments in major social areas in this country.

U.S. Bureau of the Census. *Statistical Abstract of the United States.* Washington, D.C.: Government Printing Office, 1978-

Published annually, this work summarizes statistics in a wide variety of subjects. Data on the older population is scattered throughout the book. At the beginning of each section, there is a guide to government and private statistical publications.

U.S. Congress. Senate. Special Committee on Aging Report. *Developments in Aging.* Washington, D.C.: Government Printing Office, 1963. (Consists of two volumes since 1976.)

Published annually since 1965, this report consists of issues on aging and "summarizes and analyzes the Federal policies and programs" for older persons. Each year Chapter One in volume one contains an excellent up-to-date demographic summary of the elderly population.

White House Conference on Aging, 1981. *Chartbook on Aging in America* and Supplement. Washington, D.C.: Government Printing Office, 1981.

Contains past, present, and projected demographic information on the economic and social roles of the elderly. Printing errors require the use of a supplement.

PART 8

OFFICES, ASSOCIATIONS, AND CENTERS ON AGING

Chapter 23

STATE, REGIONAL, AND FEDERAL OFFICES

A. State Offices on Aging

ALABAMA

Commission on Aging
502 Washington Ave.
Montgomery, AL 36130

ALASKA

Older Alaskans Commission
Pouch CMS-0209
Juneau, AK 99811

ARIZONA

Aging and Adult Administration
1400 West Washington
Phoenix, AZ 85007

ARKANSAS

Office on Aging
Department of Human Services
Donaghey Building
Little Rock, AR 77201

CALIFORNIA

Department of Aging
1020 19th St.
Sacramento, CA 95814

COLORADO

Aging and Adult Services Division
Department of Social Services
Room 504
1575 Sherman St.
Denver, CO 80203

CONNECTICUT

Department on Aging
80 Washington St.
Hartford, CT 06106

DELAWARE

Division of Aging
1901 North Dupont Highway
New Castle, DE 19720

DISTRICT OF COLUMBIA

Office on Aging
Office of the Mayor
1424 K St., N.W.
Washington, DC 20005

FLORIDA

Aging and Adult Services
Department of Health
and Rehabilitation
1323 Winewood Blvd.
Tallahassee, FL 32301

GEORGIA

Department of Human Resources
Aging Section
878 Peachtree St.
Atlanta, GA 30309

HAWAII

Executive Office on Aging
1149 Bethel St.
Honolulu, HI 96813

IDAHO

Idaho Office on Aging
State House
Boise, ID 83720

ILLINOIS

Department on Aging
421 East Capital Ave.
Springfield, IL 62706

INDIANA

Commission on Aging and Aged
115 N. Pennsylvania Ave.
Indianapolis, IN 46204

IOWA

Commission on Aging
Jewett Building
914 Grand Ave.
Des Moines, IA 50319

KANSAS

Kansas Department on Aging
610 West 10th St.
Topeka, KS 66612

KENTUCKY

Division for Aging Services
Department for Social Services
275 East Main St.
Frankfort, KY 40601

LOUISIANA

Office of Elderly Affairs
P. O. Box 80374
Baton Rouge, LA 70898

MAINE

Bureau of Maine's Elderly
Department of Human Services
State House - Station 11
Augusta, ME 04333

MARYLAND

Office on Aging
State Office Building
301 West Preston St.
Baltimore, MD 21201

MASSACHUSETTS

Department of Elder Affairs
38 Chauncy St.
Boston, MA 02111

MICHIGAN

Offices of Services to the Aging
101 S. Pine St.
P. O. Box 30026
Lansing, MI 48909

MINNESOTA

Minnesota Board on Aging
Metro Square Building, Room 204
St. Paul, MN 55101

MISSISSIPPI

Mississippi Council on Aging
802 N. State St.
Jackson, MS 39201

MISSOURI

Division on Aging
Broadway State Office Building
P.O. Box 1337
Jefferson City, MO 65102

MONTANA

Community Services Division
Department of Social and
Rehabilitation Services
P.O. Box 4210
Helena, MT 59601

NEBRASKA

301 Centennial Mall South
P.O. Box 95044
Lincoln, NE 68509

NEVADA

Division on Aging
Department of Human Resources
505 East King St.
Carson City, NV 89710

NEW HAMPSHIRE

New Hampshire State Council
on Aging
14 Depot St.
Concord, NH 03301

NEW JERSEY

Division on Aging
363 West State St.
Trenton, NJ 08625

NEW MEXICO

State Agency on Aging
224 E. Palace Ave.
LaVilla Rivera
Santa, Fe, NM 87501

NEW YORK

Office for the Aging
Empire State Plaza
Agency Building 2
Albany, NY 12223

NORTH CAROLINA

Division of Aging
Department of Human Resources
708 Hillsborough St.
Raleigh, NC 27603

NORTH DAKOTA

North Dakota Department of
Human Services
State Capital Building
Bismarck, ND 58505

OHIO

Ohio Commission on Aging
50 West Broad St.
Columbus, OH 43215

OKLAHOMA

Special Unit on Aging
Department of Human Services
P.O. Box 25352
Oklahoma City, OK 73125

OREGON

Senior Services Division
Human Resources Department
313 Public Service Building
Salem, OR 97310

PENNSYLVANIA

Department of Aging
Barto Building
231 State St.
Harrisburg, PA 17101

RHODE ISLAND

Department of Elderly Affairs
79 Washington St.
Providence, RI 02903

SOUTH CAROLINA

Commission on Aging
915 Main St.
Columbia, SC 29201

SOUTH DAKOTA

Office of Adult Services
and Aging
Richard F. Kneip Building
700 N. Illinois St.
Pierre, SD 57501-2291

TENNESSEE

Commission on Aging
715 Tennessee Building
535 Church St.
Nashville, TN 37219

TEXAS

Texas Department on Aging
P.O. Box 12786
Capital Station
Austin, TX 78711

UTAH

Utah Division of Aging
and Adult Services
150 West North Temple
Salt Lake City, UT 84102

VERMONT

Office on Aging
103 S. Main St.
Waterbury, VT 05676

VIRGINIA

Office on Aging
830 East Main St.
Richmond, VA 23219

WASHINGTON

Bureau of Aging and Adult
Services, Department of Social
and Health Services OB-43G
Olympia, WA 98504

WEST VIRGINIA

Commission on Aging
State Capital
Charleston, WV 25305

WISCONSIN

Office of Aging
Department of Health and
Social Services
1 West Wilson St.
Madison, WI 53702

WYOMING

Commission on Aging
Hathaway Building, First Floor
Cheyenne, WY 82002

B. Regional Offices of the Administration on Aging

REGION 1 (Conn., Maine, Mass.,
N.H., R.I., Vt.)

J.F. Kennedy Federal Building
Room 2007
Boston, MA 02203

REGION 2 (N.J., N.Y.)

26 Federal Plaza
Broadway and Worth St.
New York City, NY 10278

REGION 3 (Del., D.C., Md., Pa.,
Va., W.Va.)

P.O. Box 13716
3535 Market St.
Philadelphia, PA 19104

REGION 4 (Ala., Fla., Ga., Ky.,
Miss., N.C., S.C., Tenn.)

101 Marietta Tower
Suite 903
Atlanta, GA 30323

REGION 5 (Ill., Ind., Mich.,
Minn., Ohio, Wis.)

300 S. Wacker Dr.
Chicago, IL 60606

REGION 6 (Ark., La., N. Mex.,
Okla, Tex.)

1200 Main Tower Building
Room 2000
Dallas, TX 75202

REGION 7 (Iowa, Kan., Mo. Neb.)

601 E. 12th St.
Kansas City, MO 64106

REGION 8 (Col., Mont., N. Dak.,
S. Dak., Utah, Wyo.)

19th and Stout Sts.
Federal Office Building
Denver, CO 80202

REGION 9 (Ariz., Calif.,
H.I., Nev.)

50 U.N. Plaza
San Francisco, CA 94102

REGION 10 (Alas., Id.
Oreg., Wash.)

Third and Broad Building
2901 Third Ave.
Seattle, WA 98121

C. Federal Offices Associated with Aging

ACTION
806 Connecticut Ave., N.W.
Washington, DC 20525

ADMINISTRATION ON AGING (AOA)
Department of Health
and Human Services
330 Independence Ave., S.W.
Washington, DC 20201

BUREAU OF LABOR STATISTICS
441 G Street, N.W.
Room 1539
Washington, DC 20212

CENTER FOR STUDIES OF THE MENTAL HEALTH OF THE AGING (NIMH)
National Institute for
Mental Health
5600 Fishers Lane
Rockville, MD 20857

FEDERAL COUNCIL ON AGING
300 Independence Ave., S.W.
Room 4620, North Bldg.
Washington, DC 20201

NATIONAL CENTER FOR
HEALTH STATISTICS
3700 East-West Highway
Center Bldg., Room 1-57
Hyattsville, MD 20782

NATIONAL INSTITUTE
ON AGING (NIA)
National Institute of Health
9000 Rockville Pike
Bethesda, MD 20205

SELECT COMMITTEE ON AGING
House Annex #1, Room 712
Washington, DC 20515

SOCIAL SECURITY
ADMINISTRATION
Department of Health
and Human Services
6401 Security Blvd.
Baltimore, MD 21235

SPECIAL COMMITTEE ON AGING
U.S. Senate
Dirksen Office Bldg.
Room G-33
Washington, DC 20510

STATISTICAL INFORMATION
POPULATION DIVISION
Bureau of the Census
Washington, DC 20233

VETERANS ADMINISTRATION
810 Vermont Ave., N.W.
Washington, DC 20420

Chapter 24

GERONTOLOGICAL ASSOCIATIONS

ACTION FOR INDEPENDENT MATURITY
1909 K St., N.W.
Washington, DC 20049

AGING IN AMERICA
1500 Pelham Parkway S.
Bronx, NY 10461

AMERICAN AGING ASSOCIATION
College of Medicine
University of Nebraska
Omaha, NE 68105

AMERICAN ASSOCIATION FOR ADULT AND CONTINUING EDUCATION
1201 16th St., N.W.
Washington, DC 20036

AGING RESEARCH INSTITUTE
342 Madison Ave.
New York, NY 10017

AMERICAN ASSOCIATION FOR GERIATRIC PSYCHIATRY
230 N. Michigan Ave.
Chicago, IL 60601

AMERICAN ASSOCIATION OF HOMES FOR THE AGING
1050 17th St., N.W.
Washington, DC 20036

AMERICAN ASSOCIATION OF RETIRED PERSONS
1909 K St., N.W.
Washington, DC 20015

AMERICAN COLLEGE OF NURSING HOME ADMINISTRATORS
4650 East-West Highway
Bethesda, MD 20014

AMERICAN FEDERATION FOR AGING RESEARCH
335 Madison Ave.
New York, NY 10017

AMERICAN FOUNDATION FOR AGING RESEARCH
117 Tucker Hall
University of Missouri
Columbia, MO 65211

AMERICAN GERIATRICS SOCIETY
10 Columbus Circle
New York, NY 10019

AMERICAN HEALTH CARE ASSOCIATION
1200 15th St., N.W.
Washington, DC 20005

AMERICAN LONGEVITY ASSOCIATION
1000 W. Carson St.
Torrance, CA 90509

AMERICAN SOCIETY FOR GERIATRIC DENTISTRY
1121 W. Michigan Ave.
Indianapolis, IN 46202

ASOCIACION NACIONAL PRO PERSONAS MAYORES
1730 W. Olympic Blvd.
Los Angeles, CA 90015

ASSOCIATION FOR GERONTOLOGY IN HIGHER EDUCATION
600 Maryland Ave., S.W.
Washington, DC 20024

ASSOCIATION FOR HUMANISTIC GERONTOLOGY
1711 Solano Ave.
Berkeley, CA 94707

CENTER FOR THE STUDY OF AGING
706 Madison Ave.
Albany, NY 12208

CITIZENS FOR BETTER CARE IN NURSING HOMES, HOMES FOR FOR THE AGED AND OTHER

AFTER-CARE FACILITIES
960 Jefferson Ave.
Detroit, MI 48207

CLUB FOR PHILATELY IN GERONTOLOGY
2525 Centerville Rd.
Dallas, TX 75228

CONCERNED SENIORS FOR BETTER GOVERNMENT
1346 Connecticut Ave., N.W.
Washington, DC 20036

DAUGHTERS OF THE ELDERLY BRIDGING THE UNKNOWN TOGETHER
645 S. Rogers
Bloomington, IN 47401

DIVISION OF ADULT DEVELOPMENT AND AGING, AMERICAN PSYCHOLOGICAL ASSOCIATION
1200 17th St., N.W.
Washington, DC 20036

ELDER CRAFTSMEN
135 E. 65th St.
New York, NY 10021

FOSTER GRANDPARENTS PROGRAM
806 Connecticut Ave.
Washington, DC 20525

FLYING SENIOR CITIZENS OF U.S.A.
96 Tamarack St.
Buffalo, NY 14220

GERONTOLOGICAL SOCIETY OF AMERICA
1411 K St., N.W.
Washington, DC 20005

GOLDEN RING COUNCIL OF SENIOR CITIZENS CLUBS
218 40th St.
New York, NY 10018

GRAY PANTHERS
3635 Chestnut St.
Philadelphia, PA 19104

GREEN THUMB, INC.
1401 Wilson Blvd.
Arlington, VA 22209

HEARTLINE/NATIONAL ASSOCIATION OF OLDER AMERICANS
129 N. Cherry
Eaton, OH 45320

HELP THE AGED
1010 Vermont Ave., N.W.
Washington, DC 20005

INSTITUTE FOR RETIRED PROFESSIONALS
New School for Social Research
66 W. 12th St.
New York, NY 10011

INTERNATIONAL ASSOCIATION OF GERONTOLOGY
Duke University Medical Medical Center
Durham, NC 27710

INTERNATIONAL CENTER FOR SOCIAL GERONTOLOGY
600 Maryland Ave., S.W.
Washington, DC 20024

INTERNATIONAL FEDERATION ON AGEING
1909 K St., N.W.
Washington, DC 20049

INTERNATIONAL SENIOR CITIZENS ASSOCIATION
11753 Wilshire Blvd.
Los Angeles, CA 90025

INTERNATIONAL SOCIETY OF PRERETIREMENT PLANNERS
P.O. Box 287
Iowa City, IA 52244

LEADERSHIP COUNCIL OF AGING ORGANIZATIONS
925 15th St., N.W.
Washington, DC 20005

LEGAL COUNSEL FOR THE ELDERLY
1909 K St., N.W.
Washington, DC 20049

LEGAL RESEARCH AND SERVICES FOR THE ELDERLY
925 1st St., N.W.
Washington, DC 20005

LEGAL SERVICES FOR THE ELDERLY
132 W. 43rd St.
New York, NY 10036

MEXICAN-AMERICAN GERIATRICS SOCIETY
81 Cutts Rd.
Durham, NH 03824

NATIONAL ALLIANCE OF SENIOR CITIZENS
101 Park Washington Ct.
Falls Church, VA 22046

NATIONAL ASSOCIATION FOR HUMAN DEVELOPMENT
1620 Eye St., N.W.
Washington, DC 20006

NATIONAL ASSOCIATION FOR HISPANIC ELDERLY
1730 W. Olympic Blvd.
Los Angeles, CA 90015

NATIONAL ASSOCIATION OF AREA AGENCIES ON AGING
600 Maryland Ave., S.W.
Washington, DC 20024

NATIONAL ASSOCIATION OF HOME CARE
205 C St., N.E.
Washington, DC 20002

NATIONAL ASSOCIATION OF MATURE PEOPLE
Box 26792
Oklahoma City, OK 73126

NATIONAL ASSOCIATION OF OLDER AMERICANS
12 Electric St.
West Alexandria, OH 45381

NATIONAL ASSOCIATION OF STATE UNITS ON AGING
600 Maryland Ave., S.W.
Washington, DC 20024

NATIONAL CAUCUS AND CENTER ON THE BLACK AGED
1424 K St., N.W.
Washington, DC 20005

NATIONAL CENTER ON ARTS AND THE AGING
600 Maryland Ave., S.W.
Washington, DC 20024

NATIONAL CENTER ON RURAL AGING
600 Maryland Ave., S.W.
Washington, DC 20024

NATIONAL CITIZENS COALITION FOR NURSING HOME REFORM
1311 L St., N.W.
Washington, DC 20005

NATIONAL COMMITTEE ON ART EDUCATION FOR THE ELDERLY
Culver Stockton College
Canton, MO 63435

NATIONAL COUNCIL FOR HOMEMAKER-HOME AIDE SERVICES
67 Irving Pl.
New York, NY 10003

NATIONAL COUNCIL OF SENIOR CITIZENS
925 15th St., N.W.
Washington, DC 20005

NATIONAL COUNCIL ON BLACK AGING
Box 8813
Durham, NC 27707

NATIONAL COUNCIL ON THE AGING
600 Maryland Ave., S.W.
Washington, DC 20024

NATIONAL GERIATRICS SOCIETY
212 W. Wisconsin Ave.
Milwaukee, WI 53203

NATIONAL HOMECARING COUNCIL
235 Park Ave.
New York, NY 10003

NATIONAL HOSPICE ORGANIZATION
1901 N. Fort Myer Dr.
Arlington, VA 22209

NATIONAL INDIAN COUNCIL ON AGING
P.O. Box 2088
Albuquerque, NM 87103

NATIONAL INSTITUTE OF SENIOR CENTERS
600 Maryland Ave., S.W.
Washington, DC 20024

NATIONAL INSTITUTE ON ADULT DAYCARE
600 Maryland Ave., S.W.
Washington, DC 20024

NATIONAL INSTITUTE ON AGING, WORK AND RETIREMENT
600 Maryland Ave., S.W.
Washington, DC 20024

NATIONAL ORGANIZATION FOR WOMEN, TASK FORCE ON THE OLDER WOMAN
3800 Harrison St.
Oakland, CA 94611

NATIONAL PACIFIC/ASIAN RESOURCE CENTER ON AGING
811 First Ave.
Seattle, WA 98104

NATIONAL RETIRED TEACHERS ASSOCIATION
1909 K St., N.W.
Washington, DC 20049

NATIONAL SENIOR CITIZENS LAW CENTER
1424 16th St., N.W.
Washington, DC 20036

NATIONAL SUPPORT CENTER FOR FAMILIES OF THE AGING
P.O. Box 245
Swarthmore, PA 19081

NEW ENGLAND GERONTOLOGY ASSOCIATION
15 Garrison Ave.
Durham, NH 03824

NORTHEASTERN GERONTOLOGICAL SOCIETY
Rhode Island College
600 Mount Pleasant Ave.
Providence, RI 02908

RETIRED SENIOR VOLUNTEER PROGRAM
806 Connecticut Ave., N.W.
Washington, DC 20525

SENIOR ADVOCATES INTERNATIONAL
1825 K St., N.W.
Washington, DC 20006

SENIOR COMPANION PROGRAM
806 Connecticut Ave., N.W.
Washington, DC 20525

SENIOR PAC
1424 16th St., N.W.
Washington, DC 20036

SENIORS FOR ADEQUATE SOCIAL SECURITY
136 W. 91st St.
New York, NY 11024

SERVICE CORPS OF
RETIRED EXECUTIVES
822 15th St., N.W.
Washington, DC 20416

SOUTHERN GERONTOLOGICAL
SOCIETY
P.O. Box 3183
University of South Florida
Tampa, FL 33620

URBAN ELDERLY COALITION
600 Maryland Ave., S.W.
Washington, DC 20024

VACATIONS FOR THE AGING
AND SENIOR CENTERS
ASSOCIATION
225 Park Ave., South
New York, NY 10003

WESTERN GERONTOLOGICAL
SOCIETY
833 Market St.
San Francisco, CA 94103

Chapter 25

UNIVERSITY CENTERS AND INSTITUTES

ALABAMA

Center for Aging
University of Alabama
Birmingham 35294

Center for the Study of Aging
University of Alabama
University 35486

ARIZONA

Committee on Gerontology
University of Arizona
Tucson 85721

CALIFORNIA

Aging Health Policy
Center
University of California
San Francisco 94143

Andrus Gerontology Center
University of Southern
California
Los Angeles 90089-0191

Center for Education
in Gerontology
University of Santa Clara
Santa Clara 95053

Center on Aging
San Diego State
University
San Diego 92182-0273

CONNECTICUT

Center for the Study
of Aging
University of Bridgeport
Bridgeport 06601

Gerontology Programs
and Center
The University of Connecticut
Storrs 06268

DISTRICT OF COLUMBIA

Center on Aging
Catholic University
Washington 20064

Institute of Gerontology
University of the
District of Columbia
Washington 20009

Institute of Gerontology
Federal City College
Washington 20001

COLORADO

Institute of Gerontology
University of Denver
Denver 80208

FLORIDA

Center for Gerontological
Studies
University of Florida
Gainesville 32611

Center for Studies
on Aging
Eckerd College
St. Petersburg 33733

Center on Aging
University of Miami
Coral Gables 33124

Institute on Aging
The College of Boca Raton
Boca Raton 33431

Multidisciplinary Center
on Gerontology
Florida State University
Tampa 33612

Suncoast Gerontology Center
University of South Florida
Tampa 33612

GEORGIA

Gerontology Center
Georgia State University
Atlanta 30303

Gerontology Center
University of Georgia
Athens 30602

ILLINOIS

Gerontology Center
University of Evansville
Evansville 47702

Gerontology Center
University of Illinois
Chicago 60680

INDIANA

Indiana University Center
on Aging
Indiana University
Bloomington 47405

Institute of Gerontology
Ball State University
Muncie 47306

KANSAS

Center for Aging
Kansas State University
Manhattan 66506

Gerontology Center
University of Kansas
Lawrence 66045

Gerontology Institute
Washbarn University of Topeka
Topeka 66621

University Gerontology Center
Wichita State University
Wichita 67208

KENTUCKY

Gerontology Center
University of Louisville
Louisville 40292

Multidisciplinary Center
of Gerontology
University of Kentucky
Lexington 40536-0230

LOUISIANA

Institute of Gerontology
Northeast Louisiana
University
Monroe 71209

MARYLAND

Center on Aging
University of Maryland
College Park 20742

MASSACHUSETTS

Center on Aging
University of Massachusetts
Amherst 01003

Gerontology Center
Boston University
Boston 02215

Institute on Health and
Long Life
Southeastern Massachusetts
University
North Darmouth 02747

The Policy Center on Aging
Brandeis University
Waltham 02254

University Center
on Aging
University of Massachusetts
Medical Center
Worcester 01605

MICHIGAN

Center for Aging
Education
Lansing Community
College
Lansing 48901-7211

Institute of Gerontology
University of Michigan
Ann Arbor 48109

Institute of Gerontology
Wayne State University
Detroit 48202

Older Population Resource
Center
Delta College
University Center 48710

MINNESOTA

All-University Center
on Aging
University of Minnesota
Minneapolis 55455

MISSOURI

Center for Aging Studies
University of Missouri
Columbia 65211

Institute of Applied
Gerontology
Saint Louis University
St. Louis 63103

Center for Gerontological
Studies
Southwest Missouri
State University
Springfield

Institute of Applied
Gerontology
Saint Louis University
St. Louis 63103

NEBRASKA

Gerontology Programs
University of Nebraska
Omaha 68182

NEW JERSEY

Gerontology Center
Kean College of
New Jersey
Union 07083

Institute on Aging
Rutgers University
New Brunswick 08903

NEW YORK

All-University Gerontology
Center
Syracuse University
Syracuse 13210

Institute of Gerontology
Utica College of
Syracuse University
Utica 13502

Brookdale Center on Aging
Hunter College
New York 10010

Brookdale Institute
on Aging
Columbia University
New York 10025

Center for Geriatrics
and Gerontology
Columbia University
New York 10032

Center for the Study
of Aging
State University of

New York at Buffalo
Buffalo 14214

Center for the Study
of Aging and Dying
State University of
New York, College
at New Paltz
New Paltz 12561

Ringel Institute
of Gerontology
State University of
New York at Albany
Albany 12222

Institute on Gerontology
Malloy College
Rockville Centre 11570

Multidisciplinary Center
on Aging
Adelphia University
Garden City 11530

Third Age Center
Fordham University
New York 10023

Yeshiva University
Gerontological Institute
Yeshiva University
New York 10033

NORTH CAROLINA

Center for Study of Aging
and Human Development
Duke University
Durham 27710

OHIO

Center for Studies in Aging
University of Toledo
Toledo 43606

Center on Aging and
Health Care
Western Reserve University
Cleveland 44106

Gerontology Center
Kent State University
Kent 44242

Gerontology Council
University of Cincinnati
Cincinnati 45221

Institute for Life-Span
Development and Gerontology
University of Akron
Akron 44325

Scripps Foundation
Gerontology Center
Miami University
Oxford 45056

University Center on Aging,
Research, Education and
Service
Wright State
Dayton 45401

OKLAHOMA

Gerontological Institute
East Central University
Ada 74280

Gerontology Center
University of Oklahoma
Oklahoma City 73190

OREGON

Center for Gerontology
University of Oregon
Eugene 97403

Institute on Aging
Portland State University
Portland 97207

PENNSYLVANIA

Gerontology Center
Pennsylvania State
University
University Park 16802

Gerontology Institute
Marywood College
Scranton 18509

Institute on Aging
Drexel University
Philadelphia 19104

Institute on Aging
Temple University
Philadelphia 19123

RHODE ISLAND

Gerontology Center
Rhode Island College
Providence 02908

TENNESSEE

Center for Life
Cycle Studies
Memphis State University
Memphis 38152

Cole Interdisciplinary
Council on Aging
The University of Tennessee
Knoxville 37916

Council for the Study of
Aging and Society
The University of Tennessee
Chattanooga 37402

TEXAS

Center for Studies in Aging
North Texas State University
Denton 76203

Institute on Gerontology
Tarleton State University
Stephenville 76402

UTAH

Rocky Mountain Gerontology
Center
University of Utah
Salt Lake City 84112

VIRGINIA

Center for Gerontology
Virginia Polytechnic
Institute and State
University
Blacksburg 24061

Gerontology Center
Norfolk State University
Norfolk 23504

Virginia Center on Aging
Virginia Commonwealth
University
Richmond 23298

WASHINGTON

Institute on Aging
University of Washington
Seattle 98195

WISCONSIN

McBeath Institute
on Aging
University of Wisconsin
Madison 53706

WEST VIRGINIA

Gerontology Center
West Virginia University
Morgantown 26506

INDEX